Dōgen Studies

KURODA INSTITUTE
Studies in East Asian Buddhism

STUDIES IN CH'AN AND HUA-YEN,
edited by Robert M. Gimello
and Peter N. Gregory

Studies in East Asian Buddhism, no. 2

Dōgen Studies

Edited by
·William R. LaFleur

UNIVERSITY OF HAWAII PRESS
HONOLULU

The Kuroda Institute for the Study of Buddhism and Human Values is a non profit, educational corporation, founded in 1976. One of its primary objectives i to promote scholarship on Buddhism in its historical, philosophical, and cultura ramifications. The Institute thus attempts to serve the scholarly community b providing a forum in which scholars can gather at conferences and colloquia. T date, the Institute has sponsored six conferences in the area of Buddhist Studies The present volume is the outgrowth of the third such conference, held at Tasa jara in the fall of 1981. Volumes resulting from other and future conferences, a well as individual studies, are also planned for publication in the present series.

Library of Congress Cataloging-in-Publication Data
Main entry under title:

Dōgen studies.

   (Studies in East Asian Buddhism ; no. 2)
   Includes bibliographies.
   1. Dōgen, 1200–1253—Addresses, essays, lectures.
I. LaFleur, William R. II. Series.
BQ9449.D657D65   1985   294.3'927'0924   85–16427
ISBN 0–8248–1011–2

Contents

Dōgen in the Academy

William R. LaFleur

Some of us may live to see Japanese customs
pervading our land.
                                    —Josiah Royce (1908)

The context

The induction of Dōgen into the modern academic world, or perhaps more accurately, the academic world's first real engagement with
Dōgen came about 1924 when Watsuji Tetsurō (1889–1960) published a
provocative essay entitled "Shamon Dōgen."[1] It was this essay that to
many of Watsuji's contemporaries seemed to rescue Dōgen from what
they considered to be his entrapment for nearly seven centuries in the sectarian embrace of the Sōtō school. Watsuji insisted that Dōgen no longer
should be thought of as belonging exclusively to the monastic community. Claiming, instead, that Dōgen "belongs to mankind," Watsuji with
this declaration initiated the non-sectarian study of this thirteenth-century figure and in effect commenced what are called Dōgen Studies
[*Dōgen kenkyū*] in modern times.

As one way of exploring what it might possibly mean to say that
Dōgen "belongs to mankind," the Kuroda Institute held a conference on
Dōgen at Tassajara Springs, California from October 8 to 10, 1981. The
essays of this volume are a part of its result. Asked to edit these, I
decided first to reread Watsuji's essay in order to grasp how Watsuji saw
the relationship between Dōgen and the academic community. I came
away from this reading with the distinct impression that, at least in some
ways, my task would have been easier if I had been writing in 1924 rather
than 1983. To Watsuji the task before him was quite clearly defined. He
was immensely impressed with the quality of Dōgen's writings and quite
critical of the Sōtō monks for their readiness to accept a flawed and
sketchy account of their own founder. He censured them for their total
lack of interest in history, writing:

There may be some who defend themselves by saying that they have entered
the Zen life for the sake of their own enlightenment and that the gaining of a

historical understanding of Dōgen is not their main goal. But then I wonder
why it is so important that *he* be the founder of their school and why his
individual personality is the core of their organization.[2]

In the face of such apathy about who Dōgen really was and what he
really wrote, Watsuji held that the study of such things in the academic
world was now of fundamental importance.

He also saw it as a relatively uncomplicated procedure. Compared
to the wide range of approaches used in today's academy, those of Watsuji's time were much more limited and, as a result, scholars working
then had what now seems to us to be a long-lost confidence that they
could quite simply differentiate truth from error. Their assurance about
such things was very strong and straightforward. Watsuji quite easily
assumed that he and his colleagues would be able to carve out of their
materials a Dōgen quite different and at the same time more accurately
portrayed than the Dōgen revered but at that time little read or bothered
about in the Sōtō school itself. The time had come, he felt, to "free"
Dōgen from centuries of basically blind, hagiolatrous treatment. Textual
analysis and the historical reconstruction of the past—something Watsuji
himself did to some degree in his essay—were heady enterprises in the
1920s and were entered into by academics with little doubt about their
own ability to peel off all encrustations and locate the structure of truth
beneath.

By contrast, the ambience in academia today is quite different.[3] The
very success of modern scholarship has meant an incremental proliferation of methodologies and these now vie with one another as separate
ways of looking for the "underlying truth" in the texts and data of history. So many rival claims, however, have caused a sharp drop in the confidence that any—or even all of them together—can ever gain access to
the real truth about something. In this the academic world of Japan
today is not unlike that of the West and, as a consequence, the interest in
Dōgen is no longer something confined to one or two closely related disciplines. One book recently published there, *Gendai shisō to Dōgen*
[Contemporary thinking and Dōgen] demonstrated quite clearly that
Dōgen studies are no longer the private preserve of philologists, Buddhologists, and historians; persons in medicine, in psychiatry, and in the
study of society are also nowadays quite ready to study the *Shōbōgenzō*
for insights into their respective disciplines and for help in knowing
where these might move in new and fruitful directions.[4] Naturally, however, with all this proliferation of methodologies, the identification of the
"real" Dōgen becomes more and more problematic.

The essays of this book certainly reflect much of this development,
even though we here still lag far behind our Japanese colleagues in studies such as these. When the Kuroda Institute convened the Tassajara

Conference on the Significance of Dōgen, its purpose was to recognize that Dōgen studies even in the West have grown considerably in the last two decades, but that, since continued interaction is much more difficult among like-interested scholars here than it is in Japan, more is needed. Our distances are greater and our resources more limited. The assemblage of scholars at Tassajara reflected not only this development of Dōgen studies but also the progressive widening of approaches now taken to understand Dōgen and his significance.

In thinking about this introductory essay, I asked myself how I might deal with this diversity. I decided not to ask the reader to "tolerate" the variety of approaches and viewpoints—as if they were unfortunate or some kind of indication that Dōgen studies in the West are undeveloped or unfocussed. My own judgment is that the variety of approaches in this book is a very positive sign, something that points to the fact that Dōgen studies here are not only deepening in terms of primary engagement with the texts themselves but also broadening in terms of the variety of disciplinary specialists who, somewhat like their Japanese counterparts writing in the *Gendai shisō to Dōgen* volume, are beginning to explore Dōgen from relatively new points of view. In addition, I simply find a certain intellectual fascination in the fact that such a variety of disciplines implicitly or explicitly contend with one another in order to make their own claims upon Dōgen and what he "means."

What follows in the remainder of this introductory essay, then, has been devised to fit the format of a round-table discussion on Dōgen, one in which I try to provide a context for the other essays by exploring some of the assumptions and implications in current debates on this topic. I wish to make it clear, however, that what follows is in a real sense a fiction and not the direct product of the scholars' conversations at Tassajara in 1981. There was, of course, a good deal of discussion there and it lasted for three days; but what follows is not a record in the usual sense. The reader, therefore, should not spend any time trying to figure out whether the characters in the following fictional discussion bear any resemblance to the writers of any of the essays that comprise the remainder of this volume. Any such resemblance would be coincidental and not very important.

The point, of course, is that this is fiction which tries to be true—true, at least, to the contours of certain current debates among us. It is offered with the hope that, at least to some degree, it teases out and plays with the multiplicity and diversity of "Dōgens" that appear when scholars like ourselves—that is, scholars in 1983 rather than 1924—insist upon looking at Dōgen in the context of the academy *of our own time*. And that academy is, I think, one in which even within single disciplines such as history, philosophy, or sociology there will be a surprisingly wide variety of approaches. In fact, I am quite willing to let the "representatives" of the disciplines wobble on their pivots and shift in their alliances while they talk about Dōgen. That is to say, I think that Stephen Toulmin's description of the academic disciplines as "shifting conceptual populations" is accurate;[5] moreover, because I believe that such an academy is, in fact, an honest and healthy one, I find it interesting to see how sustained intellectual engagement with Dōgen's writings permits and even encourages such freedom to move and interact in new ways. For the various academic disciplines too there may be some value in studying the self —that is, the usually presumed and asserted "self" of each discipline— and to do so with a readiness to lose that self if and when necessary.

The conversation

CONVENER: As you know, our purpose here is to give each of you a chance to share the ways in which your several disciplines nowadays tend to look at Dōgen and then to see what happens when we respond to one another's approaches. I assume that those of you basically interested in philosophy will see somewhat of a different Dōgen than those who are historians—and so on. I will merely intervene from time to time to keep the discussion moving—and to make points which I simply can't resist making. Let's begin with one of our philosophers and see what kind of enterprise "Dōgen Studies" has become when he engages in it.

FIRST PHILOSOPHER: Well, we have to be candid and admit from the outset that Dōgen is not likely to be a name with which most philosophers in the West are acquainted. Not having been in the tradition of thinking that began with the ancient Greeks, Dōgen never had the chance to provide even one of the famous "footnotes to Plato," so naturally there are many among the academic philosophers of the West who wonder why the writings of this thirteenth-century Japanese should even be classified as "philosophical"! The situation, as most of you know, is very different in Japan, where interest in the thought of Dōgen has been found within the universities—sometimes fairly strongly so—ever since Watsuji introduced the topic there and it was picked up with even more philosophical intensity by Tanabe Hajime. Part of that interest may stem from a certain national pride on the part of those Japanese who study him. But another part also arose, I suspect, precisely because in Dōgen it was hoped that the basis might be found for a traditionally "Eastern" but at the same time philosophically sophisticated approach to life—something of an alternative to the philosophies of the "West" then being avidly studied and mastered by Japanese scholars. Remember that Watsuji himself had been specializing in Kierkegaard and Nietzsche studies before he made his sudden turn back towards his own tradition and took up Dōgen. My impression is that, even among my own colleagues in philosophy in the West, those who have showed an interest in Dōgen have usually been scholars distressed by the cultural provincialism of Western philosophy. But, perhaps because Dōgen is not a name our academic colleagues are likely to know, those of us who are Dōgen enthusiasts within the philosophy departments of universities here have had to spend a good deal of energy showing that Dōgen's thought is very sophisticated, integrated, and worked out in great detail—even though on the surface he uses language-forms that are quite different from the usual discourse of Western philosophers.

FIRST HISTORIAN: Yes, but that's precisely where I see a problem. As a historian I begin to get suspicious when I hear talk about Dōgen's "Thought"—that is, as something in the singular rather than in the plural. The term "Dōgen's thoughts" is, of course, awkward but to me as a historian it is more accurate. This happens, I suspect, because when I and many of the people in my discipline look at the *Shōbōgenzō* and other writings attributed to Dōgen, we notice not so much a neatly and architectonically constructed philosophical edifice but a man of the thirteenth century who in the course of his life and varied experiences really had a whole succession of ideas about things—and these often seem to have changed quite a bit! Dōgen was, after all, a man of his times and was deeply influenced by things such as rivalry with other Zen teachers of the time, the possibility or impossibility of official patronage, and the ever-changing views of what Ch'an or Zen had been in China. We should, I think, accept the fact that Dōgen was bound to be influenced by such things and that he seems at times to have changed his mind, made reversals, and gone off in quite new directions. As a historian, I am most interested in these changes and their place in the course of Dōgen's life. That's why talk about Dōgen's "Thought" makes me nervous. Is its unified structure really there? Or is it something we ourselves are projecting on to the *Shōbōgenzō* and his other works?   *New historicism*

SECOND PHILOSOPHER: I must confess that I feel quite close to this way of doing things—even though I am a philosopher, not a historian. I have to admit that the older way of doing what was often called "comparative philosophy" is something with which I no longer can identify very readily. I don't wish to caricature it, but I fear that the comparisons of "East" and "West" that took place under that rubric over the years now leave me quite cold. They often seemed oblivious to all of history and to culture—especially to the way in which a particular philosopher of the past was engaged with the very particular questions specific to his age and the possibilities of expression within it. What was often called "comparative philosophy," I am afraid, often seemed to want to show that, except for very minor and inconsequential differences, a thorough analysis of the thought of "X" will prove that he was a Chinese Leibniz, that of "Y" makes him the Indian Wittgenstein, and that of "Z" suggests beyond doubt that he was really the Japanese Descartes. Doing comparative philosophy in this way was to do it on a grand scale but it ignored every kind of history. I am now more inclined to accept Richard Rorty's insistence that philosophers ought no longer do their work in a way so unconcerned about history; he claims that "the common message of Wittgenstein, Dewey, and Heidegger is a historicist one."[6] And this is, I would suggest, a message also for those of us interested in philosophy that originated outside the ambit of the West. As an exercise in this newer mode of "comparative philosophy"—if the term can still be used—I much prefer Herbert Fingarette's way of handling a figure such as Confucius; Fingarette took account of the vast cultural and historical gap between ancient China and the questions asked by philosophers in the modern West and, by adjudicating these difference in discourse, nevertheless made Confucius and his concerns seem intelligible and philosophically significant.[7] I am in favor of doing something like that with and for Dōgen—if we can.

TEXTUAL CRITIC: That's interesting but I fear that usually when people wish to stress the importance of historical factors they quickly assume that these are "external" influences—that is, things that impact a figure such as Dōgen from *outside*. For me a thinker and that thinker's texts are influenced also by his or her earlier writings. In fact, I would stress that the author of the *Shōbōgenzō* was not only a thinker but also a writer. That is to say, he was bound to be self-conscious about what was gradually unfolding as his oeuvre and himself often keenly aware when there were gaps and inconsistencies in his own work. And, being human, he would probably wish to cover the tracks of these problems or "rectify" these in one way or another over the years; that is, he would wish to "create" the semblance of a unity and a consistency of structure even when it was not there. History, at least in my view, involves the impact not only of external events upon a given writer's work—the kinds of things the political and institutional historian likes to point to as the "real" determinants!—but is also the subtle effect wrought by his or her earlier works upon a writer's later program. My own reading of Dōgen would suggest that there is a considerable amount of this kind of thing in his writing.

FIRST HISTORIAN: As a historian I appreciate this but it leaves me, I am afraid, still ambivalent. On the one hand I applaud your readiness to see Dōgen's thinking or his "program of writing" as complex and other than cut from whole cloth. But I find that your approach will force us to become easily satisfied with the fact that a large part of Dōgen's oeuvre consists of Dōgen's own "projections" onto his earlier work—that is, a magnificent piece of writing but largely self-contained. In this way his text easily becomes a "textual meditation" on itself. External events—power plays, land deals, rivalries, wars, and the like—become, at least in terms of their effect on the text, unknowable and ultimately unimportant for you. My problem with this approach is that, if it is so, then *everything* becomes a kind of "writing" and everything becomes equally true! There is a kind of hearty and maybe even attractive solipsism in this. But I worry that it may also be a sophisticated excuse for scholarly laziness. It has become easy nowadays to deride the naive assumptions of Auguste Comte and the overly simple canons of positivist historiography, but I fear that much of this has become all too easy an exercise in disdain. I wish to hold out for the possibility that there is still something of value in that approach. I'm still interested in trying to sort out facts from fabrications—and Dōgen is as good a place as any to be at work.

SOCIOLOGIST: With your permission I would like here to interject a few remarks that arise from my perspective as a sociologist. It is extremely interesting to me that all of you—whether historians or philosophers—have thus far been assuming that Watsuji's act of "rescuing" Dōgen from entrapment in the Sōtō school resulted in giving Dōgen over to those to whom he *properly* should belong, namely, those of us engaged in academic pursuits. You seem to assume that for some reason or other the religious community claiming a primary allegiance to him had usurped him or was wrong in claiming its right to interpret him and the significance of his life. Now I wish to make it clear that I don't want to turn back the clock of history or even suggest that Watsuji did not begin something very important. I merely want to say that we academics should not leave the Sōtō school or today's Zen practitioners bereft of any right whatsoever to Dōgen! Nor should we assume that the "interpretation" or explanation is something that ought only take place within the academic venue. It may be true, of course, that over the centuries the Sōtō people enshrined Dōgen as holy founder and neglected to study the *Shōbōgenzō* as we today think it ought to have been studied. But, I am afraid that our strictly textual analyses proceed on the assumption that the best interpretation of Dōgen happens when we scholars, as so many individuals working in our private studies and with our books and commentaries, pore over the writings of Dōgen as another individual writing in the thirteenth century. This portrays the matter as something that is carried directly by books alone over a seven-century chasm between one individual and another. From my perspective as a sociologist you are all forgetting that texts in some sense arise *within communities* and, especially in a case such as this, continue to be embodied in the ongoing community attached to that text or its author. And, incidentally, our interpretations as scholars also arise within a community, the academic community—even though we much prefer to forget this fact and conceive of ourselves as individual researchers, somehow "uncontaminated" by the shifting intellectual fashions of our day and the sometimes almost sectarian allegience such trends and "schools" often demand in the academy.

CONVENER: Do you mean it's time to turn Watsuji on his head? That we ought now to give Dōgen back to the intentional religious community from which Watsuji wanted to rescue him, a community which today exists not only in Japan but also to some extent in the West as well?

SOCIOLOGIST: Some might say that. I myself would be satisfied merely with the recognition among us that we are not the only ones who "own" Dōgen, some realization that the religious community too has a right to its own interpretation of him and his significance. Dōgen, after all—and we ought not forget this!—was first of all interested in the formation of the Zen community and its perpetuation through time. His great emphasis upon the "bodily" expression of Buddhahood implies, I think, not only that he has something to say about the "mind/body" problem of contemporary philosophy but also that his conception of Buddhahood includes man's corporate—that is, his social and communal—nature.

FIRST PHILOSOPHER: In this connection I want to come back to defend Watsuji a bit and state that in my understanding the "practice" of Zen is not limited to what can be done within such primary religious communities. Modern philosophy in Japan has, of course, taken many forms. But certainly one of the most important has been that of the so-called Kyoto school, the works of which I've been trying to understand for some years now. As many of you know, the influence of Buddhism on this school was considerable; it was somewhat covert in the writings of Nishida Kitarō (1870–1945), the founder of the school, but has become much more overt in recent decades—especially in the writings of Hisamatsu Shin'ichi, Nishitani Keiji, Ueda Shizuteru, and Abe Masao. In some of these the influence of Dōgen is especially clear. But here is where I think that those of us who are Western readers of the writings of this school easily make a mistake. The importance of Zen and Dōgen for the Kyoto school has not been, I would suggest, merely because these provide "Eastern" or "Buddhist" views on problems that are long-standing problems within the world of philosophy. My own reading of the connection between Zen and the Kyoto school is quite different. It has to do with the fact that the philosophers connected with this school have insisted that the proper work of philosophy is that of examining *the* fundamental issue having to do with life and death. Work on this problem is, they have held, the real work of philosophy. And this requires a rigorous probing, self-examination, and thoroughgoing penetration! It is instructive to notice how important words like these are in Kyoto school writings. And it is, then, no mere coincidence that the closest analogue to all of this is that of Zen practice. Comparative philosophy wants to know what the Buddhist "view" on a panoply of problems might be; the Kyoto school, adopting much more of Zen's way of turning the question around, often asks why the discussion of these "problems" has become merely a way of avoiding *the* problem, that of life and death.

CONVENER: But isn't this what philosophy has always been about? Why was Dōgen needed to remind philosophers to do what they were already doing?

FIRST PHILOSOPHER: Perhaps it is what philosophy had once been! But I think the reason why the Kyoto school during the past few decades has really stressed the importance of Zen and Dōgen has been the obvious fact that much of Japanese philosophy, somewhat in imitation of trends in the West, had begun to turn away from the larger, more difficult problems of human existence and had begun to focus upon smaller, more readily and empirically soluble ones. Like the natural sciences, philosophers wanted "results"—even if this meant narrowing the scope of their concerns and eliminating entirely the older, much more difficult questions with which philosophy had long dealt. It was this abandonment of the older, more fundamental problem that worried the Kyoto school and it is why, since this was the basic problem of Zen practice according to Dōgen, he had such an intrinsic appeal to the Kyoto philosophers.

CONVENER: But wouldn't it have been easier and more direct for those so concerned to have simply joined one of the monastic communities where this was already the ordinary practice?

FIRST PHILOSOPHER: I don't think so. This is why Watsuji had a point; the existence of a monastic community is not itself a guarantee that Dōgen will be rightly understood and remembered. Ossification was and always will remain a danger for such communities; Watsuji and others seemed to feel that the study of Dōgen in the academic context could prevent or at least serve as a partial check against this.

SECOND PHILOSOPHER: And isn't there also simply the danger in a religious community that old concepts and ways of thinking will be revered simply because they are there and are the tradition? To me one of the interesting developments within the Kyoto school is what might be called a Buddhist revision of traditional Buddhist teachings. Nishitani, for instance, in his *Shūkyō to wa nanika* did not hesitate to subject the traditional understanding of transmigration to a rigorous analysis and go on to suggest that it might reasonably be regarded as "mythic" from the viewpoint of modern man.[8] I don't see this kind of thing as very likely to occur outside of the academic world and the freedom it gives to make such a move.

SECOND HISTORIAN: You seem to be suggesting that the real grappling with Dōgen and his concerns takes place in the academic world. But isn't it pretty clear that Dōgen, at least in the last phase of his life at Eihei-ji, insisted that the true practice of Buddhism is something that takes place in separated, strictly monastic communities? This is obviously an area in which the renewed study of Dōgen's own writings in our time has produced a problem for those of the Sōtō school who want to hold to the important role of the laity in Zen.[9] But you seem to be advocating that in the modern world the role of the monastic community may be no longer viable—that Dōgen is now better understood within the walls of the university or, at least, that there one is still able to probe the basic question of the meaning of life and death.

SOCIOLOGIST: I would simply add the observation that it is not at all easy to decide what is and what is not appropriate for so-called "modern" man and modern society. While some Buddhist thinkers in Japan may be ready to say that the monastic community is hopelessly medieval and has outlived its usefulness in the modern world, individuals in the contemporaneous West may be very ready to see the formation of such communities here as precisely what is needed to rescue our lives from a hopeless enmeshment in the fractured nature of modern life. As a sociologist I may be seeing all these things somewhat differently, but, given lots of other developments in our society, I am not at all surprised to see the growing interest in Dōgen as a growing interest in a form of Buddhist monastic or semi-monastic community life. In addition, to ignore what is happening in our own time and in our own society is to pass up a valuable way of gaining insight into what may have been even the original dynamic and appeal of a charismatic figure such as Dōgen in the thirteenth century.

CONVENER: But is it really Dōgen and his kind of Zen that is being established in the West in our time or is it something which, in spite of the community's desire to claim "transmission" across oceans, time and cultures, is really something entirely different? I'd be especially happy to hear what an anthropologist thinks of this problem.

ANTHROPOLOGIST: I, of course, can't speak for all anthropologists, but I can give my own view. I happen to be one of those anthropologists who is impressed with the relative strength and cohesiveness of what we call a given culture and the fact that the movement of ideas and religious philosophies from one culture to another is usually much more difficult than the transfer of tangible and technological cultural artifacts. One of the mistakes we often make is one of assuming that, because a robe, a bowl, a mandala, or a holy icon have made it across a mountain range or an ocean, somehow or other the exact meaning and usage of that material object have also made the transition. I doubt this very much. Even with the best linguistic training and attention to transcultural problems, the "translation" of something like Dōgen's view of things into twentieth-century American ears and minds will, I am afraid, be spotty, fragmentary, and haphazard at best. Although I hear the book has its critics and much of its expertise is different than my own so I can't really judge it, I like Hajime Nakamura's *Ways of Thinking of Eastern Peoples.*[10] Nakamura is a Buddhologist rather than an anthropologist but he has a viewpoint which made sense to me when I read it. That is, he stressed the internal integrity and cohesiveness of each of the following Asian cultures—India, China, Tibet, and Japan. I am no expert on the liguistic matters involved but I was interested in his view that the cultural predispositions of Dōgen as a Japanese so strongly influenced him that while he was in China he only would—maybe even only could!—hear and understand those things for which he was predisposed. That is, the Zen he received was a Zen that "fit" into the cultural and intellectual presuppositions of the Japanese. I suspect that is true. What becomes important then is not what Dōgen received from Ju-ching—which may not have been so much after all—but what he in fact shared with his Japanese contemporaries such as Nichiren and Shinran—even though there may have been no direct contact with them, and Dōgen himself would have disavowed it as unimportant. With Nichiren and Shinran he shared certain cultural predispositions, problems, and forms of expression and these were the "common sense" of that particular cultural context. Being the kind of anthropologist I am, this strikes me as probably correct.

CONVENER: Does that mean that we ought to be completely unconcerned about whether or not Dōgen's understanding of Buddhism—or Nichiren's for that matter—was in any sense authentic or orthodox?

ANTHROPOLOGIST: Well, it would be nice, of course, if we could show that it were somehow authentic or orthodox. But it seems highly unlikely to me that, having passed through the history of many centuries and having already been filtered into and then through the Chinese mind, there was really much left of some presumed "original" Buddhism that could have passed to Dōgen. You understand, of course, that in my view cultures—especially in intellectual and religious matters—are rather opaque, maybe even obdurate. They don't allow for the easy passage we would like them to provide. Of course, we *want* them to be permeable—especially when we ourselves are standing at the end of the line of transmission or of textual reception.

CONVENER: Doesn't this mean that you end up being much more interested in Dōgen, who—however unintentionally—really gave expression to certain modes of *Japanese* thinking rather than to Buddhism per se? This has, from my impression, been a major theme in the writing of many Japanese Buddhologists. But I have always assumed that this was influenced by a bit too much Japanese concern for detecting what is uniquely Japanese—and have disregarded it as such. But now you are suggesting that, at least from your point of view, it has validity, a validity inasmuch as *each* culture is uniquely structured, and that at least your kind of anthropology would support its likelihood.

ANTHROPOLOGIST: Well, who is to say there ever was a "Buddhism per se"? It seems to me that we must admit that even what used to be called "primitive Buddhism" or "original Buddhism" was embedded in a particular language and had Indian cultural suppositions from the outset. The existence of a primitive—by which people often seem to have meant a "culture free"—Buddhism seems to have been largely the projection of European students of Buddhism in the nineteenth and early twentieth centuries.

SECOND HISTORIAN: Yes, but our awareness of multiple cultures and their differences within the world should not betray us into thinking that Dōgen had a similar notion of culture and cultures. Here is where I again want to insist upon attention to the categories and problematics of Dōgen's own era. Certainly in going to China, Dōgen experienced it as "different" and he may even have contemplated an even greater "strangeness" in the Sanskrit texts and Indian people he may have encountered while in China. But a sense of strangeness does not imply a *concept of cultures*—especially not one of cultural relativity. Dōgen's own education had not included courses in cultural anthropology and I would maintain, in addition, he would not have been inclined to approve of our notions of cultural relativity. The texts of his own writings seem very clear on this point. They show a single-minded concern about the Buddhist Dharma, not some kind of curiosity concerning how that Dharma might be differently understood in different cultures. For Dōgen the concept of *upāya* or *hōben* did not seem to imply a cultural relativity in the meaning and application of that Dharma. He claims, of course, to have been gravely disappointed in the practice of the Buddhists he met in China—with the important exception of Ju-ching. But this was not because their Buddhism was strangled by too much Chinese culture; it was because their practice was lax. To Dōgen it was a human problem, not a cultural one. Orthopraxis for him was not a matter that had to be altered by passage through cultural filters and adapted to cultural variations. As historians and even as anthropologists it seems important to me that we notice when persons or peoples share or do not share our own notions of history and of culture.

LINGUIST: I am not so certain about that. I think we must take into account not only what you claim to be no overt interest in cultural relativity on Dōgen's part, but also his deliberate decision to compose the *Shōbōgenzō* in Japanese rather than Chinese. Wouldn't the fact that he made such a decision, something very much at variance with his contemporaries' practice of writing Buddhist treatises in Chinese, argue strongly that he wanted to make an accommodation to being "Japanese" at this level, probably the most basic level of all? After all, what can be more basic in terms of cultural awareness than the choice to move what had usually been written in classical Chinese, a kind of "ecclesiastical Latin" for Japanese clerics at that time, into the vernacular of his own people? Isn't this to communicate—even if implicitly—a deep sense of cultural awareness and the desire to translate Buddhism into a totally Japanese form?

TEXTUAL CRITIC: Ah, but there is good reason to question just how "easily communicable" Dōgen's Japanese was and is. Even for his contemporaries it had nothing of the cozy familiarity that Luther's German had, for instance, for his countrymen.

FIRST PHILOSOPHER: I can vouch for that! Some years ago I thought I had learned classical Japanese quite well . . . but then later I tried reading Dōgen! I go along totally with those scholars who say the text of the *Shōbōgenzō* looks like Japanese but really must be called something like "Dōgen-ese." It is very idiosyncratic, to say the least.

TEXTUAL CRITIC: But that's a very important point—Dōgen's intentional difficulty! And it's a point recognized by Japanese scholars who deal with medieval Japanese literature.[11] I would like to return to something I said earlier, namely, that we should not be overly conscious of the role of "outside" influence upon Dōgen or even of exactly how "Japanese" his thinking is. To me it is a fascinating and extraordinarily rich text because of its verbal and linguistic finesse. Dōgen seems to have been a very self-conscious writer; his rhetoric is marvelous and, from everything I can detect, the text has a texture, and that texture is remarkably consistent throughout.

FIRST PHILOSOPHER: But is that just an accident or some kind of literary "spit and polish" that he added to what he wanted to say? I would maintain that this was due to the depth of his religious and philosophical penetration of ultimate issues. Dōgen's style is evidence of his freedom and his freedom is the freedom of the enlightened mind. It is shown on every page. The religious profundity is patent for anyone to see and it clearly shows up in his capacity to "play" with language. His language is that of a man in *samādhi*.

FIRST HISTORIAN: Yes, but the problem—at least as someone rather neo-positivist like myself sees things—is that, while our textual critic's analysis fits in very well with contemporary philosophy's sensitivity to the language of various thinkers, it turns out once again to present Dōgen as a "systematic" thinker. It sees all his rhetorical devices as part of a *verbal fabric* and, as such, lays heavy emphasis upon the structure in it all. My problem is that when I look at the text with the kind of training I have had in reading such things I am boggled by the surprising discontinuities, flips, and reversals in the course of Dōgen's writing. Not only that. There is also the very serious problem of whether or not he understood his Chinese mentor Ju-ching while in China. As most of you know, Takasaki Jikidō has taken special notice of the fact that the key phrase in Dōgen, *shinjin datsuraku* ("dropping off body and mind"), is one that *never* appears in what we have of Ju-ching's writings.[12] Takasaki goes on to suggest that there may have been a serious linguistic misunderstanding between the master and his disciple—as it were, something of a language breakdown between the Chinese mouth and the Japanese ear. Ju-ching's phrase probably was not "dropping off body and mind" but simply "dropping the dust from the mind."

SECOND HISTORIAN: Yes, but James Kodera questions that interpretation, noting that, although the two phrases are homonyms in Japanese, they are not so in Chinese, the language Ju-ching would certainly have used.[13] Kodera goes on to suggest that Dōgen's phrase is in some ways "better" than that of his master. If I understand Kodera correctly, he says that Ju-ching's expression aims at the restoration of the original state of the mind by removing defilement from it, but Dōgen's expression assumes nothing to which an original state of purity needs to be restored.

FIRST HISTORIAN: That is interesting but it overlooks, I think, the fact that the *Hōkyō-ki,* a work which purports to be Dōgen's own later "record" of his earlier days in China, attributes the "cast off body and mind" phrase not to himself originally but to Ju-ching!

LINGUIST: Wouldn't that mean either that a very serious problem of interlinguistic communication occurred precisely at the point at which Dōgen was receiving his master's most important teaching or—and this may be even more disturbing!—that Dōgen in later life, when at the point of recollecting and writing down his "record" of his long-past days in China, *imagined* that Ju-ching must have said "cast off body and mind"? In this latter case we would have to say that Dōgen didn't really receive the transmission but rather appears to have invented it.

FIRST HISTORIAN: Yes, that's the problem. Of course, there is also the possibility that the *Hōkyō-ki* was much less Dōgen's work than that of his immediate disciples. But in either case there is something deeply problematic, at least to a historian like myself, at precisely that point where there is supposed to have been the most vital link between master and disciple.

TEXTUAL CRITIC: I hope you will pardon me but, to tell truth, I don't find that either surprising or disturbing. To come back to something I was saying earlier, Dōgen, after all, was a writer in addition to being a Zen master. I guess I simply expect a writer to be a writer. Therefore, even when a writer purports to be giving us something that he himself called "reliable" as a record or as history, there will always be some fictionalizing and fabrication in it. It's inevitable! Borges noted that great poets create their own precursors and the contemporary literary critic Harold Bloom—in books such as *The Anxiety of Influence* and *A Map of Misreading*—has been giving us brilliant analyses of how much misunderstandings and fabrications work in literature and why they are such a necessary part of being truly creative.[14] If great poets must create their own precursors, so too, I imagine, great Zen masters must create their own ancestors and patriarchs!

CONVENER: But then, if I correctly understand what you are saying, what are usually called the great patriarchs of Buddhism and of Zen were to a great extent the product of later fabrications, even of storytelling—in spite of the great emphasis within the tradition upon correct and authentic "transmission" of the Dharma, an emphasis that continues to the present day.

TEXTUAL CRITIC: According to what I have read, this has been quite apparent for some time already. The close checking of actual documents by persons really concerned about documentation has shown that there was a good deal of this within the tradition. The "history" of the transmission of Zen to the Sixth Patriarch is, I suspect, a classic case.[15] The connection between Ju-ching and Dōgen may be merely another instance. The thing I wish to stress, however, is that it is not necessary to bring some kind of moral judgment to bear on all of this. It is also why I think my approach is different from that of the historian. Unlike people in my discipline, he adopts something of the role of a detective trying to sort through the evidence to find the "truth" under the skillful obfuscations and evasions created by people wanting us not to know it; his discipline is propelled by a certain moral energy. Mine is more low-keyed and maybe it is less purist in its view of what writing—even the historiographical variety—is likely to be. Frankly, we regard historiography— even its most modern forms—as itself another form of writing and, therefore, of storytelling. As a consequence, people in my discipline would *expect* the ancient Zen masters to have "played" with the truth a bit and we will even admire them for the skill and creativity of their fictions. From everything I can tell Dōgen was a writer in this sense.

ANTHROPOLOGIST: I have a hunch that there is even some suggestion of this in the manner in which people in the Zen tradition have always been somewhat skittish about any attempt to describe "transmission of the Dharma" as if it were some kind of "thing" that were being passed down from one person to another and could, by examination, be declared more or less intact. Some teachers of Zen speak, for instance, of the circularity and reciprocity of transmission. I don't know exactly what is meant, for instance, by the phrase "direct transmission from mind to mind"—at least I don't know what someone involved in that transmission means by it. I can, however, at least make an outsider's judgment concerning it and say that such language is what we might call "boundary-marking" language. It functions to seal off a certain area of experience as very unlike even its closest analogues in the experience of other people. It says: "Don't come in here wearing the clumsy, dirty boots of 'ordinary' understandings and interpretations! This is something special and, unless you shed your usual categories of understanding, you'll never be able to grasp what this means." Some of my colleagues in anthropology have begun to mold their methodology to accommodate the importance of this. Jacques Maquet, for instance, has felt no reluctance in being what he calls an "observing participant" in the meditations and religious life of Buddhist communities both in Asia and North America.[16] There is this sense among certain anthropologists that the old stance of supposed "objectivity" was precisely that: a stance and nothing more. It really created a distance and therefore a distortion—or, more seriously, an unacknowledged distortion—in what was being observed.

SECOND HISTORIAN: But isn't that to say that you have to be *in* the line of such a transmission or, at least, be involved in Zen practice itself in this case to be able to understand exactly what is meant here? Doesn't it imply that all the structures of interpretation which we academics offer up are nothing but futile attempts? And isn't this to suggest that each of us in our own way has been looking merely at our own finger pointing to the moon rather than at the moon itself?

FIRST PHILOSOPHER: If by that you mean that some actual practice of Zen might complement and may even give further focus to our academic understanding, I have no problem. But if you are suggesting that we academics should drop our own studies of Dōgen and merely learn of him in the context of *zazen* and under the tutelage of "teachers" in the official line of transmission, I am afraid I will hold out for the continuation of interpretations through books and the older mode of cross-reference and open critiques. The academic study of Dōgen is still, I think, too tender and fragile a flower to be already abandoned. We have only just begun! To my mind the current anomie in the academy ought not to inhibit our studies but, on the contrary, should make the study of Dōgen perhaps even more fascinating than we had thought it to be.

SOCIOLOGIST: I concur with that. I maintain that the practicing community's understanding must be listened to and respected but there is always an acute danger of ossification there. People who are busily involved in doing *zazen* and working on kōans will not, in fact, have a lot of time for reading the *Shōbōgenzō*—or even the *Zuimonki*. While I am ready to champion the right of community to interpret its master, I would hate to see the Zen community on this side of the ocean do what the one in Japan appears to have done some centuries ago, namely enshrine and then treat Dōgen with benign neglect. And Dōgen, as has been forcefully noted here, is difficult. For spare-time or "easy" reading there is always the vast, eclectic, and all too accessible supermarket of English language books on "Eastern religions" and popular Zen—all of these things infinitely easier than Dōgen! This, in my opinion, argues for the need of a separate, continuous, and academic study of Dōgen—for a long time to come!

CONVENER: Are you suggesting that the future of Dōgen studies will be most safe if we have *two* fingers . . . and work at keeping both of them pointing at the moon?

The credits

In the convening of the Tassajara conference it was recognized from the beginning that it would be impossible to include all the Western scholars who have been working on Dōgen and thinking about his significance. It was hoped that the conference would represent different points of view and, in order to make this a certainty, the range of scholarly interests was as wide as the budget could let it be. The facilities, food, and hospitality provided at Tassajara Springs by the San Francisco Zen Center were wonderful and stimulating for our discussions. The setting of a monastic community in the mountains made the participants speculate that maybe they had gotten as close as possible to Eihei-ji while still remaining in California. In addition to the conferees who contributed the papers in the following pages, Professor Yasuaki Nara of Komazawa University, the author of an extremely interesting paper entitled, "Kaigai kara mita Dōgen" [Dōgen seen from abroad],[17] added much to our sense of there being, in fact, an ocean-crossing community of scholarly interest in our topic. Likewise, Professor Masatoshi Nagatomi of Harvard shared with us much of his knowledge as a Buddhologist and his own perspective on Dōgen in the Kamakura period. Monks and lay practitioners from the San Francisco Zen Center and from the Zen Center of Los Angeles kindly listened in while we scholars, loquacious as ever, did all the talking.

Taizan Maezumi Roshi and Richard Baker Roshi focused much of the discussion, however, during one especially memorable evening when the scholars and the practitioners sat in a circle to share their mutual interpretations of Dōgen. The Kuroda Institute and its director at that time, Michael Soule, sponsored and coordinated the conference and made it possible. An anonymous benefactor helped us meet the travel and other expenses involved. In the editing of these papers Peter Gregory, the present director of the Kuroda Institute, was an invaluable help to me—as were my UCLA colleagues Robert S. Kirsner and Jacques Maquet. I certainly also am very grateful to Tai-wo Kwan, who not only prepared the glossary but also helped immeasurably in many details of the editing process. Stuart Kiang of the University of Hawaii Press gave advice and editorial assistance at many points along the way.

Finally, there will be propriety in a note to the reader concerning translations and textual apparatus. Persons already familiar with Dōgen studies in the West know that we are still many years away from having a complete and definitive translation of Dōgen's complete works. Individual scholars, some of whom are represented here, have done translations of certain portions of Dōgen's writings and naturally have their own individual preferences when it comes to matters of how exactly to translate into English portions of the thirteenth-century master's prose or, for that matter, even the titles of various of the fascicles of the *Shōbōgenzō*. These are matters about which the scholars here represented often feel quite strongly—since they touch on their own individual ways of interpreting Dōgen. Therefore, in editing these essays I have not tried to impose a uniformity of translation and terminology on these contributors since such would be premature at this stage of our studies and contrary to their exploratory and investigative purpose. Being definitive in that sense will have to be the task of another book—at another stage in our studies.

Perhaps for similar reasons we are in a stage where certain words of Indian origin have over the years become sufficiently known to get entered into our own dictionaries—words such as sangha, nirvana, samsara, dharma, mahayana, hinayana, theravada, and sutra. These words, without the diacritical marks they once possessed, have now become English words and to me there seems no need to "re-alienate" them here. Other words of Asian origin have, to the best of our abilities, been rendered with proper diacriticals.

Four works in the footnotes will appear repeatedly and have been abbreviated in the following manner:

DZZ 1 and *DZZ* 2 refer respectively to the two volumes of the *Dōgen zenji zenshū* edited by Ōkubo Dōshū (Tokyo: Chikuma Shobō, 1969–70).

SSZ refers to the twenty volumes of the *Sōtō shū zensho* (Tokyo: Kōmeisha, 1929–38).

T refers to the standard version of the Chinese Buddhist canon, the *Taishō shinshū daizōkyō* in eighty-five volumes (Tokyo: Taishō Issaikyō Kankōkai, 1924–34).

EB refers to the new series of *The Eastern Buddhist*.

Notes

1. Reprinted as a chapter in Watsuji's "Nihon Seishinshi Kenkyū" in Abe Yoshishige et al., eds., *Watsuji Tetsurō Zenshū* (Tokyo: Iwanami Shoten, 1977), vol. 4, pp. 156–246. For a more full account of modern Japanese scholarship on Dōgen, see Hee-Jin Kim, *Dōgen Kigen: Mystical Realist* (Tucson: University of Arizona Press, 1975), pp. 1–9.
2. Ibid., p. 161.
3. A very different approach to hagiographical writing, for instance, can be seen in the various essays included in Frank E. Reynolds and Donald Capps, eds., *The Biographical Process: Studies in the History and Psychology of Religion* (The Hague and Paris: Mouton, 1976). In these essays the hagiographical element is detected in varied kinds of writing and is not merely "peeled off" but is itself made the subject of interest and study.
4. Kagamishima Genryū and Tamaki Kojirō, eds., *Gendai shisō to Dōgen* (Tokyo: Shunjūsha, 1981). See also the way Dōgen's thinking is stretched to invite both philosophical and psychological research in Yuasa Yasuo's important study *Shintai: Tōyōteki Shinjinron no Kokoromi* (Tokyo: Sōbunsha, 1977).
5. Stephen Toulmin, *Human Understanding: The Collective Use and Evolution of Concepts* (Princeton: Princeton University Press, 1972), pp. 336ff.
6. Richard Rorty, *Philosophy and the Mirror of Nature* (Princeton: Princeton University Press, 1972), p. 9. Here I must apologize to the reader for appending footnotes to a text that purports to be oral conversation but then this is, after all, a fabrication and there seems to be no good reason to deny the reader access to its sources. Although the conversation is a fiction, the notes, to be sure, refer to real books and essays.
7. Herbert Fingarette, *Confucius—The Secular as Sacred* (New York: Harper & Row, 1972).
8. This important work now exists in English translation: Keiji Nishitani, *Religion and Nothingness*, translated with an introduction by Jan Van Bragt (Berkeley, Los Angeles, and London: University of California Press, 1982).
9. See Shibata Dōken, *Dōgen Zenji no Zaike kyōka* (Tokyo: Shunjūsha, 1979).
10. Nakamura Hajime, *Ways of Thinking of Eastern Peoples: India, China, Tibet, Japan* (Honolulu: University of Hawaii Press, 1964).
11. For an excellent literary analysis of Dōgen's language see Yasuraoka Kōsaku, *Chūseiteki Bungaku no Tankyū* (Tokyo: Yūseidō, 1960), pp. 96–139.

12. Takasaki Jikidō and Umehara Takeshi, *Kobutsu no Manebi: Dōgen* (Tokyo: Kadokawa Shoten, 1969), 43–52.

13. Takashi James Kodera, *Dōgen's Formative Years in China: An Historical Study and Annotated Translation of the Hōkyō-ki* (London and Henley: Routledge and Kegan Paul, 1980), pp. 106–107.

14. Harold Bloom, *The Anxiety of Influence: A Theory of Poetry* (London, Oxford, and New York: Oxford University Press, 1973) and *A Map of Misreading* (New York: Oxford University Press, 1975).

15. See Philip B. Yampolsky, *The Platform Sutra of the Sixth Patriarch* (New York and London: Columbia University Press, 1967).

16. Jacques Maquet, "Bhāvanā in Contemporary Sri Lanka: The Idea and Practice," in Somaratna Balasooriya et al., eds., *Buddhist Studies in Honor of Walpola Rahula* (London and Vimamsa: Gordon Fraser, 1980), pp. 139–153.

17. Nara Yasuaki, "Kaigai kara mita Dōgen" in Kagamishima and Tamaki, op.cit., pp. 244–276.

Recarving the Dragon:
History and Dogma in
the Study of Dōgen

Carl Bielefeldt

We should go beyond our love for the carved
dragon to love the real dragon. We should learn
that both the carved and the real dragon have the
power to bring on clouds and rain.

—Shōbō genzō zazen shin *

There seems little doubt now that Dōgen has arrived in the West. The thin trickle of Western-language publications that began after World War II has broadened into a veritable stream. For those engaged in this publication, it is heartening to note that, whatever the fluctuations of public interest in Zen Buddhism, books and articles on this relative latecomer to the market continue to attract attention. For those convinced of his importance, it is satisfying to find that, as a result of this attention, Dōgen has quite suddenly emerged as one of the better-known Buddhist figures, and that he now keeps company with the likes of Nāgārjuna and Vasubandhu in Western discussions of Asian thought. For those enamored of his spiritual message, it is inspiring to realize that the burgeoning intellectual interest in Dōgen's teaching has been matched by a remarkable growth in the number and size of Western Zen groups dedicated to putting the teaching into practice. Yet if it is time now to celebrate the successful arrival of Dōgen in the West, it may also be time to pause a bit and reflect on how this has come about and what, in fact, has arrived.

From this side of the Pacific, it may seem that we are actively importing Dōgen as a new addition to our postwar trade in Zen Buddhism; from the other side, it sometimes looks rather more as if he were being dumped on us by the power of Japanese scholarship. For the fact is that in Zen studies Japanese scholarship is powerful, and in Japanese scholarship Dōgen is popular. Whether or not he himself ranks with Nāgārjuna, Western students of Dōgen (and indeed, with one or two notable exceptions, of Zen in general) have not ranked with their counterparts in Indian Buddhology. For whatever reasons, Zen studies simply have not yet attracted many trained Western scholars capable of—or interested in—original research in primary sources, and as a result, have been heavily dependent on the works of Japanese. Our delay in appreciating Dōgen itself is surely not unconnected with the fact that D. T. Suzuki wrote almost nothing on this Zen master, nor is it mere coincidence that the spate of English translations of Dōgen's works has followed upon the recent appearance of the first modern Japanese versions. If we are thus dependent on Japanese scholarship, it behooves us to bear in mind its character and the image of Dōgen it is providing us.

There is not, of course, one Japanese image of Dōgen. The sheer volume of publication, both scholarly and popular, devoted to him has assured a considerable variety of treatments. Still, among these, two general types have been particularly prominent in this century. One deals with Dōgen the philosopher, seeking to translate his thought into modern —i.e., Western—terms and sometimes to apply it to Western philosophical issues or compare it with one or another Western philosophical position. This approach enjoyed some popularity in the years before the war and still seems able to find here and there a free spirit willing to try his hand. More common today is the study of Dōgen as Kamakura Buddhist figure, a treatment that views him in Japanese context and attempts to relate his work to religious and other cultural characteristics of late antiquity and the early middle ages. This approach is an extension of a more general postwar interest in the reevaluation of Japanese intellectual history; and indeed, there is an angle from which both these treatments of Dōgen can be seen as reflexes of the shifting strategies in modern Japan's continuing search for its national origins.

The question of Dōgen's significance for modern Japan I shall leave to others better qualified to comment; what I want to note here is simply that these Japanese presentations of him as philosopher and medieval thinker, however important in the establishment of his reputation there, have relatively little immediate appeal in the West. To be sure, the philosophical approach in itself promises to find a ready market; and in fact, we are already witnessing the first efforts by Westerners to appropriate this line of inquiry. But the very accessibility of the approach means that Japanese scholarship has less to offer us; for once they seriously set to work on Dōgen, it is unlikely that many Westerners will look to Japan for philosophical guidance. On the other hand, Japanese work on intellectual history suffers from the opposite sort of weakness: its audience is limited to a small group of Japanologists. This approach to Dōgen has had almost no impact in the West, nor will it until such time as we have become considerably more interested in, and sophisticated about, Japanese cultural history. In the meantime, it is not Dōgen the medieval Japanese that attracts us but Dōgen the Zen master.

Those familiar with the Japanese literature on Dōgen will have noticed that the two approaches I have mentioned here account for only a small fraction of the whole. Of the remainder, most can be roughly described as concerned in one way or another with Dōgen the Zen master

—that is, are works of scholars of Zen Buddhism, who treat Dōgen first of all as a representative of that tradition. Not only do these works dominate numerically but their influence often permeates all Dōgen studies; for it is here that one finds most of the technical experts in Dōgen, the researchers who provide the basic textual, biographical, and doctrinal information on which the philosopher, cultural historian, and others depend. In one sense, this is perhaps as it should be; for Dōgen saw himself simply as a follower of the Buddha, and until the twentieth century no one seems to have seen him as more than a Zen master. Indeed, if the truth be known, most have seen him as less; for until this century, Dōgen's significance was limited almost entirely to his role as the founder of the Sōtō school. This fact is important for understanding modern Japanese Zen scholarship on Dōgen.

Given the centrality of Zen in medieval Japanese culture and the reputation of Dōgen as one of Japan's greatest Zen masters, it would be easy to conclude that his influence has been widespread. This does not seem to be the case. Prior to modern times, there is little evidence that Dōgen's teachings had much impact beyond the confines of his own school. This school maintained few prominent monasteries in the major urban centers, and its institutions were excluded from the higher ranks of the official *gozan* monastic system so influential in the dissemination of Zen culture. While that system was active in the publication of many Zen texts, Dōgen's writings were not widely circulated. To be sure, some minor works—such as the *Eihei Gen zenji goroku* and *Gakudō yōjin shū* —were printed early on, but the Japanese *Shōbō genzō,* by far the most important source for the study of Dōgen, was not published until the nineteenth century. In fact, throughout most of the medieval period this collection seems to have been regarded as a kind of house document, to be carefully guarded—if not necessarily studied—by the monks of the Sōtō order.

The modern emergence of Dōgen from the relative obscurity of the Sōtō monastic community had its origins in that community itself. Like much else in Japanese Buddhology, the groundwork for Dōgen studies was laid by the sectarian scholars of the Tokugawa period. It was these men—Manzan Dōhaku (1634–1714), his disciple Menzan Zuihō (1683–1769), and others—who began the work of collecting, comparing, and editing manuscripts, of evaluating the sources for Dōgen's biography, and of writing the commentaries to Dōgen's works. In the process, they fixed the orthodox Sōtō teaching and established Dōgen as its ultimate authority. Thus when he finally made his entry onto the wider Japanese scene, he appeared first in his role as founder and chief theorist of Sōtō Zen. Nor did the importance of that role end with his subsequent transformation into philosopher and medieval thinker; for if these new versions of Dōgen have continued to depend on the findings of Zen scholarship, that scholarship itself has continued to reflect the interests of sectarian tradition.

It was no mere idiosyncrasy that led the Rinzai layman D. T. Suzuki to dismiss the Sōtō master Dōgen with few, mostly negative words; for until quite recently, almost no one from that tradition has cared to do much more. Zen scholarship in Japan is primarily the work of men who belong to one or another of the Zen churches, and inevitably it tends to divide along sectarian lines. Particularly in the case of Dōgen, whose historical significance is linked so closely to a single tradition, the field has belonged almost exclusively to Sōtō adherents, many of whom were raised in temples and are themselves ordained in the order. It is not surprising, therefore, that despite valiant efforts to transcend the limits of the old sectarian scholarship, the influence of Tokugawa dogmatics has persisted. Menzan's interpretations of Dōgen still find their way into the annotation of the latest editions, into the most modern dictionaries, and inevitably, into the studies and translations based on such materials. Thus, in the face of considerable real progress, the orthodox image of Dōgen has been preserved largely intact. It is this image, an antique, so to speak, from the early Edo, that we are now importing.

While we have been importing Dōgen, the Japanese have begun work on a new model. In part this is the result of pressure brought to bear on traditional positions by the historians to whom I have referred; in part it is the product of the recent discovery of Dōgen by non-Sōtō Zen specialists, who are unimpressed by—and sometimes antagonistic toward—Sōtō apologetics. More broadly seen, it represents one aspect of a general development of contemporary Zen studies toward a more critical approach based on modern philological and historiographic principles. This development owes much to research in the Tun-huang manuscripts of early Chinese Ch'an, documents that have forced scholars to become sensitive to textual and historical problems and gradually to recognize the extent to which our view of Ch'an and Zen history has been informed by sectarian traditions. Prompted by such recognition, Zen studies have embarked on a wide-ranging reevaluation of the history and literature of the school. That process has just begun, but already it has begun to reach Dōgen. To date its most important fruit has been the renewed efforts to collect, publish, and evaluate the manuscripts of the *Shōbō genzō* and other documents by and about Dōgen. This is an essential first step, one which will make possible much more sophisticated textual and historical inquiry. At the same time, that inquiry itself has begun to make some headway, and while it may still be too soon to see just where it will lead, already it has raised some interesting new questions about the historical Dōgen and his Zen message.

I do not want here to review the recent literature on Dōgen or to explore the full range of issues addressed by that literature. Instead, I

shall limit myself to the example of a single such issue, that of the historical origins of Dōgen's Zen. This example should serve well in several
ways. First, the subject is of intrinsic interest, because it is crucial to an
understanding of Dōgen, both of his career and of his Zen teachings. It is
also of historical importance for the central role it played in the formation of Sōtō ideology and, therefore, can serve to indicate something of
how that ideology affects our image of Dōgen. Finally, because of its
importance, the topic has attracted the attention of recent scholarship;
through it, then, we can get a glimpse of the sorts of questions that are—
and are not yet—being raised for the Sōtō tradition. Let us begin with a
brief rehearsal of how that tradition has depicted the origins of Dōgen's
Zen.

If modern writers, both Japanese and Western, have often been
attracted to Dōgen's metaphysics and have held him up as one of Japan's
first and foremost philosophers, his own followers have appreciated him
more as the consummate theoretician of Zen practice. For the Sōtō tradition, at least since Menzan, what distinguishes "Dōgen Zen" is not so
much its doctrines of "being-time," impermanent Buddha nature, and so
on, as its teachings of the unity of Buddhist practice and enlightenment
(shushō ittō) and the attendant meditation known as "just sitting" *(shikan taza)* in which that unity is realized. And while the philosophers may
tend to deduce such religious teachings from Dōgen's metaphysical
theories—or the intellectual historian to reduce them to patterns of
Kamakura Buddhist soteriology—Sōtō commentators have seen them as
the very "eye of the true *dharma*" *(shōbō genzō),* the essence of the Buddha's wisdom historically transmitted through the lineage of the Zen
patriarchs. Whatever else this may mean, it means that, for them, Dōgen
did not invent his Zen but, rather, discovered it in China.

According to his traditional biography, Dōgen's discovery of the
true *dharma* was the culmination of a long religious search, and his doctrine of enlightened practice the solution to the theological issue that had
motivated that search. As a Tendai novice on Mt. Hiei, we are told,
Dōgen was troubled by the question of how to understand Buddhist
practice, given the Mahayana doctrine of inherent enlightenment. Unable to find a Tendai teacher who could solve this problem, he was led to
Zen and, eventually, to the school's monasteries on the continent. There,
at first, he had little better luck, for the Ch'an school in the thirteenth
century had lost the original spirit of the religion: its great monasteries
were corrupted by secular interests and dominated by the followers of the
Lin-chi master Ta-hui Tsung-kao (1089–1163), whose utilitarian approach to religious practice, based on the generation of a sudden insight
through the practice of *k'an-hua,* or contemplation of the *kung-an,*
ignored the very premises of Dōgen's search. After several years of study
under the leading Lin-chi prelates of his day, Dōgen was ready to admit

defeat and return to Japan. At this point, he met the new abbot of Ching-te ssu at T'ien-t'ung shan, the Ts'ao-tung master Ju-ching.

T'ien-t'ung Ju-ching (1163–1228) was different from the other masters of the Southern Sung. Indeed, he was an outspoken critic of the Ch'an of his day: he resisted the growing secularization of the school's institutions and advocated a strict monastic routine; he lamented the shallow understanding of his contemporaries and called for a return to the ancient ways of the patriarchs. He rejected the current Lin-chi emphasis on *k'an-hua* and, in its place, advocated the meditation of just sitting, in which the practitioner, by abandoning his conscious efforts to acquire Buddhahood, "sloughs off," as he said, "body and mind" *(shin-jin datsuraku)* and abides in his inherent enlightenment. Here was the answer to Dōgen's quest. In the summer retreat of 1225, upon hearing Ju-ching's teaching of *shinjin datsuraku,* he himself sloughed off body and mind. He was twenty-five years old. Two years later, when he parted from his master to return to Japan, he did so as the certified successor to the Ts'ao-tung lineage of Ju-ching; and upon arrival on his native soil, he immediately set about disseminating Ju-ching's teachings and laying the foundations for Japanese Sōtō Zen.[1]

Such in barest outline is the traditional account of the origins of Dōgen's Zen. Whatever we may say of its details, it is clear that the account involves at least two historical claims: (1) that Dōgen's Zen represents the expression of his acceptance at T'ien-t'ung shan of the teaching of his master, Ju-ching; and (2) that this teaching preserved a unique form of Buddhism, different from (and superior to) that which had developed in the contemporary Lin-chi tradition. Behind this history, it should be recognized, stands the ideology of the *shōbō genzō,* which holds that true Buddhism is nothing but the expression of the enlightened mind itself, and that, therefore, such Buddhism does not undergo historical development, but only preserves, or recapitulates through the lineage of the patriarchs, what was known to Śākyamuni himself. Because Dōgen's Zen is the *shōbō genzō,* he must have acquired it all at once and in toto through his encounter with Ju-ching; because the Sung Lin-chi tradition no longer preserved the ancient ways of the Buddhas and patriarchs, Ju-ching stands alone as Dōgen's sole link to the *shōbō genzō.*

The fact that the historical account is bound to an ideological position does not, in itself, render it false. By the same token, the fact that evidence for the account, as we shall shortly see, can be found in Dōgen's own writings does not establish its adequacy as history. For Dōgen was not a historian. His presentation of Ju-ching as the sole representative of the patriarchal lineage and of himself as the faithful transmitter of Ju-ching's teachings clearly tells us something important about Dōgen's religion, but it is not clear that it tells us much about the historical circumstances—at least as these are understood by the secular historian—under which he adopted that religion. As they have come to realize this, some modern investigators have begun to step back from Dōgen's religion and to weigh his presentation against other kinds of historical evidence. The motives for this have not only been methodological. For once Dōgen had emerged as a major—and a characteristically Japanese—religious thinker, his interpreters could hardly rest content with the image of him as mere transmitter of Chinese tradition: they have needed to establish what was original in his Zen. This has led them most immediately to the question of what he did and did not take from his master.

For some years now it has been recognized that the question of Ju-ching's teachings and their influence on Dōgen is highly problematic. The problem stems from the nature of our sources. Whatever importance he may have had for Dōgen, the fact remains that Ju-ching was not a significant figure in the history of Chinese Ch'an. Consequently, the standard histories of the school do not preserve his teachings. What is preserved, outside Dōgen's own writings, is limited to two brief records of his sayings, purportedly collected by his Chinese disciples but extant only in Japanese editions of the seventeenth and eighteenth centuries. Despite its late date, there is reason to believe that at least some of this material is authentic; and if it is, it raises serious questions about the historical adequacy of Dōgen's presentation of Ju-ching's teachings. For the Ju-ching found here bears scant resemblance to Dōgen's "former master, the old Buddha" *(senshi kobutsu)*. This Ju-ching never mentions the crucial doctrines of *shikan taza* and *shinjin datsu-raku* and puts no particular emphasis on meditation practice, let alone on its identity with the *shōbō genzō*. He does not assert his Ts'ao-tung heritage, nor is he critical of the Lin-chi tradition. He displays no marked dissatisfaction with current styles of Ch'an and, indeed, is rather difficult to distinguish from the bulk of Southern Sung abbots Dōgen so despises.[2]

If some intellectual historians have welcomed the Ju-ching texts as evidence for Dōgen's originality, sectarian scholars have sometimes been troubled by them for the same reason. Unfortunately, neither has yet subjected them to the sort of detailed critical study that alone might determine their historical value. But if we must, therefore, continue to use these texts with care, this very fact reminds us that we need to be equally critical in our use of Dōgen's writings, bringing to bear on their interpretation what we know of their provenance and textual histories. An obvious case in point here is the *Hōkyō ki*, Dōgen's own record of Ju-ching's teachings.

This interesting little work purports to contain the private instructions given to Dōgen by his master during the former's stay at T'ien-t'ung shan (hence its title: "Record from the Pao-ch'ing [era of the Sung, 1225–1227]"). Among these instructions are some that accord well with the characteristic features of Dōgen's own Zen, a fact often used in arguments for his fidelity to his master. Yet to the extent that the *Hōkyō ki* represents Dōgen's work, such use clearly begs the question. The assumption has been that the text preserves a set of notes, taken down more or less verbatim at T'ien-t'ung, but the evidence for this is not strong. On the contrary, we know from a colophon to the text that the work is a posthumous edition made by Dōgen's chief disciple, Koun Ejō (1198–1280), from papers he claims to have discovered among his master's personal effects. It is quite possible, therefore, that the material we now have—even if it owes little to Ejō's editing—could have been composed or revised well after the period it purports to record.[3]

The question of the provenance of the *Hōkyō ki* is particularly important because our earliest reliable sources for Dōgen's teachings date from several years after his return from China. To be sure, his biographers have generally held that his famous meditation manual, the *Fukan zazen gi,* was composed in 1227, almost immediately upon that return; and on these grounds the work has often been seen as a kind of manifesto of the Zen teachings he brought back from T'ien-t'ung. But in fact, neither of the extant versions of this text can be reliably dated earlier than 1233, some years after Dōgen had begun to establish himself as an independent Zen teacher. Hence, if the evidence of the *Hōkyō ki* is inconclusive, we simply do not know how much of Dōgen's Zen was learned in China and how much developed after his return to Japan.[4]

While the lack of reliable early sources makes it possible thus to doubt the traditional account of the origins of Dōgen's Zen, such doubt by no means rests merely on argument *ad ignorantiam.* For the critical reading of Dōgen's texts has also provided evidence of a positive sort that his teachings underwent real—indeed striking—development during the course of his ministry. The texts in question are primarily those of the *Shōbō genzō.* This collection, widely regarded as Dōgen's magnum opus and a masterpiece of religious writing, is often treated as a single work; but it must be remembered that it is no more than a random collection— or more properly, several such collections—of independent texts, and that the composition of these texts, the bulk of which were first presented in the form of lectures, spans a period of some two decades, covering almost the entirety of Dōgen's teaching career. Fortunately, most bear colophons recording the dates of their composition. Hence, while important questions about the origin of the several redactions of the *Shōbō genzō* certainly remain, it has been possible to establish a fairly exact chronology of their component texts.[5]

When the *Shōbō genzō* is read with an eye for its chronology, it becomes apparent that, on several topics, Dōgen changed his views quite radically. This is not to deny that there may be a constant vision, or set of premises, underlying the whole; but it must be admitted that the changes are sufficiently pronounced, and the views involved sufficiently impor-

tant, that it becomes difficult indeed to maintain the picture of a mono-
lithic system of religious teachings. Rather, as is now gradually becoming
acknowledged, it is necessary to speak at least of an early and a late (if
not a middle) Dōgen. It need hardly be emphasized that this way of
speaking tends to undermine the traditional story of how Dōgen arrived
at his religion. Interestingly enough, the very motifs associated with that
story are among the topics on which he seems to have changed his mind.

Our earliest example of Dōgen's Zen teachings is probably the
Bendō wa ["Talks on pursuing the way"], thought to have been written
in 1231. From that date, over the next decade, in addition to composing
over a dozen of the vernacular texts collected in the *Shōbō genzō,* he
wrote several important Chinese works, including such influential pieces
as the *Fukan zazen gi, Gakudō yōjin shū,* and *Tenzo kyōkun.* These early
works already display some of the religious themes characteristic of
Dōgen's mature teachings. What they do not show is the kind of historical doctrine that underlies the traditional account of how he acquired
such teachings. To be sure, Ju-ching is mentioned and identified as
Dōgen's teacher, but he is mentioned only rarely and is hardly singled out
for special praise, let alone held up as the sole living representative of the
true *dharma.* Nor does Ju-ching's Ts'ao-tung heritage have any particular claim to the transmission of that *dharma.* On the contrary, as we shall
see, the emphasis, if any, is on the more common notion that the *shōbō
genzō* has been handed down in all the traditions of Ch'an.[6]

Around 1240–1241, Dōgen seems to have begun work in earnest on
the texts of the *Shōbō genzō,* and the next four years saw the composition of over two thirds of the material in that collection. They also wit-
nessed the emergence of a number of new themes in Dōgen's teachings.
One of these is an exaggerated emphasis on his Chinese master. Beginning in 1241, Ju-ching suddenly starts to appear regularly in Dōgen's
writings, and by 1243, he has come to dominate the *Shōbō genzō.* In the
twenty-five texts dated from the latter year, he is cited fully three dozen
times. In these citations, for the first time he becomes closely identified
with the doctrines of *shikan taza* and *shinjin datsuraku* and is now regularly quoted as the authority for various criticisms of contemporary
Ch'an. Dōgen's praise of his master becomes increasingly hyperbolic.

The important *Gyōji* ["Sustained practice"] fascicle, of 1242,
devoted to edifying examples of great Ch'an practitioners, reserves a
long, final section for Ju-ching. Here for the first time Dōgen attributes
to his master the doctrine that Zen practice is sloughing off body and
mind, achieved through just sitting; he goes on to declare that only Ju-
ching, of all contemporary Chinese masters, has understood this doctrine
and laments the fact that he is unappreciated in his own land.[7] A similar
refrain appears in many of the works composed during the succeeding
months. In the *Butsudō* and *Bukkyō* texts, of the following year, Ju-

ching again stands alone against all Sung Ch'an, and Dōgen wonders how the Chinese could think that T'ang masters like Lin-chi I-hsüan (d. 866) and Te-shan Hsüan-chien (782?–865), let alone contemporary masters, are his equal (*DZZ* 1:380, 409, 413). The *Baika,* from the same period, is taken up almost entirely with Dōgen's master, of whom it is said there has been no one of his stature before or after (*DZZ* 1:460); he is "the old Buddha among old Buddhas" (*DZZ* 1:462). Similarly, in texts from the following weeks, we learn that there has not been an old Buddha like Ju-ching in China for the last two or three hundred years (*Henzan, DZZ* 1:492), and that no one during the last four or five hundred years has so thoroughly grasped the "eye of the Buddhas and patriarchs" (*Zanmai ō zanmai, DZZ* 1:539).

The new emphasis on the uniqueness of Ju-ching coincides with a new sense of the limits of the historical transmission of the *shōbō genzō.* This aspect of Dōgen's Zen, perhaps because it is embarrassing to modern ecumenical sensitivities, has not been well reported. On the contrary, most recent interpreters have presented Dōgen as envisioning a universal religion, based solely on the Buddhism of Śākyamuni and transcending all historical sectarian division. As evidence, they can cite his repeated emphasis on the true *dharma* as the sufficient criterion for orthodoxy and his explicit rejection, particularly in the *Butsudō* ["Way of the Buddha"] text of the *Shōbō genzō,* of the very notion of a distinct Zen school —not to mention the five houses *(goke)* into which it is commonly divided. Yet if such sentiments appear on the surface to reflect a refreshingly ecumenical spirit, just below that surface moves a specter of a very different sort. For as is perfectly clear from the *Butsudō* text itself, Dōgen's position, far from affirming a catholic appreciation of diverse forms of Buddhism, is intended precisely to limit the true religion to a single historical tradition.

Already in his earliest writings it is clear that Dōgen considers the *Shōbō genzō* a historical reality, preserved only in the Zen tradition he has now brought from China. The *Bendō wa* opens with a rehearsal of that tradition.

> The Great Master Śākyamuni transmitted the *dharma* to Kāśyapa at the assembly on Vulture Peak. It was then correctly passed from patriarch to patriarch down to the Worthy Bodhidharma. He proceeded to the kingdom of Cīnasthāna [i.e., China], where he transmitted the *dharma* to the Great Master Hui-k'o. This was the first transmission of the *Buddha-dharma* in the Eastern Land. (*DZZ* 1:730)

Buddhist texts, Dōgen goes on here to say, may have existed in China before the advent of Bodhidharma, but no one understood them; it was only after his arrival that the pure *Buddha-dharma* spread there.

Lest his audience miss the point, he concludes with the hope that this same *dharma* will now spread in Japan.

In the *Bendō wa,* Dōgen traces the "single transmission" *(tanden)* of the *dharma* down to the Sixth Patriarch, Hui-neng (638–713). He then proceeds to describe the subsequent history of the faith.

> The Sixth Patriarch had two "supernatural feet" *(jinsoku)*: Huai-jang of Nan-Yüeh and Hsing-ssu of Ch'ing-yüan. Both carried on the transmission of the Buddha seal, becoming the teachers of men and gods. As their two factions developed, they opened five gates: the schools of Fa-yen, Kuei-yang, Ts'ao-tung, Yün-men, and Lin-chi. Today in the Great Sung, it is the Lin-chi school alone that dominates everywhere. The five houses differ, but they all [bear] the one Buddha mind seal. (*DZZ* 1:730)

Later, in the *Butsudō,* Dōgen would claim that, though he had himself once thought to investigate "the dark import of the five schools," after studying under Ju-ching, he had realized that the term "five schools" was a "corrupt expression" (*DZZ* 1:380); but here, in his earliest extant work, it is clear that Dōgen, like more of his Ch'an contemporaries, still believed that after Hui-neng the single line of Zen patriarchs split into several lineages, each transmitting the orthodox *dharma.* The same belief is expressed in the *Fukan zazen gi,* of 1233: "From the Western Heavens [i.e., India] to the Eastern Land, the patriarchal teaching opened five gates. All equally maintain the Buddha seal, while each enjoys its own style of teaching" (*DZZ* 2:4). As late as 1240, Dōgen continues to emphasize the five houses of Ch'an. In the *Den'e,* from that year, he declares that the custom of transmitting the Buddhist robe from patriarch to patriarch as a sign of the *shōbō genzō* did not end with Hui-neng but was preserved for subsequent generations by the founding patriarchs of the five schools (*DZZ* 1:289).

By 1243, as we have seen, when he wrote the *Butsudō,* Dōgen had changed his mind and come to reject the notion of five orthodox houses. In its stead, he had begun to preach a more radical doctrine, which extended the the single transmission of the *shōbō genzō* beyond the Sixth Patriarch to his disciple Ch'ing-yüan and the line of his descendants leading to Tung-shan Liang-chieh (807–869), founder of the Ts'ao-tung school. This new doctrine appears, in fact, in the conclusion of the *Butsudō* text itself. After examining the origins of the various Ch'an traditions, Dōgen observes,

> The treasury of the eye of the true *dharma* of the Old Buddha [Hui-neng] was correctly transmitted only to the Eminent Patriarch Ch'ing-yüan. Even if we concede that [Hui-neng] had two "supernatural feet" equally possessed of the way, the Eminent Patriarch [Ch'ing-yüan] represents the sole pace of the true supernatural foot *(shō jinsoku no doppo)*. . . . The Great

Master Tung-shan was the legitimate successor *(tekishi)* in the fourth generation after Ch'ing-yüan. He correctly received the transmission of the treasury of the eye of the true *dharma* and opened the eye of the marvelous mind of *nirvana (nehan myōshin)*. There is no other transmission; there is no other school. *(DZZ* 1:385–386.)

The first signs of this startling new doctrine appear in 1241, coincident with the new emphasis on Ju-ching. At the outset of that year, in a little document called *Busso* ["The Buddhas and patriarchs"], Dōgen set down the lineage of the *shōbō genzō*. It opens with the traditional set of seven Buddhas, twenty-eight Indian patriarchs, and six Chinese patriarchs; but now Dōgen proceeds from Hui-neng to list seventeen masters from Ch'ing-yüan through Tung-shan to Ju-ching. The list is followed by a note: "During the summer retreat of the first year of the Pao-ch'ing era of the Great Sung [1225], attending upon the Great Teacher, my former master the Old Buddha of T'ien-t'ung, I, Dōgen, completed my obeisance to this Buddha and patriarch. It was 'but one Buddha to another' *(yui butsu yo butsu)."* *(DZZ* 1:456)

Two months later, Dōgen composed the *Shisho*, in which he argues that the true transmission of the *Buddha-dharma* must always be accompanied by a formal rite of succession *(shihō)* and certified by a proper document of succession *(shisho)*. He goes on to describe several such documents, from various lineages, that he himself saw while on the continent, and he expresses his appreciation for all. However, at the close of the text, he introduces a remarkable new element: the certificate of succession of "our Tung-shan tradition" *(waga Tōzan monka)* is different from that of Lin-chi and the others, for it is based on a document written in the mingled blood of Hui-neng and Ch'ing-yüan. This is the procedure for the certificate of succession followed by the First and Second Patriarchs and handed down from the Seven Buddhas. "Only the Eminent Patriarch Ch'ing-yüan . . . obtained such certification; no other patriarch could do so. Those who know of this fact say that the *Buddha-dharma* was correctly transmitted only to Ch'ing-yüan." *(DZZ* 1:345)

The new emphasis on the lineage of Ch'ing-yüan, Tung-shan, and Ju-ching now becomes a standard feature of Dōgen's account of the orthodox transmission of the *shōbō genzō*. The *Busshō,* from the end of 1241, speaks of the maintenance of Śākyamuni's teachings through twenty-eight Indian and twenty-three Chinese generations; these teachings have been correctly transmitted for 2190 years, during fifty generations, down to "my former master, the teacher Ching of T'ien-t'ung."[8] The *Menju,* of 1243, opens with the famous legend of the first transmission of the *shōbō genzō* on Vulture Peak. It then goes on to describe the subsequent tradition.

This is the meaning of the treasury of the eye of the true *dharma* personally bequeathed *(menju)* from Buddha to Buddha and patriarch to patriarch. It was correctly transmitted from the Seven Buddhas to the Worthy Kāśyapa. From Kāśyapa it was bequeathed twenty-eight times down to the Worthy Bodhidharma. Descending to Cīnasthāna he personally bequeathed it to the Worthy Hui-k'o, the Great Master P'u-chüeh, Great Patriarch of the True School. Through five transmissions it reached the Great Master Ta-chien Hui-neng of Ts'ao-ch'i shan. Through seventeen bequests it reached my former master, the Old Buddha of T'ien-t'ung, renowned Mt. T'ai-po of Ch'ing-yüan county of the Great Sung.

The transmission of the *shōbō genzō* does not stop with Ju-ching. Dōgen goes on here:

On the first day of the fifth month of the first year of the Pao-ch'ing era of the Great Sung, I, Dōgen, first offered incense and made obeisance at the Terrace of Sumeru (Miao-kao t'ai) [at Ching-te ssu] to my former master, the Old Buddha of T'ien-t'ung. On that occasion, when my former master, the Old Buddha, saw me for the first time, directly and personally bequeathing [the *shōbō genzō*] to me, he said, "The *dharma* personally bequeathed from Buddha to Buddha and patriarch to patriarch is [hereby] realized. This is [Śākyamuni's] holding up a flower on Vulture Peak; it is [Hui-k'o's] attainment of the marrow on Sung-shan; it is the transmission of the robe [to Hui-neng] on Huang-mei; it is the personal bequeathal of Tung-shan. This is the personal bequeathal of the treasury of the eye of the Buddhas and patriarchs. It exists only within our chambers *(go oku ri);* others have never even dreamt of it."[9]

Having thus succeeded to the lineage of the *shōbō genzō,* Dōgen can now speak, as he does later in this text, of "the seven Buddhas and fifty-one generations." *(DZZ* 1:448) In the *Baika,* from the same period, we read of the "seven Buddha patriarchs, twenty-eight patriarchs of the Western Heavens, and six patriarchs together with the nineteen patriarchs of the Eastern Land."[10] Dōgen is now privy to an esoteric tradition of the *shōbō genzō,* secretly transmitted only among the patriarchs of the Ts'ao-tung lineage. In the *Jishō zanmai,* of 1244, he writes,

Be it known: it is under Ch'ing-yüan shan that the certificate of succession of the Buddhas and patriarchs in the Western Heavens and Eastern Lands has been correctly transmitted. From Ch'ing-yüan shan, it was correctly transmitted to Tung shan. This is known to no one else in the ten directions; only the descendants of Tung-shan know it. *(DZZ* 1:559)

On the basis of such claims to an exclusive lineage of the *shōbō genzō,* we might expect Dōgen to reject as heterodox all Ch'an masters falling outside his own tradition. In fact, he does not. Rather, the curious logical tension between the universal *shōbō genzō* and its historical instantiation is maintained, and in Dōgen's later writings we continue to find appreciations of masters from all the houses of Ch'an. There is only one that comes in for regular criticism—and this, perhaps less on the basis of its lineage than on the personal failings of its members. The house is Lin-chi, and again the criticism of it begins with the new emphasis on Ju-ching.

We have seen that in his early writings Dōgen still held to the notion of five legitimate traditions of Ch'an. The Lin-chi house was no exception. On the contrary, as late as 1242, when he wrote the *Gyōji*, Dōgen had only the highest praise for the founder of the house, Lin-chi I-hsüan. Commenting on a conversation between I-hsüan and his master, Huang-po, he applauds the sincerity of Lin-chi's practice and describes him as the "legitimate heir" of Huang-po. Indeed, Lin-chi is without peer: "Lin-chi and Te-shan are known as the 'heroes of the patriarchal seat,' but how could Te-shan approach Lin-chi? Truly one such as Lin-chi stands beyond the crowd." (*DZZ* 1:136)

Here Dōgen seems to prefer Lin-chi to his contemporary Te-shan Hsüan-chien, in the lineage leading to the Yün-men and Fa-yen schools. But already by this time he had begun to single out these two T'ang "heroes" for unfavorable treatment. In the *Butsu kōjō ji,* written only a few days before the *Gyōji,* he comments on Tung-shan's expression "what lies beyond the Buddha" *(butsu kōjō).* Introducing Tung-shan as the legitimate heir of his master, Yün-yen T'an-sheng (780?–841), and the thirty-eighth patriarch after the Tathāgata, Dōgen goes on,

> The eminent Patriarch Tung-shan is the Buddha and patriarch beyond the Buddhas and patriarchs. For while there may be many other Buddhas and patriarchs *(butsumen somen),* none has even dreamt of this saying, "beyond the Buddha." Te-shan and Lin-chi may talk about it, but they do not accede *(jōtō)* to it. (*DZZ* 1:226)

This kind of remark recurs several times in subsequent texts. In the *Butsudō,* as we have already had occasion to see, Dōgen compares Lin-chi and Te-shan unfavorably with his master, Ju-ching, and elsewhere we are told that they cannot compare with Ju-ching's own master, Hsüeh-tou Chih-chien (1105–1192) (*Mitsugo, DZZ* 1:396). In the *Kattō*, from 1243, Dōgen praises a saying of Chao-chou (778–897), commenting that his words cannot be matched by Lin-chi, Te-shan, Ta-kuei (771–853) or Yün-men (864–949) (*DZZ* 1:335). Again, the *Mujō seppō,* of the same year, concludes with the remark that only those (like Tung-shan) who are Buddhas and patriarchs master the doctrine that insentient beings preach the *dharma (mujō seppō);* it cannot be known by the likes of Lin-chi and Te-shan (*DZZ* 1:404). By 1244, these two masters have become the butt of sarcastic jokes. In the *Dai shugyō,* in commenting on the famous story that Po-chang had among his followers one who had been born 500 times as a fox in recompense for giving a false answer to a student's question, Dōgen remarks,

> [Even if his answer were wrong,] it does not necessarily follow that he fell into the body of a fox. For if it were inevitable that one becomes a fox on the basis of a false answer to a student's question, how many thousands of times more recently would Lin-chi, Te-shan, and their followers have become foxes. . . . Yet I have not heard that they have become foxes.[11]

Criticism of Lin-chi in the *Shōbō genzō* is by no means limited to such passing gibes. As early as the *Daigo,* composed in the first month of 1242, Dōgen expresses mild doubts about Lin-chi's understanding of Buddhism.[12] By 1243, he is going out of his way to attack him. The *Sesshin sesshō* contrasts the teachings of Lin-chi and Tung-shan, concluding that the former's famous expression "the true man of no rank" *(wu-wei chen-jen)* has not yet "fully penetrated" the truth (*DZZ* 1:362). In the *Butsudō,* we learn that Lin-chi in fact never understood his own master, Huang-po (*DZZ* 1:384–384); and the *Bukkyō* ["Scriptures of the Buddha"], written a few days later, pursues this point in some detail. Complaining that in recent centuries Ch'an monks have rejected the *sūtras* in favor of such formulae as Lin-chi's "four considerations" *(ssu liao-chien),* Yün-men's "three propositions" *(san chü)* or Tung-shan's "five ranks" *(wu wei),* Dōgen goes on to discuss Lin-chi himself. Recalling the famous account of his enlightenment, he complains that the story has led people to think that Lin-chi alone transmitted Huang-po's Buddhism. Such is by no means the case: Lin-chi was "not of the highest caliber" as a student and never reached the level of his master.

> Huang-po was an old Buddha transcending [the Buddhas of] past and present, more worthy than Po-chang, more brilliant than Ma-tsu. But Lin-chi had no such talents. For he never said anything original even in his dreams. He just comprehended the many and forgot the one, or reached the one and was vexed by the many. Why should anyone think that his "four considerations," and so on, have "the flavor of the way" and take them as guides to the study of the *dharma?*[13]

Dōgen's dissatisfaction with the founder of the Lin-chi house does not lead him to reject the entire tradition: he continues to have high praise for certain of Lin-chi's descendants. Still, there can be no doubt that the attack on the founder is the extension of more general criticism of the school, at least as it had developed in Sung times. Although in his early works Dōgen seems to have no particular complaints about contemporary Ch'an, the texts written after his rediscovery of Ju-ching are heavy with lamentations over the decline of the *dharma* in China and bristling with rebukes of the ignorant, illiterate, ambitious, insincere, heretical, and downright demonic monks that had come to dominate the religion there. These references are not always explicitly to members of the Lin-chi school; but as we have seen Dōgen himself point out, it was this school that held sway in the Southern Sung. By implication, it is this school that must bear responsibility.

Already before his first open attacks on Lin-chi I-hsüan himself, Dōgen was beginning to complain about the founder's contemporary descendants. In the *Zazen shin,* for example, from early 1242, "a bunch calling themselves a branch of Lin-chi" is criticized for its view that meditation is only a practice for beginners, transcended by those who recognize Zen in every act. They take this view because they lack correct transmission of the *Buddha-dharma* (*DZZ* 1:91). The perversion of transmission is the subject of criticism in the *Shisho,* written a year earlier. There we are told of "fellows styling themselves distant descendants of Lin-chi," who claim succession from a master on the basis simply of their possession of his portrait or copies of his writings. One pack of "dogs" even goes so far as to collect such possessions and trade on them with government officials for appointment to the abbacy of monasteries.[14]

Exactly who these ambitious Lin-chi prelates are, Dōgen does not tell us here, but elsewhere he is more explicit. In the *Gyōji* section on Ju-ching that we have already had occasion to cite, he singles out a certain Kuang Fo-chao as an example of one who lacks "the way-seeking mind." According to Ju-ching, this man thought that one could master Buddhism through self-understanding, without recourse to a teacher. As a result, he took no care of the monks' hall or the congregation and spent his time instead chasing after official guests. He never practiced Zen. He knew nothing of the workings of the *Buddha-dharma* and only "hungered for fame and lusted after profit." "How," asked Ju-ching, "could the *Buddha-dharma* rest in the hands of such a man? What a pity!" (*DZZ* 1:158)

This Kuang Fo-chao is better known as Cho-an Te-kuang (1121–1203), an influential master in the Yang-ch'i branch of Lin-chi. He himself served as the abbot of several major Ch'an monasteries, and his disciples held the abbacies of T'ien-t'ung and Ching-shan during Dōgen's sojourn in China. He was also the master of one of the first prominent Rinzai teachers in Japan. We shall come back to this point later on, but here we need to speak of another ambitious Lin-chi abbot, Te-kuang's own master, the renowned Ta-hui Tsung-kao. Of all the descendants of Lin-chi, it is this man that comes in for the most extended criticism in the *Shōbō genzō.*

Here again, Dōgen's early works give no inkling of what is to come, for Ta-hui does not appear in the early texts of the *Shōbō genzō.*[15] The assault on this monk begins with the *Sesshin sesshō,* in 1243. The text represents a commentary on the statement by Tung-shan that there is someone within and without who "explains the mind and explains the nature" *(sesshin sesshō).* We have already seen that Dōgen finds opportunity in this work to criticize Lin-chi I-hsüan, but his real opponent here is Lin-chi's descendant Ta-hui. Dōgen quotes the latter's comment that, whereas people nowadays seem to enjoy "explaining the mind and explaining the nature" or "discussing the dark and discussing the mysterious" *(dangen danmyō),* enlightenment comes precisely when mind and nature are both discarded and dark and mysterious are both forgotten. This remark, Dōgen says, shows that Ta-hui has understood neither mind nor nature. In fact, his position has not even gone beyond the confines of the Hinayana, let alone reached the inner mysteries of the Mahayana or the higher workings of Zen. "It is difficult to say that he has tasted the fare of the Buddhas and patriarchs."[16]

This judgment, harsh as it may seem, is mild in comparison with what we find in the following year in the *Jishō zammai* ["Samādhi of self-verification"]. We have already noted that this work, surely one of the most remarkable in the *Shōbō genzō,* advances the doctrine of the secret lineage of Tung-shan. That passage appears as the conclusion to the text, most of which is taken up with Ta-hui. After explaining that Buddhism is ultimately a matter of "self-verification" *(jishō)* and "self-awakening" *(jigo),* Dōgen warns that such expressions do not imply, as some non-Buddhists think, that one can simply study religion on one's own, without transmission from a master; nor is the self referred to here to be confused with the Hinayana notion of the five aggregates. Thereupon, he turns to Ta-hui.

Ta-hui once studied under a Ts'ao-tung master named Tao-wei (d.u.), from whom he asked a certificate of succession. The master refused, saying that he could not make a hasty bequest to one who still "lacked the eye." Ta-hui responded, "The true eye we originally possess is verified of itself and awakened of itself *(jishō jigo);* how can you say that you cannot make a hasty bequest?" Tao-wei just laughed (*DZZ* 1:556). Although this passage is presumably intended simply as an example of a misunderstanding of the expressions "self-verification" and "self-awakening," Dōgen uses it to launch an extended and vitriolic *ad hominem* attack on Ta-hui himself. After quoting a long passage to show that Ta-hui was rejected again by his subsequent teacher, Wen-chun (1061–1115), he goes on to comment. The text is too long to translate here, but it is worth a paraphrastic summary. Tao-wei, Dōgen says, was correct in his evaluation of Ta-hui; for he did not investigate Buddhism, did not produce "the great doubt," did not "break through" or "slough off" body and mind. Yet he had the audacity to seek a certificate of succession. Here is the extreme example of one who lacks "the way-seeking mind" and the "investigation of the ancients." "He knows no compunction; he has no capacity for the way; he is totally uneducated. Hungering for fame and lusting after profit, he would violate the inner chambers of the Buddhas and patriarchs." And because Ta-hui himself did not understand the teachings of the Buddhas and patriarchs, most of the followers of his tradition are "phonies"; there is not a single truly solid one among them.

Dōgen is not finished. He goes on to warn us not to believe the report of Ta-hui's subsequent enlightenment under his final master, Yüan-wu K'o-ch'in (1063–1135); for he shows no sign that he made further progress. Yüan-wu was "an old Buddha, rare even in the other world," but Ta-hui comes nowhere near him. His wisdom is nothing but a few memorized passages from the *Avataṁsaka* or *Śūraṅgama sūtras*. He confuses the *Buddha-dharma* with the view of "recluses taken by the spirits of the grasses and trees." Moreover, after Ta-hui left Yüan-wu, he never completed his training but rushed instead to become the head of great monasteries. In the end, he never clarified the great *dharma* but simply "ran his mouth."

Yet, Dōgen continues, the ignorant think that Ta-hui was the equal of the ancients. They should look to Tao-wei's opinion of him. There are many in Sung China who call themselves the descendants of the Buddhas and patriarchs but few who study and teach the truth. Ta-hui's case is a good example. And if things were bad in his day, how much worse are they now, when the monks are led by men who have no idea of the great way of the Buddhas and patriarchs. Dōgen goes on here to explain that this great way is preserved only by the descendants of Ch'ing-yüan and Tung-shan and then concludes with a parting shot at Ta-hui and his followers. Ta-hui never understood the expression "self-verification and self-awakening," much less any other *kōan*. Who, then, among those who come after him could be expected to understand? The teachings of the Buddhas and patriarchs express their very bones and marrow; these "pedestrian types" do not even get their skin.[17]

So much, then, for Dōgen's vision of the history of the *shōbō genzō*. Whatever else we may say of that vision, the dates of these texts would seem to leave little doubt that it was well over a decade after his return to Japan and at the very midpoint of his ministry that Dōgen first began to espouse the doctrine that pitted the teachings and lineage of his master against the Lin-chi tradition of Ta-hui. The relatively late and rather sudden nature of this development naturally raises the question of its proximate cause; and as the question has become more widely recognized, several scholars have in fact come forward to propose explanations. One of these is Masutani Fumio, a specialist in Japanese Buddhist literature and a long-time student as well as recent translator of the *Shōbō genzō*. In his article "Rinzai to Dōgen: Dōgen no shisō teki tenkai" ["Lin-chi and Dōgen: Dōgen's intellectual development"], in which he traces the chronology of Dōgen's attitudes toward Lin-chi, Masutani criticizes the assumption by traditional scholars of the *Shōbō genzō* that Dōgen's Zen was fully formed through his enlightenment under Ju-ching. He emphasizes instead what he calls Dōgen's "inner development" *(naiteki tenkai)*. In an ironic turn, he takes the argument directly to his opponents by basing it on their own ideology: if, as we are told, practice and enlightenment are the same, then to the extent that Dōgen continued to practice after his return to Japan, it follows that he continued to be enlightened; therefore, we should expect his understanding of Zen to develop. As a result of such development, Dōgen came to recognize the gap that existed between his own understanding and that current in China—hence, the need to clarify the difference through a criticism of the Lin-chi tradition dominant there.[18]

Whatever its premises, the conclusion that Dōgen really did change his mind on certain matters is a welcome one. Still, the question would seem to remain why he changed it when he did and why so suddenly. Masutani's emphasis here on Dōgen's inner life leaves him little room to explore how the external world might have impinged on, and directed the development of, that life; but at the end of his article, he does call attention to one historical event coincident with the first appearance of Dōgen's new doctrine. This is the arrival in Japan of a copy of Ju-ching's recorded sayings. According to the *Kenzei ki* biography of Dōgen, he received this work on the fifth day of the eighth month of 1242. He immediately presented it to the monks in his lecture, and thereafter quotations from it begin to appear regularly in his writings. It is also, as we have seen, from around this time that he became so enamored of his former master, and Masutani speculates that Dōgen's striking inner development was stimulated by his reencounter with Ju-ching through this text.[19]

The importance of the Ju-ching text for understanding Dōgen's new teachings has been reiterated recently by Yanagida Seizan. Professor Yanagida, a leading historian of Chinese Ch'an and an expert on Lin-chi, is perhaps the foremost of those non-Sōtō Zen specialists who have lately taken an interest in Dōgen. In his article "Dōgen to Rinzai," he offers a response to Masutani's piece. Recalling that the *Nyojō goroku,* at least as we know it, does not coincide with Dōgen's own presentation of his master's teachings, Yanagida suggests that it was in fact his deep disappointment with the work that touched off Dōgen's attack on contemporary Chinese Ch'an. Upon discovering that Ju-ching's leading Chinese disciples had failed utterly to grasp his message, Dōgen became convinced that he alone preserved in Japan the true *dharma* of his master, which had now been lost on the continent. The blame for the loss rested with the prevailing Lin-chi climate there—hence, the attack on Ta-hui and his followers and, by extension, on the founder of the house, Lin-chi I-hsüan himself. Yanagida goes on to remark—in a comment worthy almost of Dōgen himself—that this attack, far from representing an inner development, is an indication of the decline in Dōgen's thinking and the onset of "senility" *(rōsui).*[20]

If these two explanations do not necessarily yield the same picture of the development of Dōgen's attitude toward Lin-chi, they do share the premise that the primary factor in this attitude was his perception of the current state of Chinese Ch'an. Other scholars have taken what in some ways represents a more radical approach to interpretation, suggesting that Dōgen's new sectarianism is less a response to Chinese Buddhism than to certain historical events in Japan. One such scholar is Furuta Shōkin, a prominent historian of Japanese Buddhism with particular interest in Rinzai Zen. Furuta reminds us that Dōgen's new teachings coincide with his withdrawal from the capital area to the isolated province of Echizen. This move, he suggests, was the culmination of a growing frustration over the increasing success of the new Rinzai movement in Japan, a frustration expressed in Dōgen's writings through his sudden outburst against the Chinese background of the movement.[21]

Immediately after his return from the continent, Dōgen stayed in Heian at Kennin ji, the monastery where he had first studied Zen. After several years, he moved out, eventually to establish his own monastery, the Kōshō ji, on the southern outskirts of the capital. Although this institution seems to have prospered, after a decade, in 1243, Dōgen suddenly abandoned it, retired to distant Echizen, and built there a new monastery. The reasons for the move have never been clear. The traditional explanation has seen it as the fulfillment of Ju-ching's final instructions to Dōgen that he dwell apart from political centers and concentrate solely on the training of his disciples. Whatever truth there may be in this, it hardly explains why it was not until the middle of his career that he made the move, and recently historians have tended rather to emphasize the political pressures brought to bear on Dōgen at this time by the Tendai establishment on Mt. Hiei. Furuta also sees sectarian politics at work here; but in his case, they are Dōgen's own political ambitions.[22]

In his article "Kangen gannen o sakai to suru Dōgen no shisō ni tsuite" ["The first year of Kangen (1243) as a dividing line in Dōgen's thought"], Furuta calls attention to the fact that already in such early texts as the *Tenzo kyōkun* and *Zuimon ki* Dōgen expressed criticism of the Zen practice at Kennin ji, and he goes on to suggest that Dōgen's own community at Kōshō ji developed in conscious opposition to that Rinzai monastery. The sense of rivalry with Rinzai was brought to a climax by the arrival in Heian of Enni Ben'en (1202–1280).[23]

Like Dōgen, Enni had first studied Zen under a disciple of Yōsai and then spent several years on the continent, where he received transmission from the important Lin-chi master Wu-chun Shih-fan (1177–1249). After returning to Japan in 1241, he was active in Kyūshū and was soon invited to the capital to become the founder of the new Tōfuku ji. This great monastic complex was built by the powerful minister Kujō Michiie (1193–1252) and was intended, it is said, to rival the ancient Nara institutions of Tōdai ji and Kōfuku ji, from which it took its name. It was located on the southern edge of Heian, quite close to the site of Dōgen's Kōshō ji. Enni arrived in the capital in the second month of 1243 and, in the eighth month, officially opened Tōfuku ji. But by this time Dōgen was gone, having suddenly abandoned his monastery only weeks before.[24]

Furuta argues that the move to Echizen represents a retreat before the ascendant star of Enni. It should be remembered that, prior to the latter's appearance, Dōgen would seem to have had reason to hope for considerable political success with his mission to the capital. He was, after all, the scion of a powerful aristocratic family and well connected not only in Heian but also at the new *bakufu* headquarters in Kamakura. He could claim *dharma* descent from Yōsai and, unlike most of Yōsai's followers, several years of training under the leading Ch'an masters of China. He had intimate knowledge of the new Chinese monastic system and, within five years of his return from the mainland, had managed to establish the first independent Zen monastery in Japan. Perhaps in anticipation of things to come, he called it Kōshō ji, after the great Hsing-sheng wan-shou ssu at Ching-shan, then probably the foremost of the "five mountains" *(wu shan)* officially recognized by the government of the Southern Sung.[25]

With the decision to make Tōfuku ji the new center of Zen in the capital and the selection of Enni as its founder, whatever hopes Dōgen might have harbored for Kōshō ji were dashed. Abandoning the field, Furuta suggests, Dōgen gathered his flock and repaired to the mountains, hoping to establish there a separate Sōtō community in opposition to the swelling Rinzai tide. The new emphasis on Ju-ching and the lineage of Tung-shan and the new bitterness toward the Lin-chi tradition both first appear in the months just preceding this move and reach their zenith in the texts written shortly after Dōgen's arrival in Echizen; and it is against this historical background, Furuta argues, that these teachings must be viewed.[26]

In effect, this explanation suggests that Dōgen's new teachings, whatever their ostensible subject, tell us more about Zen in Japan than in China; and that, whatever their reputed origins, they are less a product of his enlightenment as a student on the continent than of his ambitions as a teacher—and, be it admitted, as a politician manqué—in his own country. Elsewhere, in fact, Furuta goes on to point out that throughout his sojourn in China, and even following his return to Japan, Dōgen was himself primarily associated with the very Lin-chi tradition he came to reject. His original study of Zen, we may recall, was with the Rinzai monk Myōzen, a disciple of Yōsai. Upon arriving in China with Myōzen, he made for T'ien-t'ung shan, where Yōsai had trained. Together they studied there under the Lin-chi master Wu-chi Liao-p'ai (1149–1224), a disciple of Cho-an Te-kuang. Thereafter, Dōgen traveled alone to Ching-shan to study with Che-weng Ju-yen (1151–1225), another of Te-kuang's heirs, and later sought out P'an-shan Ssu-cho (d.u.), also of the Ta-hui faction of Lin-chi. Even in his subsequent training at T'ien-t'ung shan under Ju-ching, Furuta argues, it is doubtful that Dōgen heard much of Ts'ao-tung; for, as we have seen, Ju-ching's sayings give no evidence of such teaching, and, in fact, most of this master's own associations seem to have been with Lin-chi figures. Finally, after his return to Japan, we find Dōgen back at the Rinzai monastery of Kennin ji, where he lived for several years. And when he began thereafter to establish his own following, his major disciples turn out to be monks belonging to the lineage of Dainichi Nōnin (d.u.), himself a Japanese descendant of Te-kuang. It is only after acquiring these disciples that Dōgen began to deny his Lin-chi background and assert the unique tradition of Ju-ching.[27]

This last point is particularly important, for it raises a question, often overlooked, crucial to any interpretation of Dōgen's Zen. This is the question of the audience or audiences for which it was intended. In mid-career, it appears that Dōgen suddenly decided to abandon his proselytism in the capital and lead his followers away to found an isolated religious community of his own. This decision meant that his audience would shrink from the wider Japanese Buddhist community to the much more intimate circle of those surrounding him in Echizen. Furuta's discussion of Enni and the construction of Tōfuku ji explains Dōgen's teachings from this period in terms of the political circumstances that may have driven him to this decision; but we may also see these teachings —and, indeed, the decision itself—as reflecting the constitution of the new audience of disciples on which Dōgen was to build his church.

A version of this general approach to explanation is, in fact, sometimes used to interpret another troubling innovation in Dōgen's doctrine that dates from his move to Echizen: the denial of salvation to the layman. Perhaps because of its profound implications for the modern Sōtō church, this is probably the best-known feature of the late *Shōbō genzō* texts and the one that has done most to force a wider recognition of the contradictions between the early and late Dōgen. The early Dōgen seems to minimize the distinction between monk and layman and, indeed, states explicitly that one can achieve enlightenment in lay life.[28] Once in Echizen, however, the late Dōgen reveals that it is only the monk that can truly practice and understand Buddhism. The *Sanjūshichi hon bodai bunpō* ["The thirty-seven branches of enlightenment"], from 1244, is especially adamant on this point. In discussing the traditional Buddhist virtue of right livelihood, Dōgen defines it as "going forth from the home and cultivating the path, entering the mountains and acquiring enlightenment." No layman, he says, has succeeded to this right livelihood of Buddhism or correctly transmitted the great way of Buddhism. In the lengthy discussion that follows, Dōgen rejects several lay Buddhists respected by the tradition, including the famous Ch'an figure P'an Yün (d. 808) and even the legendary Bodhisattva Vimalakīrti. No Buddhist text, no Buddhist patriarch, he goes on, has ever claimed that the layman was the equal of the monk. Even the lawless *bhikṣu*, bereft of *dharma* and wisdom, is superior to the wise layman, obedient to the percepts. The layman simply lacks sufficient "good roots." Indeed, no layman achieved enlightenment even under the Buddha Śākyamuni himself; for lay life presents too many obstacles and is, therefore, no training ground for the study of Buddhism (*DZZ* 1:511–513).

This rather vexing new doctrine, whatever its intrinsic interest, might seem to have little direct connection with our subject, but the fact that it first occurs coincident with Dōgen's new sectarianism does give one pause. One kind of explanation for the connection is suggested—though he himself does not address the matter—by Furuta's approach. The disparagement of laymen in the *Shōbō genzō* passage just cited is accompanied by a violent attack on "a bunch calling themselves Zen monks" who, for the past two or three hundred years in China, have been claiming that lay and clerical practice are the same; to kings and ministers they say that the concerns of government are one with the concerns of the Buddhas and patriarchs, thereby winning from their ignorant patrons ecclesiastic titles. Such men have never even dreamt of the great way of the Buddhas and patriarchs. Indeed, they are not men at all: they are "demons"; they are "beasts." They are "evil dogs that seek only to eat the excrement of laymen." If monks had more excrement, these dogs would undoubtedly favor the monks (*DZZ* 1:511–512).

The scatology may be new, but both the object and the style of criticism should by now be familiar; they are one with other comments on Sung Ch'an we have already seen. And like these comments, though ostensibly they have to do with China, it may be that here too we need look no further than Heian for their inspiration. Yet if this kind of explanation is provocative, it still leaves us with the content of Dōgen's teachings and the fact that he seems to contradict himself. Some interpreters have tried to escape the contradiction by emphasizing the change in Dōgen's audience: in his early years, his message was directed at a wider Buddhist—including lay Buddhist—community; in Echizen, he was instructing his own assembly of monks. In effect, then, we have here—though probably few would care to use such terms—a distinction between exoteric and esoteric teachings.

The hallowed hermeneutic of an audience-specific teaching may appeal to some among Masutani's traditionalist opponents, for whom it can serve to insulate the master from any real intellectual development: the teachings may change, but the teacher does not. But the question of Dōgen's audience has recently been raised as well by those without claim to privileged access to the constant teacher behind the teachings. One of these is Imaeda Aishin, a historian of medieval Japanese Zen who has published several biographic studies of Dōgen. Like Furuta, Imaeda emphasizes the connection between Dōgen's new doctrines and his move to Echizen; but for him, though he recognizes the importance of events in the capital, the key lies less with the opponents Dōgen left behind than with the followers he took with him. These were the monks of what is sometimes called the "Japanese [Bodhi]dharma school" (Nihon Daruma shū), the descendants of Dainichi Nōnin.[29]

Nōnin, like his better-known contemporary Yōsai, was a Tendai monk who undertook the practice of the new Ch'an Buddhism of the Sung. Unlike Yōsai, he never visited China but apparently studied on his own, presumably from Ch'an documents beginning to filter into Japan. Criticized for his lack of proper credentials, in 1189 he dispatched two disciples to the mainland with a letter requesting certification from Ta-hui's disciple Te-kuang, then abbot of A-yü-wang shan. A certificate, declaring Nōnin the fifty-first patriarch in the lineage of the Buddha Śākyamuni, was duly granted; along with it, it seems, came other insignia of succession, including a robe and a portrait of the master.

Despite the somewhat unorthodox manner of his certification, Nōnin seems to have been quite successful in promoting his new brand of Buddhism. Whether or not he was publicly recognized in court as the "First Patriarch of the True School of Bodhidharma," as his descendants were later to claim, we know that he was sufficiently prominent to be sought out as a Zen teacher by Benchō (1162–1238), one of Hōnen's leading disciples, and later to be singled out, along with Hōnen himself, for criticism by Nichiren. But the success was not without its costs, for it brought him to the attention of the Tendai establishment. In 1194, prompted by a petition from Mt. Hiei, the court enjoined Nōnin's proselytizing activities.

Nōnin was not the only Rinzai master at this time to run afoul of the establishment: the order proscribing his Zen teachings included the name of Yōsai, who had recently returned from China and just arrived in the capital. Yōsai fought back with his famous treatise, the *Kōzen gokoku ron* ["Promotion of Zen for defense of the nation"], in which he argued for the orthodoxy of his Buddhism and sought to distinguish it from what he considered the antinomian heresies of Nōnin's Zen. In the end, as we know, Yōsai prevailed: he was invited to Kamakura by the *bakufu* government and eventually returned to the capital in triumph as the founding abbot of the government-sponsored monastery of Kennin ji.

His competitor Nōnin was less fortunate. According to one source, he was assassinated on orders of a relative, the powerful Taira general Kage-kiyo. More likely, he lived on for some years as an active teacher. But in any case, he seems to have remained an outsider, never gaining official support nor forming any alliance with Yōsai's more prosperous Zen movement. Still, he did not die without *dharma* issue.[30]

Nōnin's Zen was kept alive outside the capital by his disciple Kakuan (d.u.), who withdrew to Yamato, and by the latter's disciple Ekan (d. 1251?), who established himself in Echizen. Another of Ka-kuan's monks was Koun Ejō. According to tradition, he first visited Dōgen while the latter was still at Kennin ji. In 1234, the year after the opening of Kōshō ji, he joined the community there, and, by 1237, had become the head monk *(shuso)*. In 1241, Ekan joined Ejō at Kōshō ji, bringing with him from Echizen his own disciples Gikai (1219–1309), Giin (1217–1300), Gien (d. 1314), and others. These men were to become the nucleus of Dōgen's new community and the founding fathers of his church: two years later they would accompany him to Echizen and, after his death in 1253, would take over his monastery there and begin the work of spreading his Zen.[31]

Why the descendants of Nōnin converted to Dōgen, we do not know. It is possible that his community represented for them a Zen alternative to Yōsai's Rinzai tradition at Kennin ji, against which they may have continued to feel animosity. Both Furuta and Imaeda suggest it was, in part at least, a matter of lineage; for, as we have seen, Dōgen had studied under disciples of Nōnin's Chinese master, Te-kuang. In any case, by 1241, Dōgen had suddenly become the leader of an outcast band of Rinzai monks and, whether or not for this reason, soon found himself, like Nōnin before him, under attack from Mt. Hiei. Like Yōsai before him, he fought back, but his apologia of 1243, the *Gokoku shōbō gi* ["The meaning of the true *dharma* for the defense of the nation"], was rejected by the court. When he withdrew from the capital in the seventh month of that year, he was headed for Ekan's home base in Echizen.[32]

In several of his works on Dōgen, Imaeda emphasizes the impact of the Dharma school audience on the development of Dōgen's new teachings. It is, of course, immediately following their conversion that the emphasis on Ju-ching and the criticism of Lin-chi begin. Imaeda points out that this criticism is selective: of recent representatives of his house, it is only the Ta-hui faction that comes under attack; and of Ta-hui's many disciples, it is only Nōnin's master, Te-kuang, that is explicitly singled out. The new teachings, then, represent a project in the reeducation *(sai kyōiku)* of the Dharma school disciples, which sought to convince them of the failings of Nōnin's tradition and establish them firmly in Dōgen's Zen.[33]

The Dharma school factor may help to explain not only Dōgen's general disparagement of the Lin-chi school but also some of his specific complaints against contemporary Ch'an. It may be, for example, that behind the repeated criticisms of the independent, self-awakened Zen student lurks the image of the autodidact Nōnin, and that the extreme emphasis on correct transmission—and especially on the direct, personal bequest *(menju)* from master to disciple—is an echo of the old doubts about Nōnin's claim to Zen succession.[34] More importantly, perhaps, the conversion of the Dharma school monks may provide a key to the origin and purpose of the *Shōbō genzō* writings themselves.

If the arrival of Nōnin's followers marks the beginning of Dōgen's new teachings, it also coincides, as we have seen, with the rather sudden increase in production of the texts associated with the *Shōbō genzō*. Moreover, it should be noted that it is particularly in these vernacular pieces—and much less in Dōgen's formal essays and collected sayings in Chinese—that we find the exclusive emphasis on the Ts'ao-tung lineage and the harsh criticism of Lin-chi Ch'an. This fact may help us to understand why the *Shōbō genzō* texts were subsequently treated as secret by the Sōtō school and why, when the school finally decided to make them public, their printing was opposed by the Tokugawa authorities. It also suggests that these texts may have had a particular didactic purpose not necessarily limited to the philosophical teachings for which they are now most appreciated. We do not know when Dōgen first conceived of a collection of his vernacular writings. It now appears that he originally used the title *Shōbō genzō* for a collection, made in 1235, of 300 *kōan* cases drawn from the Chinese Ch'an literature. Presumably this work was inspired by Ta-hui's famous *kung-an* collection of the same name. Whether Dōgen was already influenced in this by contact with Ejō and his Dharma school colleagues, we cannot say; but it is possible, as Yanagida Seizan has pointed out, to see the subsequent proliferation of *kōan* commentaries that comprise the vernacular *Shōbō genzō* as the record of Dōgen's instruction to his new band of disciples in the reading and interpretation of the Chinese texts of their tradition.[35]

There is no need here to argue the relative merits of these different interpretations; nor, for that matter, are we obliged to choose among them, for they are not necessarily mutually exclusive. But we are obliged to recognize that all of them—and also, let us not forget, some of the evidence they interpret—raise questions for Sōtō tradition and, hence, for our current image of Dōgen. Perhaps the most immediately obvious of these questions is biographical. The literature on Dōgen—and not only that by Sōtō apologists—regularly depicts him as a model of the unworldly Buddhist monk and presents his life as the unfolding of a detached search for ultimate truth and a singleminded devotion to matters of the spirit. He has been encapsulated, as it were, in a kind of immaculate hagiographic shell, sterilized within from any taint of meanness, doubt, pride or ambition, and protected without from the dirt of secular history. To be sure, this is the kind of shell in which most great figures of Zen tradition tend to live, and in most cases we do not know enough of their biographies to lead them out; but in Dōgen's case, it now appears we already know too much not to do so. Whether or not, once he comes out, we shall see him as less of a man for it, we shall at least begin to see him as a man.

Historical questions about Dōgen's motives and the circumstances that might have influenced his life may be uncomfortable for those who look to him as a spiritual model, but they do not explain away his Zen. This may be obvious, but it is also easy to forget and, in fact, seems sometimes to be forgotten by both critics and defenders of the tradition. Perhaps this is a reflection, in part, of the extent to which Dōgen has been revered as the founder of the Sōtō school and his image linked to Sōtō ideology: the reverence tends to incite the irreverent historian to reductionist attack; the ideology tends to compel the pious believer to obscurantist defense. It is probably no accident that, among the examples of historical explanation we have seen here, the two least complimentary to Dōgen are proposed by scholars—Yanagida and Furuta—with background in the Rinzai tradition; it is also fallacious—and ultimately self-defeating—for Sōtō apologists to dismiss their explanations, as they sometimes have, simply on these grounds. In any case, the fact remains that neither side has yet addressed with any rigor the question of just how the new historical approaches to Dōgen will affect our understanding of his Zen. As a consequence, while some chinks may have opened in his traditional image as a man, except for a minor crack here and there, the edifice of the orthodox Tokugawa account of Dōgen's teachings has remained largely intact. Yet if that account cannot simply be replaced by historical reduction, neither can it long remain unscathed by historical revision.

We have seen that the traditional view of the origins of Dōgen's Zen emphasizes his original experience of *shinjin datsuraku,* the enlightenment that justifies and gives unity to all his subsequent teachings. Behind this emphasis, I have suggested, is the notion of the *shōbō genzō:* if Dōgen's enlightenment represents his succession to the *shōbō genzō,* it must be one with the understanding of his master; and if his teachings are the expression of the *shōbō genzō,* they must somehow constitute a coherent whole. To this extent the fact—if fact it be—that Dōgen's understanding differs markedly from that of Ju-ching raises considerable doubt about the adequacy of the *shōbō genzō* not only as a historical but also as a theoretical model for interpreting his Zen. More importantly, the fact that Dōgen may have changed his views during the course of his ministry calls into question not only the ideology of the *shōbō genzō* but the very notion of "Dōgen Zen" itself; it obliges us to bracket the assumption of a unified religious message and reexamine his entire corpus to determine anew what he did and did not say.

A case in point here is provided by the other major claim of the tradition, that Dōgen's Zen teaching of just sitting was unique to his school and differed sharply from the *kung-an* practice of Ta-hui and his Lin-chi followers. That view became orthodox after Menzan, but it was not always so clear. It was not so clear to Tokugawa Sōtō scholars like Tenkei Denson (1648–1735), against whom Menzan argued and whose accommodations with Rinzai were denounced as heresies; it was not so clear to the Sōtō monks of the Muromachi period, who continued to study Rinzai Zen and to transmit secret *kōan* study guides, often attributed to Dōgen or Ju-ching; it was apparently not clear to some of Dōgen's immediate followers, who continued for several generations to claim descent from both Dōgen and Ta-hui. The question naturally arises, then, whether it is as clear in Dōgen himself as the orthodox account would have it. There is no doubt that Dōgen came to criticize Ta-hui's Buddhism: of that, we have seen sufficient evidence from his own writings. What we have not seen—and what is difficult to find in those writings— is evidence that he criticized it on the specific religious grounds assumed by the later tradition. Thus, quite apart from the question—itself obviously problematic—of whether the tradition has adequately pictured the religion of Dōgen's Lin-chi opponents, it remains to be demonstrated that it has correctly interpreted Dōgen's own religion.

The revision of the traditional account of the origins of Dōgen's Zen thus strikes at the very heart of Sōtō dogmatics. If the spiritual significance of this account is not always obvious to us today, in the early Tokugawa, the twin themes of Dōgen's fidelity to the Buddhism of his master and of that Buddhism's superiority to the tradition of Lin-chi were crucial religious issues for the founders of modern Sōtō. These men were faced, in most general terms, with two major tasks: the reformation of the institutions of the church and the clarification of its dogmatic bases. The former task was focused especially on the matter of succession. The custom had grown up within the medieval church of recognizing *dharma* succession on the basis not only of one's certification by one's master but also of one's association with a monastery. This system, known as *garan bō* ("monastic *dharma*," as opposed to *ninpō*, "individual *dharma*"), allowed a monk to claim descent from more than one master and to change his lineage by moving his residence. Since one's status in the church and eligibility for appointments tended to hinge on the question of lineage, the opportunity for corruption was great. The problem was exacerbated by the reorganization of the Sōtō monastic system carried out by the Tokugawa government during the early decades of the seventeenth century. The new system, by shifting power away from the old centers of the church in Hokuriku to monasteries in the Kantō region, touched off a predictable scramble for realignment.

In response to this situation, Menzan and others associated especially with the old Hokuriku center of Daijō ji sought a reform of the system of succession that would do away with the *garan bō* and prevent the conversion of lineage. Though they ultimately won some measure of recognition for their movement from the secular authorities, in the process they touched off a theological debate within the church. When the dust settled, the followers of Menzan had been driven to a rather radical position: the transmission of the *dharma* was not dependent on the state of the mind of the recipient but solely on the act of formal certification by a master. No disciple could serve two masters: once he had been certified, his lineage and, hence, his religious loyalties were fixed. This was not only a normative but a historical truth; for no patriarch of the Sōtō tradition, whether in China or Japan, had ever confused these loyalties and claimed to transmit the *dharma* of more than one master.

If this emphasis on fealty to the lineage developed in service to institutional reform, it also had another job to do: it reminded the Sōtō monk of his loyalties to the house as a whole. Though today there is very little interaction between Sōtō and Rinzai, in medieval times this was not necessarily the case. Even among Dōgen's most prominent disciples there were those, as we have seen, who claimed descent from both houses; and throughout the subsequent centuries, monks of his lineage continued to be strongly influenced by the more conspicuous Rinzai tradition. Indeed, the Edo renaissance of Sōtō itself was stimulated by the arrival, in 1654, of the Chinese Lin-chi master Yin-yüan (Ingen; 1592–1672) and the subsequent development of the so-called Ōbaku school of Zen. Like their Rinzai contemporaries, Sōtō monks—including Menzan himself—went to study this new Ming style of Lin-chi. Partly in reaction to such foreign competition, both Sōtō and Rinzai became more sensitive to their own native traditions and to the need to revitalize them. They also became more sensitive to each other. Lamenting the long neglect of Dōgen's Zen and the intrusion of Rinzai elements into his tradition, Menzan and others turned back to the founder in an effort to uncover the roots of Sōtō and demonstrate its historical and ideological integrity as a distinct house of Zen. One of the first orders of business was to differentiate the house from the more prominent one next door and to ground that differentiation in the life and teachings of Dōgen.

Menzan and the other founders of the Tokugawa orthodoxy may thus have had their own reasons for appreciating the traditional account of the origins of Dōgen's Zen. But they did not wholly invent it. Whether or not their intepretations of his teachings are always adequate, there is no doubt that they are drawing on his own historical vision: Dōgen himself, as we have seen, casts himself in a sacred history of the patriarchate of the *Shōbō genzō*. To that extent, he is himself to blame if the historical account of the origins of his Zen became part of a theological position. He is also partly to blame, then, if that position is now threatened by historical revision. For as we know too well, once a historical claim becomes an article of faith, that faith is subject to historical evidence. This issue has yet to be faced by his modern apologists, and it thus remains to be seen whether they will be able to salvage the faith and make it compatible with modern historical consciousness.

It may or may not be a defect in Dōgen's religion that it is bound to a particular sacred history, but it is surely a defect in historical scholarship if it allows that fact to determine its results. This was not yet a clear issue for the early Sōtō scholars, who were themselves engaged in writing sacred history. Such, in one form or another, was the style of Tokugawa Buddhist scholarship in general, a style that has done much to provide the popular images of Dōgen, Shinran, Nichiren, and Kūkai, and to fix the mix of genealogical register and ideological handbook that often still passes for the history of Japanese Buddhism. Modern scholarship in Japan is now turning away from that style, but the process takes time. Meanwhile, the old way persists and finds its way abroad. It is one of the ironies of our age that we who invented the historical understanding of religion may one day have to reimport it from Japan.

Notes

*   *DZZ* 1:91–92. The author would like to thank Elizabeth Kenny for assistance in the preparation of this paper.

1.   The basic outlines of this account are provided by early biographies such as the *Sanso gyōgō ki* ["Chronicle of the acts of the three patriarchs"] (*SSZ* 1:1–9), *Denkō roku* ["Record of the transmission of the light"] (*T* 2585), and *Kenzei ki* ["Kenzei chronicle"] (*SSZ* 2:15–32). Examples of modern elaborations can be found in Takeuchi Michio, *Dōgen,* Jinbutsu sōsho 88 (Tokyo: Yoshikawa Kōbunkan, 1962), pp. 35–185; and in Ōkubo Dōshū's influential *Dōgen zenji den no kenkyū* ["Studies in the biography of the Zen master Dōgen"] (rev. ed., Tokyo: Chikuma Shobō, 1966), pp. 74–173. English versions appear in Hee-Jin Kim, *Dōgen Kigen: Mystical Realist* (Tucson: University of Arizona Press, 1975), pp. 23–46; and in James Kodera, *Dōgen's Formative Years in China* (Boulder: Prajñā Press, 1980), pp. 16–78.

2.   See *Nyojō oshō goroku* ["Recorded sayings of the teacher Ju-ching"] (*T* 2002A) and *Tendō san Keitoku ji Nyojō zenji zoku goroku* ["Further recorded sayings of the Ch'an master Ju-ching, of the Ching-te monastery, Mt. T'ien-t'ung"] (*T* 2002B). Though the latter text in particular is rather dubious, the former preserves material appearing in a collection of the sayings of Ju-ching used by Dōgen himself, a point to which I shall return below. While the *Nyojō goroku* does not mention Dōgen's doctrine of "body and mind sloughed off," it does contain the phonically similar but theologically distinct expression "mental defilements sloughed off" *(shinjin datsuraku),* a fact that has led to speculation that Dōgen's enlightenment was based on a misunderstanding of Chinese. This and other problems in the interpretation of Dōgen's relationship to Ju-ching have been discussed at some length by Kagamishima Genryū, in "Nyojō to Dōgen" ["Ju-ching

and Dōgen"], in *Dōgen zen no shisō teki kenkyū,* ed. by Kurebayashi Kōdō (Tokyo: Shunjūsha, 1973), pp. 249–278; and in *"Nyojō goroku to Hōkyō ki"* ["The *Recorded sayings of Ju-ching* and the *Pao-ching record"*], *Sanshō,* special issue no. 50 (Nov., 1975), pp. 77–83. Kagamishima is one of those within the Sōtō tradition that appreciates Dōgen's Zen as a Japanese development *(Nihon teki tenkai)* of Ju-ching's teachings; see, e.g., his "Dōgen zenji to Sōchō zen" ["The Zen master Dōgen and Sung-dynasty Ch'an"], *Nihon bukkyō nenpō* 26 (1960), pp. 57–72; repr. in Kagamishima, *Dōgen zenji to sono monryū* (Tokyo: Seishin Shobō, 1961), pp. 7–27.

3. For Ejō's colophon, see *DZZ* 2:388. If the *Hōkyō ki* includes material similar to that found elsewhere in Dōgen's writings, it also contains several passages that would seem to run counter to the spirit of his mature teachings. Interestingly enough, Sōtō scholars have sometimes welcomed these passages as evidence of the early provenance of the work—the argument being that they would not have escaped later editing. Having thus established to their satisfaction the authenticity of the *Hōkyō ki* account of Ju-ching's teachings, they then ignore these doctrinally troublesome entries and emphasize those that agree with their view of Dōgen.

4. I shall discuss the *Fukan zazen gi* in detail in another context, but it is worth noting here that the 1233 text reveals an approach to meditation somewhat different from the later, vulgate version used in traditional interpretations of Dōgen's Zen.

5. A convenient chronological chart of the *Shōbō genzō* texts can be found in Zen bunka gakuin, ed., *Gendai yaku Shōbō genzō,* (Tokyo: Seishin Shobō, 1968), pp. 224–225.

6. Ju-ching does appear with some frequency in the *Shōbō genzō zuimon ki,* Ejō's record of Dōgen's teachings said to date from the Katei era (1235–1237); but even here he is hardly more prominent that the Rinzai figure Yōsai (1141–1212), founder of Kennin ji (where Dōgen first studied Zen) and master of Dōgen's first Zen teacher, Myōzen (1184–1225). In any case, as a historical source, the *Zuimon ki* text, which may have been edited by Ejō's followers, suffers from the same kind of weaknesses as the *Hōkyō ki.*

7. *DZZ* 1:158. A version of the famous saying (which also occurs in the *Hōkyō ki* [*DZZ* 2:377]) first appears, without specific attribution, in the *Bendō wa* (*DZZ* 1:731).

8. *DZZ* 1:14. Bodhidharma is traditionally counted as both the twenty-eighth Indian and first Chinese patriarch—hence, the total of 50.

9. *DZZ* 1:446. Dōgen reasserts his succession to Ju-ching's *dharma* at the end of this text (*DZZ* 1:450).

10. *DZZ* 1:461. Dōgen is presumably counting the Sixth Patriarch twice, after the model of Bodhidharma. This still leaves us with only eighteen names in the list of masters ending with Ju-ching.

11. *DZZ* 1:545–546. A similar disparaging comment on Lin-chi and Te-shan appears in several manuscripts of the *Soku shin ze butsu* (*DZZ* 1:44 n.). If authentic, this would put Dōgen's criticisms of Lin-chi as early as the fifth month of 1239.

12. There he quotes a saying of Lin-chi, which he identifies as the "skin, flesh, bones and marrow" of the true tradition. Nevertheless, he encourages his audience to go beyond Lin-chi's saying to study "the action cherished by the patriarchs" (*DZZ* 1:83).

13. *DZZ* 1:409–410. Dōgen goes on here to criticize Yün-men mildly, but when he comes to Tung-shan's "three paths" *(san lu)* and "five ranks," he rejects their use on quite different grounds: they are "not in a realm known to illiterates *(zusan).* They correctly transmit the essential message and directly

indicate the Buddha's action; by no means are they the same as [the teachings of] other traditions" (*DZZ* 1:410).

14. *DZZ* 1:341. The text goes on to contrast such men with Dōgen's own master and to cite Ju-ching's criticism of them.

15. He is mentioned only in Ejō's *Zuimon ki,* where in fact he is praised as a dedicated practitioner (*DZZ* 2:489).

16. *DZZ* 1:359. Dōgen goes on at the end of the text to say that not only Ta-hui but no one outside the lineage of Tung-shan truly understands his saying. Those in other traditions have not even dreamt of it; it has been correctly transmitted only among Tung-shan's "legitimate heirs" (*DZZ* 1:361).

17. *DZZ* 1:557–559. Additional criticisms of Ta-hui appear in the *Ō saku sendaba,* from 1245, where Ju-ching is quoted as lamenting the fact that he is more honored than his Ts'ao-tung contemporary Hung-chih Cheng-chüeh (*DZZ* 1:595); and in the *Jinshin inga,* of the late, twelve-fascicle *Shōbō genzō,* where Dōgen suggests that his teachings tend toward the heresy of naturalism (*DZZ* 1:680).

18. In Masutani, *Rinzai to Dōgen* ["Lin-chi and Dōgen"] (Tokyo: Shunjūsha, 1971), pp. 15–89; see especially pp. 33–37.

19. Ibid., pp. 82–89. For the *Kenzei ki* dating of Dōgen's receipt of the Ju-ching text, see *SSZ* 2:23a. Dōgen's presentation of the work is recorded in the *Eihei kōroku* (*DZZ* 2:26).

20. *Risō* 513 (Feb., 1976), pp. 74–89; see especially pp. 81–83. Yanagida suggests in passing here that the *Hōkyō ki* represents "Dōgen's *Tanni shō*"— i.e., was composed precisely to correct current misinterpretations of Ju-ching's teachings.

21. The general notion that Dōgen's attack on contemporary Chinese Ch'an was in part an indirect criticism of Japanese Rinzai was suggested many years ago by Morita Yoshizō, in "Dōgen no Nansō zenrin kan ni tsuite" ["On Dōgen's view of the Ch'an community in the Southern Sung"], *Shikan* 12, (1937), pp. 74–100; see especially p. 76. Morita, however, seems to have been unaware of the chronology of the attack.

22. For Ju-ching's admonitions, see *Kenzei ki* (*SSZ* 2:21a). On the conflict with Hiei zan, see Ōkubo, *Dōgen zenji den no kenkyū,* pp. 184–196.

23. Furuta, *Nihon bukkyō shisō shi no sho mondai* (Tokyo: Shunjūsha, 1964), pp. 145–160; see especially pp. 154–155. For Dōgen's criticisms of Kennin ji, see *DZZ* 2:300, 461.

24. According to the *Kenzei ki* (*SSZ* 2:23), Dōgen left Kōshō ji for Echizen on the sixteenth of the seventh month (August 3) of 1243, a date corroborated by other evidence.

25. Dōgen is usually said to be the son of the minister Michichika, in the Koga branch of the Murakami Genji; more likely his father was Michichika's son Michitomo. Kōshō ji was supported by, among others, Kujō Noriie. This man was the brother of Enni's patron, Michiie, and Furuta suggests that, given his brother's loyalties, he may have encouraged Dōgen to withdraw from the capital.

26. Dōgen's withdrawal from Heian did not necessarily mark a severance of his secular connections. There is some evidence that the new monastery he built in Echizen was founded as a memorial temple *(bodai ji)* for the late Shōgun Sanetomo and his politically powerful mother, Hōjō Masako. He called the monastery Daibutsu ji (later changed to Eihei ji), a name that has given rise to speculation that he intended it to become the rival of Tōfuku ji and a center of public worship. The site was on the domain of Dōgen's patron, the

influential *bakufu* retainer Hatano Yoshishige. Presumably through the intervention of this man, in 1247 Dōgen traveled to Kamakura for an interview with the Shōgun Tokiyori, an avid student of Zen and supporter of Enni. The trip seems to have come to naught, and within a few months we find Dōgen back at his monastery in Echizen.

27. Furuta, *Shōbō genzō no kenkyū* ["Studies in the *Shōbō genzō*"] (Tokyo: Sōbunsha, 1972), pp. 2–15.
28. See especially the *Bendō wa, DZZ* 1:741–742.
29. This name for the school was popularized by Ōkubo Dōshū, who was among the first to explore its importance for Dōgen; see his extended study in *Dōgen zenji den no kenkyū*, pp. 406–446, on which the following is largely based.
30. For a discussion of Yōsai's criticism of Nōnin, see Yanagida Seizan, "Yōsai to *Kōzen gokoku ron* no kadai" ["Yōsai and issues in the *Kōzen gokoku ron*"], in Ichikawa Hakugen et al., eds., *Chūsei zenke no shisō, Nihon shisō taikei* 16 (Tokyo: Iwanami Shoten, 1972), pp. 467–471. Nōnin's assassination is reported by the *Honchō kōsō den* ["Lives of eminent monks of Japan"] (*Dai Nihon bukkyō zensho* 102, p. 273), but the references to him in both Benchō's biography and Nichiren's writings indicate that he outlived Kagekiyo, who died in 1196.
31. Ejō became the second abbot of Eihei ji, and Gikai and Gien both became his disciples. A dispute over which would succeed him led to a split in the church that was not healed until modern times. Gikai's faction, led by his most important disciple, Keizen Jōkin (1268–1325), was largely responsible for the subsequent expansion of Sōtō in Hokuriku. Giin also became Ejō's disciple and, after a pilgrimage to China, was active in Kyūshū.
32. The *Gokoku shōbō gi* is not extant. The notice in the *Keiran shūyō shū* by which its existence is known is quoted and discussed in Ōkubo, *Dōgen zenji den no kenkyū*, pp. 191–196.
33. *Chūsei zenshū shi no kenkyū* ["Studies in the history of medieval Zen"] (Tokyo: Tokyo Daigaku Shuppankai, 1970), pp. 27–36. See also Imaeda's *Dōgen to sono deshi* ["Dōgen and his disciples"] (Tokyo: Mainichi Shinbunsha, 1972), pp. 111–115; and *Dōgen: Zazen hitosuji no shamon* ["Dōgen: Monk of single-minded (devotion to) meditation"], NHK bukkusu 225 (Tokyo: Nihon Hōsō Shuppankai, 1976), pp. 129–140.
34. The *Menju* text, it may be noted, concludes with a long postscript arguing against the notion that one could claim descent from a master he has never met (*DZZ* 1:451–453). Tamamura Takeji, though he accepts the notion that Dōgen's view of the Ta-hui faction was influenced by Ju-ching, has suggested that he might also have inherited from Myōzen a prejudice that dates back to Yōsai's conflict with Nōnin; see his "Eihei Dōgen no Rinzai shū ni taisuru kanjō" ["Eihei Dōgen's feelings toward the Rinzai school"], *Nihon rekishi* 47 (April 1952), pp. 26–31.
35. See Yanagida, "Kana *Shōbō genzō* no himitsu" ["The secret of the vernacular *Shōbō genzō*"], *Tenbō* 210 (June 1976), pp. 44–61. Yanagida suggests that the original *Shōbō genzō* collection (popularly known as the *Sanbyaku soku* [*DZZ* 2:201–252]) was intended as a textbook for Dōgen's new Dharma school disciples, a view that would assume considerable contact with them prior to their formal conversion in 1241. The date for the collection, 1235, is provided by the colophon of a preface attributed to Dōgen.

"The Reason of Words and Letters": Dōgen and Kōan Language

Hee-Jin Kim

We are told by his biographers that Dōgen, while studying Buddhism on Mt. Hiei as a teenage initiate, was greatly troubled by the question: "As I study both the exoteric and the esoteric schools of Buddhism, they maintain that man is endowed with the Dharma-nature by birth. If this is the case, why had the buddhas of all ages—undoubtedly in possession of enlightenment—to seek enlightenment and engage in spiritual practice?"[1] We are also told that Dōgen on Mt. Hiei, the most respected center of Buddhist studies in those days, could find no one who could satisfactorily answer this question, and not to be daunted, Dōgen resolved to pursue his religio-philosophical quest in distant China. Notwithstanding the controversy surrounding the historical authenticity of this account, numerous students of Dōgen continue to see this perplexity as the central issue in his life and thought, expressed most effectively in his *Shōbōgenzō:* Method and Realization.[2]

While Dōgen's question is couched in religious rhetoric, its implications are more broadly philosophical, and give rise to a series of related questions. To restate the dilemma: If man is originally enlightened, hence already absolutely free, pure, and perfect, why does he have to exert himself at all in life? What is the significance of the intellectual, moral, and religious endeavors that occupy human existence? And, what is the meaning of existence?

From a specifically Mahayana Buddhist perspective, the quest here is directed toward the principle of absolute emptiness, which is none other than the truth of the Buddha-dharma. That is to say, it has to do with the dialectical relationship between nonduality and duality, between equality and differentiation, between original enlightenment *(hongaku)* and acquired enlightenment *(shikaku).* Is it in fact possible for man in absolute freedom to live at once duality and nonduality? If so, how is he able to accomplish it?

Dōgen relentlessly pursued the rationality of the Buddha-dharma throughout his life. Nonwithstanding the multitude of contradictory and disconcerting elements of his life and thought, which, incidentally, are no small matters for students of Dōgen, the cogency of Dōgen the man and the thinker seems to lie above all in his single-minded exploration and explication of the Buddha-dharma's rationality. In this respect, Dōgen reveals both his religious devotion and his critical, analytical genius.

Dōgen's life and thought were the fruition of much questioning and exploration, and his *Shōbōgenzō* was the quintessence of his work. This compilation presents Dōgen's lifelong reflections on method and realization in the Buddha-dharma, setting forth in some ninety fascicles the theme of a radically nondualistic mode of living and thinking—with variations which constantly originate from, and return to, this theme. The extensive range of its topics covers the vast territory of the Buddhist tradition with its fertile ideas and symbols. Of all Dōgen's works, the *Shōbōgenzō* is the most philosophical and methodical, differing significantly from his other writings in its approach, style, and language. While the work is firmly grounded upon his religious orientation, its tenor is preeminently philosophical.[3] Even in speaking of cleansing the body or eating a meal, Dōgen could not but be philosophical; his passion for rationality manifested itself in such apparently trivial acts as cleansing and eating.[4] For Dōgen, rationality was part and parcel of spirituality, and the *Shōbōgenzō,* as a whole, is a brilliant testimonial to this truth.

The method of Ch'an/Zen consists in *zazen* and the *kōan*.[5] This subject has usually been understood in the context of the traditions of Silent-illumination Zen *(mokushō-zen)* and Koan-inquiry Zen *(kanna-zen),* in terms of which the Sōtō/Ts'ao-tung sect and the Rinzai/Lin-chi sect in China and Japan are opposed to each other. It is generally presumed that the former employs the method of *zazen,* whereas the latter that of the kōan. This characterization of Ch'an/Zen methodology is related to the distinction between the school of original enlightenment and the school of acquired enlightenment, which roughly correspond to the Sōtō/Ts'ao-tung and the Rinzai/Lin-chi sects, respectively. While recognizing the usefulness of this conventional opposition, however, we should guard against a tendency toward oversimplifications that might fossilize these two traditions, historically as well as phenomenologically.[6]

The popular view is that Dōgen, while on the one hand advocating *zazen* in the tradition of Silent-illumination Zen, also attempted to reinterpret it radically via the practice of single-minded sitting *(shikan-taza).* This view, however, is at best deficient and, at worst, obstructive to an accurate understanding of the spirit of Dōgen's Zen. The fact is that Dōgen, nurtured primarily in the Ch'an/Zen tradition, used both methods, *zazen* and the kōan, discarding neither. His serious interest in the kōan is evidenced by the prevalence in the *Shōbōgenzō* of extensive exegeses and interpretations of carefully selected kōans from the classical sources of Ch'an/Zen. Dōgen's effort was not to destroy the kōan, but to restore it to its rightful status. As he transformed *zazen* into single-minded sitting, so Dōgen adopted the kōan as the "realization-kōan" *(genjō-kōan)*. For Dōgen, single-minded sitting and the realization-kōan were two aspects of a single methodology. In brief, *zazen* was kōan, kōan was *zazen*.

In this essay we shall examine Dōgen's treatment of the kōan, specifically, his analysis of the language and symbols of the kōan as they relate to realization *(genjō)*; our investigation will attempt to demonstrate how radical Dōgen was in his conception of linguistic activity as the ultimate spiritual freedom demanded by the Buddha-dharma. Although Dōgen's methodology has to do with areas broader than mere linguistic activity, we shall confine ourselves to this aspect of the issue, since it has not heretofore received the attention it deserves.[7]

In his treatment of the kōan, Dōgen always posits a duality of meaning: on the one hand, he deeply appreciates the legacy of the old-paradigm kōan *(kosoku-kōan)* used as an expedient to bring about enlightenment; yet he also wants to lend new significance to the realization-kōan as absolute truth dynamically present in life. It may be that Dōgen's originality lies in his radical transformation of the language of the old-paradigm kōan within the living context of the realization-kōan. In this process of appropriating kōan language, Dōgen reveals himself to be exceedingly conscious of language, and in this respect, astonishingly modern. And yet, despite the evidence of a deliberate rhetorical component in his writing, his foremost concern is ultimately rational rather than rhetorical; he believes that reason, not eloquence, is paramount for the attainment of the Way.[8]

Dōgen gives us one of the clearest statements on the language of the kōan in his explanation of Yün-men's saying "The east mountain walks over the water":

> In great Sung China today there are a group of scatterbrained people, whose number is so large that they cannot possibly be scared off by the faithful few. They would argue: "Talks such as 'The east mountain walks over the water,' Nan-ch'üan's sickle, and the like are incomprehensible utterances. The idea is that any talk concerned with all sorts of discriminating thoughts is not the Ch'an talk of the buddhas and patriarchs; only incomprehensible utterances are the talk of the buddhas and patriarchs. Therefore, Huang-po's training stick and Lin-chi's thundering shout—these exceed comprehension, and are never concerned with discriminating thought. This is known as great enlightenment prior to the time when no incipient sign has yet emerged. The past masters often employed as skillful means phrases which cut off entangling vines, but it was because [such phrases] were beyond comprehension."

People who utter such nonsense have not yet met a true master; hence, they lack the eye of proper study. They are fools not worthy of mention. . . . What these pseudo-Buddhists regard as "incomprehensible utterances" are incomprehensible only to them, not to the buddhas and patriarchs. Their lack of comprehension should never serve as an excuse not to study the path of the buddhas' and patriarchs' comprehension. If [these utterances] were ultimately incomprehensible, what they now allegedly comprehend must also be wrong. A good many such fellows abound in Sung China, and I have seen them myself. How pitiable are they who are unaware that discriminating thought *is* words and phrases, and that words and phrases *liberate* discriminating thought![9]

Here Dōgen's critique of what I would call the "instrumentalist" view— the view that kōans are incomprehensible utterances employed merely as a device to cut off intellectual entanglements or as "fingers pointing to the moon," but not the moon itself—is scathing and uncompromising.

Throughout the history of Ch'an/Zen up to the present day, the instrumentalist view of kōan language would seem to typify a deep-rooted, pervasive proclivity, if not intention, in this tradition. More recently, D. T. Suzuki advanced a similar view laden with psychological overtones, clearly delineating a major difference between himself and Zen Buddhists of the past.[10] His interpretation may be summarized as follows: The words and acts of a given kōan are arranged in such a way that they flatly violate logic and common sense. Confronted with such an incongruous and absurd discourse, the practitioner of kōan meditation is profoundly baffled, frustrated, and even amused. Any attempt to translate a kōan into intelligible discourse misses its intention altogether, because the nature of its extraordinariness is such that it does not lend itself to ordinary statement. Yet, the "illogicality" of the kōan is so highly deceptive that it initially lures the practitioner into the semblance of an intellectual solution, only then to deceive and obstruct the intellectual process the deeper one enters into that deception. This deliberate "stratagem" is designed to thwart the practitioner's tendency to seek a logical and causal meaning in the kōan, since, once discovered, that meaning will turn out to be irrelevant after all. The kōan thus functions to disturb, exasperate, and finally bankrupt the intellect with a view to allowing the mind to see things "as they truly are" in the allegedly trans-intellectual state of consciousness. In other words, the meditator, having exhausted his intellectual resources, may be said to find himself in a spiritual impasse, one which will lead him to an eventual breakdown of ordinary consciousness and to the dawning of a new transcendent awakening called enlightenment. Enlightenment is an explosive breakthrough in the state of consciousness; and it is the kōan method which is said to bring about this psychological-ontological event most effectively.[11]

There are two noteworthy aspects in the foregoing account of the kōan. On the one hand, the kōan is said to function exclusively as a device to bring forth the psychological antecedent of enlightenment in order to lead the practitioner to the ontological-soteriological phase of enlightenment; consequently, there is radical discontinuity between the psychological process and the ontological-soteriological reality. On the other hand, the kōan is deemed to be a vehicle which enables the practitioner to leap into the realm of transcendent enlightenment. It is only at that stage that the paradoxes of the kōan are dissolved in the ocean of pure experience, while as statements of logical, commonsense experience, they remain undecipherable. In neither aspect does Suzuki construe psychological, intellectual, or linguistic activities as integral to realization.[12]

Against this classical and modern background, we may be able to appreciate Dōgen better. As we have seen, Dōgen holds that the absence of cognitive relevance in the kōan, by virtue of its *apparent* illogicality, does not imply meaninglessness in "the path of the buddhas' and patriarchs' comprehension," i.e., in the rationality of the Buddha-dharma. This is because words, like deeds, have at once limiting and liberating functions, or, as Dōgen himself put it, "discriminating thought *is* words and phrases, and . . . words and phrases *liberate* discriminating thought." In other words, kōan language presents the workings of Buddha-nature, in which self-limitation and self-liberation are interfused in a paradoxical way. In spite of inherent frailties in their make-up, words are the bearers of ultimate truth. In this respect, words are not different from things, events, or beings—all are "alive" in Dōgen's thought. The dynamics of words as living forces in the context of realization, in turn, legitimates discriminating thought.

Having said this, we may still wonder whether linguistic activity, or thinking in general, can ever avoid its inherent one-sidedness and fragmentation. An utterance by definition excludes all other possible utterances. Language is ever divisive and partial, whereas reality is indivisible and whole. On this account the critics of language point out its fundamental defects and even its harmfulness to a total understanding of reality. To be sure, Dōgen is cognizant of this problem when he speaks of the 'traps and nets of words and letters' *(monji no sentei),* but his conclusions regarding language are more positive. He would say that even its natural weaknesses can be soteriologically appropriated without violating the principle of absolute nonduality/absolute emptiness. Yet how can this be done?

The shortest way to the heart of the matter lies in the notion of total exertion—the total exertion of one dharma *(ippō-gūjin),* to be precise. According to the notion of total exertion, every dharma in the world has its unique particularity, yet exists in such a way that it bears absolute significance: while being a single unique dharma, it is at once all dharmas and no-dharma. This view echoes the totalistic philosophy of Hua-yen

Buddhism, in which all is one and one is all, in mutual identity and mutual penetration. Dōgen's thought of total exertion, however, is far more dynamic than the Hua-yen approach. To illustrate with a few of Dōgen's favorite expressions, one dharma is said to "leap out" of itself *(chōshutsu),* and "leap into" itself *(chōnyū).* By leaping out and leaping into, the single dharma at once transcends and embraces all dharmas. This dharmic dynamism is characterized by another expression, *kappap-pat* or *kappatsupatchi,* which refers to the movement of a fish out of water. The relationship of individual dharmas to each other in the universal context is also quite graphically depicted in that all dharmas are described as "crashing and smashing against each other" *(chikujaku-katsujaku)* in unity and freedom. When one dharma lives out its life, all dharmas become that dharma, and there is only this one dharma in the entire universe. A dharma is never juxtaposed to others; therefore, dharmas never oppose one another in dualistic fashion. A dharma is, by definition, that particularity which transcends all forms of dualism; it is both independent of and harmonious with all dharmas. In this view, a particular actuality is never devaluated or obliterated; to the contrary, the uniqueness, freedom, and purity of the single dharma emerges unequivocally into the foreground.

The reality of total exertion is thoroughly saturated with the principle of ascesis (namely, practice or discipline), privileging the latter over vision, not in order to deny seeing, but to explicate a deeper meaning, one that seeing itself is fundamentally creating and making. That is to say, seeing presupposes the vow or resolution on the part of the seer to create a new being or a new reality; hence, it concerns itself not only with seeing things as they are but creating things as they are meant to be. This is why total exertion can properly be understood only against the background of the ascesis of *zazen.* It is to be enacted rather than envisioned. This ascesis of one dharma in total independence is itself the enactment of the samādhi of self-enjoyment *(jijuyū-zammai),* a sheer joyfulness of play *(yuge),*[13] which casts off body-mind *(shinjin-datsuraku)* and in which practice and verification are nondually one *(shushō-ittō; shushō-ichinyo).*

All in all, total exertion is Dōgen's appropriation of the traditional Mahayana principle of nonduality/absolute emptiness; it is the core of the realization-kōan and, for that matter, of single-minded sitting. The dynamics and mystery of words originate precisely from this fundamental postulate of total exertion. When language and thought are appropriated in the context of total exertion, only then can they serve realization without confronting their ultimate limitations and unlimited possibilities. Dōgen clearly recognizes the possibility that language, despite its aspect as a tool of duality, can partake of nonduality; only thus does language become "expression" *(dōtoku).*[14]

Consider the following statements:

> We should study, then, the moment when we consider the water of the ten directions in light of the ten directions. It is not only when humans and gods see water that we should study this; there is also a study in which water sees water. Because water practices and verifies water, there is a penetrating study in which water speaks of water.[15]

> Although water is manifold for various beings, it seems that there is neither original water nor various beings' water. Even so, the waters which vary according to the beings do not depend on mind or body; nor do they originate from karma; nor are they dependent on self or other. Water liberates itself through water. . . . Even within a single drop of water an incalculable number of buddha-lands are realized. Accordingly, it is not that water is within the buddha-land or that the buddha-land is within water. As for the whereabouts of water, it in fact has no relation to the three periods or to the dharma realm. Yet, for all this, water is the kōan realized.[16]

In these statements, the word "water" is not only a metaphor but a reality—a reality which transcends all discriminations, and thus redeems all thought. Language and symbols circumscribe reality; but, as living forces, they are dynamic enough to open up, constantly re-expressing, renewing, and casting off, so as to unfold new horizons of their own life. In this way language and symbols know no limits with respect to how far they can penetrate both conceptually and symbolically. Participation in these unexplored possibilities of words and letters *(monji)* constitutes kōan study.

Thus Dōgen probes the inner dynamics of concepts and symbols not as a means of intellectual speculation but as a way of realization. When linguistic experimentation and transformation are executed within the realizational milieu of total exertion, the results are truly remarkable, as we shall see shortly. Throughout the *Shōbōgenzō,* Dōgen painstakingly dissects a given passage and explores its semantic possibilities at every turn, literally turning the conventional diction upside down and inside out. The result is a dramatic shift in our perception and understanding of the original passage. One of the most rewarding aspects of translating Dōgen's *Shōbōgenzō* lies in dealing with his radical challenge to ordinary language. To Dōgen the manner of expression is as important as the substance of thought; in fact, the experimentation with language is equivalent to the construction of reality. Furthermore, Dōgen frequently puts forth deliberate, often brilliant, "misinterpretations" of certain notions and passages of Buddhism. This distortion of original meaning is due not to any ignorance of Chinese or Japanese (indeed, it testifies to a unique mastery of both) but rather to a different kind of thinking—the logic of the Buddha-dharma. Dōgen's methodology is deeply rooted in this characteristically Buddhist way of thinking.

Let us examine Dōgen's analytical methods and attempt to probe more systematically Dōgen's treatment of kōan language in the realizational context.[17] Our exposition will deal with the following topics: (1) Transposition of Lexical Components; (2) Semantic Reconstruction Through Syntactic Change; (3) Explication of Semantic Attributes; (4) Reflexive, Self-causative Utterances; (5) The Upgrading of Commonplace Notions and Use of Neglected Metaphors; (6) The Use of Homophonous Expressions; and finally, (7) Reinterpretation Based on the Principle of Absolute Nonduality/Absolute Emptiness. It goes without saying that these headings should not be seen as rigid categories. More often than not, examples drawn from the *Shōbōgenzō* will illustrate two or more of the above characteristics.

(1) Transposition of Lexical Components

This is perhaps the most frequently used procedure in Dōgen's *Shōbōgenzō*. Its model consists of reshuffling the Chinese lexical components of a given phrase or expression, say, A, B, C, D, and E of "ABCDE" in Chinese, so as to adduce, for example, "BACED," "ADCBE," and so on. The transposition of linguistic elements is intended to suggest that they are as dynamic and versatile as reality itself in their infinitely variegated configurations and possibilities. The analogy of a mosaic rearranged in multiple designs might help us here. Just as reality incessantly transforms itself, so can language act as a living force in its own right. The method of transposing lexical components attests to this view.

In his exposition on the Buddhist notion that "Mind itself is Buddha" *(sokushin-zebutsu),* Dōgen presents a classic treatment. After defining the four linguistic elements—"mind" *(shin),* "itself" *(soku),* "is" *(ze),* and "Buddha" *(butsu)*—of "Mind itself is Buddha," he reshuffles them in various ways, and gives examples of five out of the twenty-four possible combinations.

> The "Buddha" has taken up all things and let them go. Even so, they do not address themselves to the sixteen-foot golden body.
> The "itself" is the kōan: it neither anticipates its realization nor averts its dissolution.
> The "is" is the triple world from which we do not retreat and to which we do not advance; [as the triple world,] it is not mind-only.
> The "mind" is walls and partitions; still, it does not work clay or build them.
> [The buddhas and patriarchs] penetrate into "Mind itself is Buddha," penetrate into "Itself mind Buddha is," penetrate into "Itself Buddha is mind," penetrate into "Mind itself Buddha is," and penetrate into "Is Buddha itself mind." Penetration such as this is indeed "Mind itself is Buddha," and

through this, they have authentically transmitted ["Mind itself is Buddha"]
to "Mind itself is Buddha." Such an authentic transmission has continued to
the present day.[18]

The Sōtō exegetical canon has noted the twenty-four possibilities, although not their significance. Each lexical element represents a single
dharma's total exertion which is absolutely discrete from all others, yet
bears all others in it, without falling into atomism or monism. The same
holds true of each and every combination of the four elements.

As often happens in the *Shōbōgenzō,* some such modulated expressions cannot be easily rendered in intelligible statements; perhaps Dōgen
did not wish them to be reduced to conventional locutions, but rather to
be appreciated visually and aurally, as they are, like the images of a
dream. Incidentally, this fanciful, even playful trait in Dōgen's diction
has been largely overlooked by most Dōgen scholars. Far from being
nonsensical constructs, such linguistic modulations stand for the infinite
versatility of a seamless reality.[19]

Let us take another example, perhaps one of Dōgen's most difficult:

> Kuei-tsung's saying, "If your eyesight has the slightest dimness, [you will
> see] the sky flowers falling furiously" speaks of "upholding the Buddha."
> We must know, therefore, that the "furious falling of the flowers of dim-
> ness" is the realization of the buddhas, and that the "flowers and fruits of
> the emptiness of eyesight" are the "upholding of the buddhas." They bring
> the "eyesight" to realization through the "dimness." They realize the
> "flowers of emptiness" in the "eyesight"; they realize the "eyesight" in the
> "flowers of emptiness." If the "flowers of emptiness" are in your "eye-
> sight," [you will see] the "slightest dimness falling furiously"; if the
> "slightest eyesight" is in the "emptiness," [you will see] the "immense dim-
> ness falling furiously."[20]

Even in such a complex saying as this, Dōgen has transposed the linguistic elements "dimness" *(ei),* the "flowers of emptiness" *(kūge),* "falling
furiously" *(rantsui),* "eyesight" *(gen),* and "emptiness", *(kū),* all taken
from the original passage, "If your eyesight has the slightest dimness,
[you will see] the sky flowers falling furiously" *(ichiei-zaigen kūge-rant-
sui/ichiei me ni areba kūge midare ochin).* The resultant new expressions
reveal heretofore unseen dimensions of the original. Immediately after
the foregoing quote, Dōgen writes:

> For this reason, "dimness" is the presence of total dynamism; "eyesight" is
> the presence of total dynamism; "emptiness" is the presence of total dyna-
> mism; and "flower" is the presence of total dynamism. "Falling furiously"
> are a thousand eyes—the eyes that are the whole body [of Avalokiteśvara].[21]

A similar example can be gleaned from a passage in the Shohō-jissō
fascicle:

The "real" is "only a buddha"; the "nature" is "with a buddha." The "can" is "only a buddha"; the "thorough penetration" is "with a buddha." "All dharmas" are "only a buddha"; the "real nature" is "with a buddha." That "all dharmas" are authentically "all dharmas" is called "only a buddha"; that "all dharmas" are the "real nature" just now is called "with a buddha."[22]

This is Dōgen's analysis and transformation of the saying that "Only a buddha with a buddha can thoroughly penetrate all dharmas as the real nature" *(yuibutsu-yobutsu nainō-gūjin shohō-jissō/tada hotoke to hotoke to nomi sunawachi yoku shohō-jissō o gūjin su).*

It is abundantly clear that in these linguistic and symbolic transformations Dōgen acts as a magician or an alchemist of language conjuring up an infinity of symbolic universes freely and selflessly as the self-expressions of Buddha-nature. No doubt Dōgen was a matchless alchemist adroitly transforming the elements of language into insights worth their weight in gold.

Closely related to this method was Dōgen's inversion of lexical components—a technique which also uncovered new signification. For example, in his discussion of *tō-higan* ("reaching the other shore"), Dōgen transposed its elements to *higan-tō* ("the other shore's arrival" or "the other shore has arrived").[23] Thus while the original meaning of *higan,* "the other shore," i.e., nirvana, was clearly a future event attainable only at the end of countless kalpas of spiritual efforts, it was now radically transformed so that the other shore was no longer in the distance or in the future but the event of realization here and now.

Similarly in discussing *seppō* ("preaching the Dharma," "discourse on the Dharma"), Dōgen transformed this expression into *hō-setsu* ("the Dharma preaches," "the Dharma's discourse"). The net result was that the Dharma was no longer the object of preaching but the absolute subject of preaching in which preacher, preached, and preaching were all one. In Dōgen's unequivocal words: "This 'discourse on the Dharma' is 'the Dharma's discourse.' "[24]

(2) Semantic Reconstruction Through Syntactic Change

As we have already seen, Dōgen felt unconstrained by conventional Buddhist usage, or, for that matter, by secular traditions. This is clearly demonstrated by his method of arbitrarily regrouping linguistic components in a sentence, often in violation of Chinese syntactic rules. Given the expression "A-B-CDE" in Chinese, for example, Dōgen might reorganize it as "AB-CDE," jolting the conventional meaning of the original; alternately, he might single out "BC." Meaningless in isolation in its original context, with Dōgen it would take on a novel signification. Dōgen was a master of neologisms.[25] This technique involved the rearrangement of linguistic elements through syntactical reorganization (or disorganization), within a given original passage.

In the *Shōbōgenzō* Busshō, Dōgen takes the *Nirvāṇa Sūtra* passage *issai no shujō wa kotogotoku busshō ari* ("All sentient beings without exception have Buddha-nature") and shifts its syntactical components to read *issai-shujō shitsuu busshō* ("All sentient being are all existence, Buddha-nature"). The far-reaching religious and philosophical implications of such distorted readings are now well known to us.[26] First, Buddha-nature as potentiality is construed as actuality, because sentient beings do not possess but are Buddha-nature; secondly, by being placed in apposition with "all existence," sentient beings are liberated from homocentrism as well as biocentrism; and thirdly, "sentient beings," "all existence," and "Buddha-nature" are all nondually one, a notion which is described, in a different context but in typically Buddhist language, as: "though not identical, they are not different; though not different, they are not one; though not one, they are not many."[27]

The *Shōbōgenzō* abounds with such examples. In the same fascicle, Dōgen takes up Nāgārjuna's utterance *mi ni engatsusō o genzu* ("The body manifests the form of the round moon") and renders it as *shingen-engatsusō* ("The bodily actuality is the form of the round moon").[28] By so doing, Dōgen unambiguously makes explicit the realizational tenor—the bodily actuality as the dynamic presence of the round moon, which is only faintly implied in the conventional reading.

In his exposition on beholding the Buddha *(kembutsu)*, quoting *moshi shosō wa hisō nari to mireba sunawachi nyorai o miru nari* ("If one discerns that all phenomena are not phenomena, he sees the Tathāgata"), Dōgen renders it as follows: *moshi shosō to hisō too mireba . . .* ("If one discerns both all phenomenon and nonphenomenon . . . ").[29] The traditional reading stresses nondifferentiation by transcending differentiation, whereas Dōgen's underscores differentiation as nondually identical with nondifferentiation. This is in accord with his understanding of the ambiguities and contradictions of existence, a hallmark of his view of realization. Nowhere is Dōgen's acute sensitivity to the mystery of realization more clearly stated than in the following:

> The occasion [of illusion] such as this is expressed and realized as "A broken mirror never reflects again" and "A fallen flower cannot rise the tree." When a fallen flower is truly a fallen flower, even were one to ascend to the top of a hundred-foot pole, it would still be a fallen flower. Because a broken mirror is unambiguously a broken mirror, however we may think of it, it is still that "reflector" which "never reflects again." By pondering the fundamental principle describing the broken mirror and the fallen flower, we may grasp the time "when a man of great enlightenment still has illusion."[30]

Dōgen's disregard of Chinese syntactic rules, ordinarily regarded as essential to an accurate understanding of the original passages, is noteworthy. He perseveres in this syntactic violation in spite of his insistence on observing what he calls the authentically transmitted Buddha-dharma *(shōden no buppō)*. His transformation of the original significations imbibes a cultural atmosphere typically Japanese—given the context within which he operates. It is not surprising, therefore, that the *Shōbōgenzō,* and particularly its scriptural and kōan passages, are couched in the milieu of medieval Japanese language which is fundamentally different from its Chinese counterpart. Only against this linguistic backdrop do Dōgen's intentional misrepresentations become intelligible.[31]

Closely related to Dōgen's method of syntactic recontruction is his "straight" reading of Chinese Buddhist expressions. For instance, while *juki* is ordinarily understood to be the Buddha's prediction of a disciple's future enlightenment, Dōgen transfigures it into the fact of that realization in the present. This is done by rendering the passage *masani anokutara-sammyaku-sambodai o ubeshi* ("They shall attain supreme, perfect enlightenment") as *tōtoku anokutara-sammyaku-sambodai* ("They have certainly attained, supreme, perfect enlightenment").[32] The assurance of a future event is thus construed as testimony to a present one.

Elsewhere Dōgen renders *kono hō no okoru toki* ("When these dharmas arise") as *shihō-kiji.* That is to say, *shihō* ("these dharmas") and *kiji* ("the time of arising") are placed in apposition so that the entire expression now means: "These dharmas are the time of arising." What Dōgen is expressing here is the nonduality of the *time* of arising and the *event* of dharmas: "[Speaking of 'When these dharmas arise,'] the 'time of arising' is 'these dharmas,' but it is not of the twelve hours; 'these dharmas' are the 'time of arising,' yet they are not of the triple world arising in rivalry."[33] That is to say, dharmas do not move in time but *are* time; dharmas are not juxtaposed to one another in spatial spread, nor is time segmental in temporal sequence. This is a simple phrase transformed into a profoundly philosophical statement.

Another example will help illustrate the appropriateness of Dōgen's rendering of these Buddhist teachings: When expounding on the "pictured cakes" *(gabyō),* Dōgen transforms the customary reading *gabyō wa ue ni mitazu* ("The pictured cakes do not satisfy hunger") into *gabyō wa fu-jū-ki,* a straight reading of the Chinese original, thus exposing its hitherto unrecognized significance, "The pictured cakes are no-satisfaction-hunger." While the expression had negative connotations in the conventional interpretation, it is now taken to transcend the dualism of hunger and satisfaction, implying in turn that these are in themselves ultimate truth. Thus, "because the entire world and the entire dharmas are unequivocally pictures, men and dharmas are realized through pictures, and the buddhas and patriarchs are perfected through pictures."[34]

(3) Explication of Semantic Attributes

Dōgen's concern here is to probe the multiple meanings and functions of Chinese ideographs, by meticulously exploring the possible significations of a given character and speculating on their soteriological possibilities. By so doing, Dōgen goes beyond the narrow confines of traditional diction and usage, and penetrates to the intricate interior of these significations.

For example, the expression *kūge* originally meant in Buddhism "sky flowers," "flowers blooming in the sky," and, by extension, "illusory perceptions," "unrealities," etc. Yet, the word *kū* means not only "sky" but "emptiness," a pivotal notion of Mahayana Buddhism. Hence, in Dōgen's hands the term is metamorphosed from nonexistent illusory flowers to the evocative, powerful metaphor of the "flowers of emptiness."[35] With no hard-and-fast demarcation drawn between reality and illusion, all dharmas of the universe thus become flowers of emptiness. Dōgen writes:

> There are indeed a number of ways to study the flowers of emptiness: seeing by dim eyesight and seeing by clear eyesight; seeing by a buddha's eyesight and seeing by a patriarch's eyesight; seeing by the Way's eyesight and seeing by the blind's eyesight; seeing by three thousand years and seeing by eight hundred years; seeing by a hundred kalpas and seeing by immeasurable kalpas. Though each of these ways sees the "flowers of emptiness," the "emptiness" is already variegated, and the "flowers" are also manifold.[36]

In the Buddhist tradition, *mitsugo* implies secrecy and hiddenness, as opposed to manifestation and uncovering. But Dōgen finds in the *mitsu* of *mitsugo* another meaning, intimacy or an absence of hiatus between self and other, between thought and reality, between the symbol and the symbolized: it is the transparency of being to its own being. In his words: "The *mitsu* in question has the meaning of intimacy, with no hiatus whatsoever."[37]

Another significant character is *nyo,* which has the dual meaning of "like" or "resemble" on the one hand and "thusness" or "as-it-is-ness" on the other. By using this twofold meaning Dōgen maintains that likeness is thusness, that is, the nondual interfusion of the concept and the conceptualized, or of a relative and absolute meaning. *Nyoze,* which has a double meaning similar to *nyo,* is also interpreted in this way. In the Tsuki fascicle Dōgen writes:

> The "like" in the foregoing "like the moon in the water" is the "moon-in-the-water" itself. It is the "thusness of the water," the "thusness of the

moon," "within thusness," and the "thusness of within." We are not construing "like" as resemblance: "like" is "thusness."[38]

As we have seen repeatedly, metaphor, simile, parable, and the like in Dōgen are not mere instruments or vehicles of communication, but the bearers and workings of ultimate reality/truth. In this sense Dōgen views language itself as realization rather than as a mere vehicle for communicating truth.

Such an astute utilization of the dual or multiple meaning of an ideograph or expression also appears in the Baika fascicle, where *ima itaru tokoro ni* ("now everywhere") is rendered as *nikon-tōsho* ("everywhere the absolute present has arrived").[39] The original passage is taken from Ju-ching's saying "When Gautama [the Buddha] sheds his [illusory] vision, the plum blossoms of just a single branch are in the snow. Now everywhere thorns are grown, but [the blossoms] are smiling amid the spring breeze wafting madly all over."[40] By explicating its semantic attributes, Dōgen gives a religious and philosophical ultimacy to the ordinary words "now everywhere."

Another example is the word *dōtoku* ("expression") which is comprised of two Chinese characters: *dō* ("the way," "to say") and *toku* ("can," "to attain"). These sematic attributes combine to make this commonplace word extremely rich in its religio-philosophical implications. The term signifies simultaneously what is said and what can be said— expression and expressibility; at the same time, it means the Way's appropriation, making an expression the embodiment of the Way. Thus together with the notion of activity-unremitting *(gyōji)*, this notion of expression becomes one of the two foci of the inner dynamics of total exertion. Dōgen writes about this expression:

> As we hold on to these efforts throughout many months and ever so many years, we further cast off the efforts of former months and years. When we are about to cast off [these efforts], our skin, flesh, bones, and marrow alike discern the casting-off; the countries and lands, mountains and rivers likewise discern the casting-off. At this time, we set out on the path to reach the casting-off as the treasured place of ultimacy, but because this resolve to reach is in fact realization itself, there is an expression being realized even without anticipation, at the very moment of casting-off. Though neither by the power of the mind nor by the power of the body, it gives expression to itself of its own accord. Once it is expressed, we do not feel in the least any unnaturalness or strangeness about it.[41]

Expression and expressibility are so nondually interpenetrated that the Way appropriates itself ever afresh in its process of casting-off *(datsura-ku)*, ad infinitum. Language is part and parcel of this expressive and transformative process.

Dōgen also transforms such an everyday word as *arutoki* ("at a certain time," "sometimes," "there is a time," "once"), transmuting it into one of the most important notions in his thought by combining *aru* or *u* ("to be," "to have") and *toki* or *ji* ("time," "occasion"), and thus characterizing the nonduality of existence and time, expressed as "existence-time" *(uji)*.[42] Dōgen's new usage, moreover, adds a further dimension, that of an absolute present, with its rich connotations. Another common word, *kyōryaku* ("to pass through," "to experience"), is elevated to the status of a cognate notion signifying "the passage of time," by which Dōgen denotes "temporal dynamicity," "temporal movement," etc.—the dynamics of the absolute present, in and through which all time and all existence are realized. Temporal dynamicity is stated succinctly as follows:

> "Passage" is, for example, like spring. Spring has a great many features, and these are called "passage." We should study that spring "passes" without anything outside itself. For example, the "passage" of spring always "passes through" spring. "Passage" is not spring, but because it is the "passage" of spring, the "passage" perfects the Way now in spring time.[43]

This last quotation is especially pertinent for our understanding of Dōgen's view of language. As we have seen, language as he perceives it is as dynamically alive as any living being in the world; as such the perspective which the concept of temporal dynamicity affords us is as pivotal within language as it is within our existence. In essence, the interior dynamics of words and symbols amount to neither more nor less than the temporal dynamicity of existence-time.

(4) Reflexive, Self-causative Utterances

In Ch'an/Zen, the statement of identity is quite commonplace and frequently used in order to suggest the absolute nonduality of equality and differentiation, of emptiness and form, and so on. Underlying the statement of identity is the dialectical logic of identity-and-difference which appears in its classical form in the *Diamond Sūtra*.[44] Its paradigm can be stated as follows: "A is −A; therefore A is A." Thus "A" is at once negated and affirmed in dialectical fashion, through the mediation and authentication of absolute emptiness. Only then is "A" absolutely free, pure, and perfect: it attains its authenticity.

As an heir to both Mahayana and Zen Buddhist traditions, Dōgen draws heavily on this kind of expression. He has this to say in the Busshō fascicle:

> The "emptiness" in question is not the "emptiness" of "form is emptiness."
> [The true meaning of] "form is emptiness" is not that you forcibly make

"form" into "emptiness" or that you split "emptiness" so as to fabricate "form"; it is the "emptiness" of "emptiness is emptiness." This "emptiness" of "emptiness is emptiness" is "a single piece of rock in emptiness."[45]

Elsewhere Dōgen writes:

An ancient buddha said: "Mountains are mountains, waters are waters." This expression does not mean that we point to the mountains as the mountains, but that the mountains are nothing but the mountains. Therefore, we should study mountains penetratingly. When we study mountains penetratingly, this is the mountains' own efforts. Such mountains and waters, of themselves, become wise men and holy sages.[46]

As is made evident in these two quotations, the sayings "emptiness is emptiness" *(kū-ze-kū),* "mountains are mountains" *(san-ze-san),* and "waters are waters" *(sui-ze-sui)* are brought to bear upon realizational significance more forcefully and explicitly rendered than in any traditional readings. Dōgen makes his notion of total exertion unequivocal in these illustrations.

By far the most Dōgen-like expression along these lines of thought, however, is stated paradigmatically as follows: " 'Obstruction hinders obstruction, and sees obstruction; obstruction obstructs obstruction'— such is time."[47] The original reads: *Ge wa ge o sae ge o miru. Ge wa ge o ge-suru nari. Ge,* short for *keige* ("obstruction"), is used by Dōgen in his *Shōbōgenzō* in a way that deliberately distorts the conventional usage. Instead of the dualistic "inter-dharmic" juxtaposition of that which obstructs and that which is obstructed, Dōgen uses the term to denote an "intra-dharmic" dynamic[48] in which that which obstructs and that which is obstructed are one and the same dharma. As a consequence, *ge* or *keige* properly stands for the "self-obstruction" of a dharma, and by extension, the absolute uniqueness and freedom of that dharma. This example provides an excellent instance of Dōgen's freehanded attitude towards a traditional mode of expression. But more importantly, Dōgen refuses to express a dharma's ultimate existence by any predicates other than its own self-generative manner of expression. It is like a finger trying to catch itself: a whimsical simile used to suggest the only authentic approach to existence from Dōgen's realizational perspective. To put it differently, in Dōgen's writing a noun is converted into a makeshift verbal form in order to predicate that same noun. Thus the paradigm "A A-s A" (e.g., "The sky sky-s the sky") and its variants appear throughout the *Shōbōgenzō.* Dōgen's predilection for creating new forms of verbs, as we shall see presently, is founded on this supposition.

The fundamental meaning of "not-hearing" is such that when [the tongue] is obstructed by the tongue, it is "not-hearing"; when [the ear] is obstructed by the ear, it is "not-hearing"; when [the eye] is illumined by the eye, it is "not-hearing"; and when [the body-mind] is blocked by the body-mind, it is "not-hearing."[49]

Here a cluster of reflexive utterances appear in this discussion of Tung-shan Liang-chieh's statement concerning the task of going beyond the Buddha *(bukkōjōji)*. The tongue, the ear, the eye, and the body-mind are respectively in total exertion; on this account, each of their activities is said to be "not-hearing," that is, beyond hearing.

The following are additional cases in point:

> "Reaching" is obstructed by "reaching," not by "not-reaching"; "not-reaching" is obstructed by "not-reaching," not by "reaching." "Mind" obstructs "mind," and sees "mind." "Words" obstruct "words," and see "words."[50]

> By and large, many sages commonly have an inclination to the study of cutting off the roots of vines, but they do not realize that cutting vines with vines is called "cutting off," nor are they aware of entangling vines with vines, let along inheriting vines with vines.[51]

> Because the buddhas succeed one another, the Buddha-way is that which only the buddhas thoroughly penetrate, and not a single moment exists apart from the buddhas. For instance, a stone succeeds a stone; a gem succeeds a gem. A chrysanthemum succeeds [a chrysanthemum], and a pine confers the seal of verification [upon a pine]: all of which seems to indicate that the preceding chrysanthemum and the succeeding chrysanthemum are thusness, and the preceding pine and the succeeding pine are thusness.[52]

As we have touched on previously, Dōgen coins words and generates a seemingly endless multiplicity of new verbal expressions, all derived from nouns. We would probably not be mistaken to note that this procreation of verbs is greatly facilitated by the nature of the Japanese language, which allows verbs to be formed from any noun by adding the verbal suffix *su* as in *dōtoku su* from *dōtoku*. Yet we should bear in mind that it was Dōgen's religio-philosophical orientation which propelled him to take full advantage of this feature of the Japanese language. The *Shōbōgenzō* abounds with examples of this kind, of which the following are but a few: *hōtō su* (from *hōtō*, "the jeweled pagoda"); *kokū su* (from *kokū*, "the empty sky"); *uji su* (from *uji*, "existence time"); *jōroku-kon-jin su* (from *jōroku-konjin*, "the sixteen-foot golden body"); *muchū-set-sumu su* (from *muchū-setsumu*, "discourse on dream in dream"); *kyō-ryaku su* (from *kyōryaku*, "passage"); *shitsuu su* (from *shitsuu*, "all existence").

Another favorite device of Dōgen's is that of repetitive succession of the same Chinese character: e.g., *ka-ka* (*ka*, "fruit," "effect"); *tō-tō* (*tō*, "equality," "nonduality"); *butsu-butsu* (*butsu*, "buddha"); *shin-jin* (*shin*, "body"); *shō-shō* (*sho*, "birth"); *ji-ji* (*ji*, "time"). While the effects may vary with different contexts, the resultant meanings do share the conjuncture of absolute particularity conjoined with absolute universality, as in *jiji* ("each particular time," "all time"). Again the import of this kind of diction is akin to the Hua-yen Buddhist view of all-in-one and one-in-all, which is based on the notion of the "non-obstruction of an event and [all other] events" *(jiji-muge; shih-shih-wu-ai).*

In sum, Dōgen's peculiar usage of reflexive utterances may be seen to derive from his religio-philosophical outlook, which is to suggest the existence of a close correlation between the usage and the outlook. The *locus classicus* of this correlation is found in the statement on temporal dynamicity already quoted at the end of the last section: "spring 'passes' without anything outside itself."

(5) The Upgrading of Commonplace Notions and Use of Neglected Metaphors

Dōgen also manifests his sensitivity to language through his effort to revive quasi-obsolete Buddhist metaphors and symbols. In the *Shōbō-genzō,* Dōgen resurrects forgotten metaphors, infusing them with new, immediate value; in other cases, he discovers hidden meanings, while in still others, he liberates them from conventional constraints. It is most remarkable to observe Dōgen's almost tender attention to every possible nuance of meaning in even the most ordinary everyday words.

Take the metaphorical usage of the word "dream" *(mu).* In Buddhism, this word is used chiefly in association with the transience and precariousness of life, along with such images as bubbles, dew, etc. As against these stock derogatory connotations of dream, however, Dōgen declares that dream is indeed the real nature *(jissō),* i.e., ultimate reality:

> Inasmuch as the wonderful Dharma of the buddhas is communicated only between a buddha and a buddha, all dharmas of the dream state as well as of the waking state are equally the real nature. In the waking state there are arousing the mind, training, enlightenment, and nirvana; and in the dream state there are arousing the mind, training, enlightenment, and nirvana. The dream state and the waking state are respectively the real nature: no largeness or smallness, no superiority or inferiority, has anything to do with them.[53]

As Dōgen uncompromisingly holds here, man in the dream state is as creative in his soteriological activities as in the waking state.

Vine *(kattō)* is another word which is usually given pejorative connotations as an expression of "entanglement," be it of passions and desires, of words and letters, or of theories and interpretations. Dōgen, however, adopts this image as descriptive of the type of communicative relationship between master and disciple which leads to ever greater discovery and understanding of the Dharma, thereby upgrading the status of the metaphor to the level of the Dharma itself. Dōgen writes:

> For this reason, [the master's] sayings are the instances of leaping-out in which the master and the disciples participate together. [The disciples'] hearings are also the instances of leaping-out in which the master and the disciples participate together. The concerted penetration of master and disciple is the vines of the buddhas and patriarchs; the vines of the buddhas and patriarchs are the life-pulse of the "skin-flesh-bones-marrow." The Buddha's holding up a flower with winking is a vine; Mahākāśyapa's bursting into a smile is the "skin-flesh-bones-marrow."

> We should further study penetratingly: Because a vine seed has the power to cast itself off, branches, leaves, flowers, and fruits entwine the vine, and because they are all harmonious with and yet independent of each other, the buddhas and patriarchs are realized, and the kōan is realized.[54]

This is "the principle that the 'skin, flesh, bones, and marrow' intertwine as vines."[55] By implication Dōgen suggests that the very texture of the Buddha-dharma is constituted of passions and desires, conflicts and antitheses; and that reason does not exist by freeing itself from paradox any more than paradox can exist independently of the power of reason. Truth lies rather in the mysterious interpenetration of reason and paradox.

In a similar manner Dōgen elevates *gabyō* ("the pictured cakes"), *kūge* ("the sky flowers"), *mitsugo* ("intimate word"), and other terms from their deprecatory status to a prestigious one in his universe of discourse. He probes such conventional Buddhist locutions as *hiniku-kotsu-zui* ("the skin, flesh, bones, and marrow"), *dōtoku* ("expressions"), *kokyō* ("the primordial mirror"), *gyōji* ("activity-unremitting"), *genjō-kōan* ("the realization-kōan"), *zenki* ("total dynamism"), *udonge* ("the udumbara flower"), *immo* ("thusness"), *arakan* ("the arhat"), *shoaku-makusa* ("not to commit any evil"), in order to rescue them from neglect and obscurity, and so that they may function as dynamic, transformative concepts and symbols in the soteriological milieu of the Buddha-dharma. Dōgen also radically reinterprets the concepts of *jinzū* ("superknowledge"), *darani* ("charms and spells"), *tashintsū* ("the knowledge of others' minds"), *ōsaku-sendaba* ("the king asking for the saindhava"), among numerous others. As should be clear from these few illustrations, Dōgen's multifaceted genius consists in his ability to discover and rediscover the conceptual and symbolic possibilities of plain, unpretentious words and expressions.

In this connection, the following observation is in order. A medieval aristocrat in origin, Dōgen could not be other than literary and poetic in his writing, even in his most cerebral and analytic moments. It is thus not surprising that he also devotes his analytic abilities to such emotive images as *baika* ("plum blossoms"), *kōmyō* ("radiant light"), *tsuki* ("the moon"), *keisei-sanshoku* ("valley sounds, mountain sights"), *shunjū* ("spring and autumn"), *ryūgin* ("a dragon's song"), and *sansui* ("mountains and waters.") Throughout, however, his overriding concern remains unequivocally soteriological and ontological. A true alchemist of symbols, Dōgen evokes the vicissitudes of the dharmic drama of the universe through his exquisite, matchlessly poetic, and refined manipulation of language and symbols. Nonetheless, he does show a certain restraint regarding the sensuous aspects of the poetic.

In Dōgen's writing, then, the symbolism emerges as living force in its own right, or, to put it differently, the symbolized "bodies forth" in and through the symbol. It follows that likeness is thusness, simile is actuality. In short, the symbol is not a means to edification but an end in itself—the workings of ultimate truth. It is from this perspective that Dōgen may be seen to defy emphatically the traditional instrumentalist's view of "the gate of skillful means" *(hōbemmon):* "The gate of skillful means is the supreme virtue of the Buddha-fruit [of realization]."[56] What is referred to as "skillful means" *(hōben)* here is not instrument but realization itself. The means and the ends here are mediated and authenticated by absolute emptiness, and thereby realized in thusness. Therefore: "The Buddha-dharma, even if it is a metaphor, is the real nature."[57] The humble expressions adopted in Dōgen's symbolic universe are no exception in this regard.

(6) The Use of Homophonous Expressions

In his writing Dōgen frequently employs various associative techniques.

> We must know that this "east mountain's walking over the water" is the bones and marrow of the buddhas and patriarchs. "All the waters" are realized at the foot of the east mountain; consequently, "all the mountains" ride on the clouds and stride in the heavens. The peaks of "all the waters" are "all the mountains"; the ascending and descending walks [of "all the mountains"] take place over the water. Since the tips of the feet of "all the mountains" walk across "all the waters," splashing "all the waters" merrily, their walking is free everywhere, and their practice and verification are not nonexistent.[58]

Dōgen here repeats "all the mountains" *(shozan)* and "all the waters" *(shosui),* interweaving them with pertinent associations and imagery.

Consequently, the nonduality of mountain and water is vividly presented. This is but one of countless examples of poetic and ideational association which appear in the *Shōbōgenzō*.

We shall concern ourselves here with but one aspect of Dōgen's associative use of homophonous pairs to generate meaning. Dōgen says: *Shobutsu kore shō naru yueni shobutsu kore shō nari* ("Because all the buddhas are verification, all things are verification").[59] Dōgen associates *shobutsu* ("all the buddhas") with *shobutsu* ("all things"). Another example: *Butsudo akiramezareba busshi ni arazu. Busshi to iuwa busshi to iu kotonari* ("Unless we understand the Buddha-way, we are not the Buddha successors. The Buddha successors mean the Buddha children").[60] Here Dōgen relates *busshi* ("the Buddha successor") to *busshi* ("the Buddha child").

The foregoing observations shed light on a recent hypothesis advanced by Takasaki Jikidō. According to Takasaki, the term "casting off the body and mind" *(shinjin-datsuraku)* never appears in the works of Ju-ching, Dōgen's master. Another expression "casting off the mind's dust" *(shinjin-datsuraku)* does appear, however, though just once. It is possible, therefore, that Dōgen may have understood Ju-ching's "casting off the mind's dust" as "casting off the body and mind."[61] When we consider the fact that these two expressions are homophonous in Japanese, and put this idea in the context of what we have observed with respect to Dōgen's frequent use of homophonous expressions, it is not too farfetched to think that he may have hit upon this central idea of "casting off the body and mind" by way of homophonous association, which in turn triggered his religio-philosophical imagination. If this conjecture is correct, we may also speculate that Dōgen's proclivity for intentional misrepresentation may have been inspired during his student years in China (1223–1227).

Whatever the validity of such a surmise, there is no doubt about Dōgen's superb mastery of the associative technique as a means of furthering religious understanding.

(7) Reinterpretation Based on the Principle of Absolute Emptiness

⌊If there is any single principle central to Dōgen's life and thought, it is that of absolute emptiness, as appropriated in the context of realization. Let us examine some examples of his radical reinterpretation—alternately referred to as intentional misrepresentation—based on various aspects of this principle. These examples can be conveniently grouped under the following subheadings: (i) the relative seen in terms of the absolute; (ii) the future construed as the present; (iii) the transcendental and static interpreted in terms of the realizational and dynamic; (iv) differing degrees or stages of practice all conceived as verification, perfect and total; (v) a pre-enlightenment event viewed as a post-enlightenment event; (vi) imperative statements construed as declarative ones; (vii) anaology seen as identity; and (viii) interrogatives and negatives used in the context of realization. We will not provide examples for each heading, but instead limit ourselves to just a few illustrative cases in point.

> The foregoing "If you wish to know the meaning of Buddha-nature" means: "Just now you know the meaning of Buddha-nature." "You should observe the conditions of time" means: "Just now you know the conditions of time." To know this "Buddha-nature" is to know the "conditions of time." And to say "If the time arrives" means: "The time has already arrived; how can you doubt it?"[62]

The conventional reading of these expressions, whereby Buddha-nature is to be realized sometime in the future, is transformed by Dōgen to mean a realized actuality of the present.

In the Tashintsū fascicle Dōgen deals with the incident of Nan-yang Hui-chung (d. 776) and Ta-erh, a Dharma master from India, in which the former tests the authenticity of the latter's ability to know others' minds (i.e., one of the six supernormal powers). But Dōgen criticizes the popular dualistic understanding of this power, interpreting it instead in an absolute sense, such that it becomes the grasping of the absolute mind which transcends self and other, body and mind.[63]

Discussing Bodhidharma's statement "You have attained my skin, flesh, bones, and marrow" *(hiniku-kotsuzui),* Dōgen repudiates the traditional view, which sees these four as metaphors for progressive degrees of understanding or as means of hierarchically ranking Bodhidharma's four disciples, Tao-fu, Tsung-chih, Tao-yü, and Hui-k'o. Instead, he views them from the absolute standpoint of realization:

> We should know that the patriarch's saying "skin, flesh, bones, and marrow" has no bearing on shallowness or deepness. Even though [the disciples'] views may differ in terms of superiority and inferiority, the patriarch's own expression is nothing other than "You have attained me." Its fundamental meaning is that his instructions, such as "You have attained my marrow" and "You have attained my bones," are all methods to guide people. None is either more or less adequate than any other. . . . The patriarch's body-mind is such that the skin, flesh, bones, and marrow are all equally the patriarch himself: the marrow is not deepest, the skin is not shallowest.[64]

Dōgen elsewhere writes:

In the Buddha-dharma, practice and verification are one. Inasmuch as one's practice right at this moment is based on verification, a beginner's enactment of the Way is the wholeness of original verification. . . . Because it is intrinsically the verification of practice, there is no end to verification; because it is the practice of verification, there is no beginning to practice.[65]

When we compare supreme, perfect enlightenment and the budding arousal of the thought of enlightenment to each other, they are like the fire of the kalpa of destruction and the glow of a firefly. Yet, when we arouse the thought that "one ferries others across the river before he has crossed himself," they are "two but not different."[66]

The following example has to do with the well-known story of Nan-yüeh's polishing a tile:

Chiang-si Ma-tsu formerly studied under Nan-yüeh [Huai-jang], from whom he personally received the seal of the mind. This is the very beginning of [the tradition of] polishing a tile. [Thereafter] Ma-tsu resided in Ch'uan-fa-yüan and daily engaged in *zazen* for some ten years. . . . One day when Nan-yüeh visited Ma-tsu's hut, Ma-tsu was in attendance on him. Nan-yüeh asked: "What have you been doing of late?" Ma-tsu said: "These days I just sit single-mindedly." "What is *zazen* for?" said Nan-yüeh. "I sit to become a buddha," replied Ma-tsu. Then Nan-yüeh picked up a piece of tile and began to polish it against a rock by Ma-tsu's hut. Seeing this, Ma-tsu immediately inquired: "Master, what are you doing?" "I am polishing a tile," Nan-yüeh said. Ma-tsu asked: "What is polishing a tile for?" "I am making a mirror by polishing it," said the master. "How can you make a mirror by polishing a tile?" asked Ma-tsu. "How can you become a buddha by doing *zazen*?" asked Nan-yüeh.[67]

In this quotation and throughout the subsequent exposition, Dōgen suggests that the incident took place *after* Ma-tsu received the seal of the Buddha-mind from Nan-yüeh. The original source of the story, however, had presented the two events in reverse order.[68] Viewed as a post-enlightenment event, as Dōgen urges us to do, the story's significance is transformed: the emphasis is not on the futility but on the necessity of doing *zazen*. Nan-yüeh's words and acts are to warn against waiting for verification, and not against doing meditation. Becoming a buddha by sitting in meditation is impossible, because Buddhahood is not the end result but the starting point of Zen training. Hence doing *zazen* is indispensable not as a means of seeking but as the evidence of verification.

In his analysis of *shoaku-makusa* ("not to commit any evil"), which is ordinarily construed as a negative imperative, "Do not commit any evil" *(shoaku wa tsukuru koto nakare* or *shoaku wa nasu koto nakare),* Dōgen reads it as an indicative: *shoaku wa tsukuru koto nashi* or *shoaku wa nasu koto nashi* ("[The enlightened one] does not commit evil)." His message here is that *shoaku-makusa* is not to be taken as a moral imperative, whether self-imposed by autonomous conscience or inculcated by heteronomous imposition, but rather as the transformative reality of realization, whose mystery lies in one's resolve "never to commit any evil." This in turn means, however paradoxical it may sound, that realization both transcends good and evil and is at the same time profoundly involved with good and evil. In this way, for Dōgen morality and ethics, as well as language and intellect, become an integral component of spirituality.

> We must realize that when heard as "not to commit any evil," it is the Buddha's true Dharma. This "not to commit any evil" does not mean that an ordinary person first contrives and then brings about like this. When we hear the teaching of enlightenment expounded, it is heard like this. It is heard like this because it is the expression which supreme enlightenment itself is speaking. It is already the talk of enlightenment; therefore, it talks about enlightenment. Supreme enlightenment propounds itself and is heard in such a way that one is moved to desire "not to commit any evil" and to go on practicing "not to commit any evil." Where evil is no longer being committed, the power of training is realized at once.[69]

To conclude this section, let us consider Dōgen's use of negatives. Negative expressions are of course common in Zen usage: e.g., no-thought *(musō)*, no-mind *(mushin)*, no-birth *(fushō)*, no-form *(musō)*, nonthinking *(hishiryō)*. Although strikingly akin to those expressions of *via negativa* in other mystical traditions, however, the Ch'an/Zen negative method performs two functions: first, it works as the radical negation of *both* components of an antithesis, avoiding the privileging of one over the other. Thus it constantly rejects the reification of its own negating activity in any objective, referential manner. Second, it functions as an equally radical affirmation of dynamic, creative reality in the realm of dualities and antitheses.

Against this tradition, Dōgen's Zen distinguishes itself by rigorously explicating the realizational, dynamic function of negation, which, at the same time, never loses sight of its transcendental, critical function. One of the clearest illustrations of this technique involves his interpretation of *shin-fukatoku*. Usually understood as "the mind cannot be grasped," the assumption being that the mind is a transcendental object of knowledge, this expression is interpreted by Dōgen to mean that the mind *is* the unattainable and the unattainable *is* the mind. Thus the word "unattainable" *(fukatoku)* is freed of its customarily epistemological cast, and becomes the ontological-soteriological reality vibrant in the everyday mind.[70]

In the Zazenshin fascicle of the *Shōbōgenzō* Dōgen gives a fascinating account of Yüeh-shan's thinking *(shiryō)*, not-thinking *(fu-shiryō)*, and nonthinking *(hi-shiryō)*[71] Dōgen quotes the original kōan:

> After sitting, a monk asked Great Master Yüeh-shan Hung-tao: "What are you thinking in the immobile state of sitting?" The master said: "I think of not-thinking." The monk said: "How can one think of not-thinking?" The master replied: "Nonthinking."[72]

In Dōgen's rendition of this kōan, *kono fu-shiryō-tei o shiryō su* ("I think of not-thinking") is transformed into *shiryō ko fu-shiryō-tei* ("Thinking is not-thinking"). Here *fu-shiryō* is *fu no shiryō:* the not's, or should I say, the absolute emptiness's, thinking. In other words, *fu-shiryō* does not denote the absence or denial of thinking, but suggests rather the absolute truth's thinking. In the final analysis, authentic thinking is the not's thinking. By the same token, *fu-shiryō-tei ikanga shiryo sen* ("How can one think of not-thinking?") is read as: *fu-shiryō-tei ikan (no) shiryō* ("Not-thinking is the How's thinking"). "How" as an interrogative evokes a quality of absolute significance, i.e., the incomprehensible, indeterminate truth/reality, and consequently, not-thinking is equated to How's thinking. This whole complex meaning is called non-thinking *(hi-shiryō)* which is the essence of *zazen:* the "non" *(hi)* in non-thinking in Dōgen's thought emphasizes not so much the transcendence of thinking and no thinking as the dynamic realization of thinking and not-thinking in the ascesis of *zazen.* All in all, *zazen* is authentic thinking —the trinary complex of thinking, not-thinking, and nonthinking— which is none other than the most concrete reality of the self and the world.

Our investigation here is but a modest beginning in the direction of a systematic treatment of Dōgen's enormously complex linguistic universe. Yet, on the basis of the foregoing, we may affirm that language and thought are to be living realities for the practitioner of *zazen,* and to that extent, they should be the legitimate concerns of the student of Ch'an/Zen spirituality. Moreover, it is apparent that authentic linguistic activity is appropriate to the principle of absolute emptiness, and that a creative use of language is in itself the realization and expression of spiritual freedom. This point cannot be overemphasized; it has been flagrantly ignored by most students in the field of Ch'an/Zen studies. It is a golden opportunity for us, without going to the extreme of becoming apologists of Ch'an/Zen, to recognize this fascinating and important side of the tradition.

Viewed superficially, Dōgen's treatment of the kōan appears to be not so different from the traditional *teishō* of Zen Buddhism. Still, Dōgen is unique in that his commentary is based on a radically different appreciation of language. The context of realization within which he works can be fully appreciated only by paying attention to the underlying characteristics of his method, as we have suggested in this essay. The fundamental difference between Dōgen and most other commentators has to do with his awareness of the vital realizational potential of language. As Dōgen sees it, the kōan does not castigate the intellect only to supplant it with prajñā or transcendent wisdom; rather, it liberates the intellect in the direction of its own ontological and soteriological possibilities.

✕What Dōgen typically does in his *Shōbōgenzō* is to repeat a certain concept, metaphor, or image over and over again, and in this apparently redundant process, to change word order, shift syntax, indicate alternate meanings, create new expressions, and revive forgotten symbols. These linguistic activities are not building blocks for a new religious or philosophical system; they are rather like "ripples"—concentrically reaching out from, and returning to, the ascesis of *zazen*—which explicate and reinforce Dōgen's primordial belief in absolute emptiness. Linguistic activities are claimed to be the very workings of *zazen*, of nonthinking itself. It is in this respect that the language of the old-paradigm kōan becomes a living force operative in the working of the realization-kōan, and what is more, that, in the truest sense, kōan becomes *zazen*, and *zazen* becomes kōan.

⌊ Dōgen was a superb master of language, appreciating it not for its rhetorical use-value, but rather for its appeal to reason and rationality. For Dōgen, the interior and exterior of language were the very fabric of existence. His scrupulous and categorical respect for language stemmed directly from this sense of its identity as existence itself. Yet, this respect for language did not prevent him from constantly experimenting with it and challenging its ordinary locution with a view to the creation of a more humane, compassionate world. To him method was realization; rationality was spirituality; and reason and ascesis redeemed each other. Such a view of language was the fruition of his quest for the "reason of words and letters" *(monji no dōri)*.

Notes

1. Hee-Jin Kim, *Dōgen Kigen—Mystical Realist* (Tucson: University of Arizona Press, 1975), p. 25.
2. Concerning the historical and doctrinal background of this question, see ibid., pp. 25–27.
3. This is not intended to slight the poetic dimension of Dōgen's thought: he was a poetic thinker. See note 8 below.
4. Kim, op. cit., pp. 234–252.
5. With respect to these two methods of Ch'an/Zen, see Philip Kapleau, *The Three Pillars of Zen,* revised and expanded edition (New York: Anchor Press, 1980); Katsuki Sekida, *Zen Training: Methods and Philosophy*

(Tokyo and New York: Weatherhill, 1975); etc. For a history of the kōan tradition, see Isshū Miura and Ruth F. Sasaki, *Zen Dust: The History of the Koan and Koan Study in Rinzai (Lin-chi) Zen* (New York: Harcourt, Brace & World, 1966), pp. 3–76; Furuta Shōkin, "Kōan no rekishi-teki hatten-keitai ni okeru shinri-sei no mondai," in Miyamoto Shōson, ed., *Bukkyō no kompon shinri* (Tokyo: Sanseidō, 1956), pp. 807–840. As to the problem of classification of kōans, see Kajiya Sōnin, "Kōan no soshiki," in *Kōza Zen* 7 (Tokyo: Chikuma shobō, 1968), pp. 263–270; Miura and Sasaki, op. cit., pp. 46–72. For the inner dynamics of kōan meditation, see D. T. Suzuki, *Essays in Zen Buddhism,* Second Series (London: Rider, 1950), pp. 17–188.

6. Heinrich Dumoulin, *A History of Zen Buddhism* (New York: Pantheon Books, 1963), pp. 132–136, as regards these two strands of Ch'an. Needless to say, the history of Ch'an/Zen is much more complex than here described. This paragraph should serve only to facilitate our understanding of the structural aspects of Dōgen's methodology.

7. In this connection we should bear in mind that, despite the prevailing Ch'an/Zen principle of "a special tradition outside scriptures" *(kyōge-betsuden; chiao-wai-pieh-ch'uan),* Dōgen considered the sutras to be as much an integral part of the Buddha-dharma as the kōans. Thus our observations relative to the kōans apply to Dōgen's conception of the sutras as well.

8. See Dōgen, *Shōbōgenzō zuimonki* 3:17 (*DZZ* 2:449–450); 3:14 (*DZZ* 2:447–448). Paradoxically, Dōgen was eloquent in his writings, especially in the *Shōbōgenzō.* Yet his eloquence was accompanied by a profound emotional resonance which is the essential part of poetics. Thus, for all his admonitions against play with words, he was deeply poetic and, as a medieval Japanese, he could not have been otherwise. To Dōgen, to philosophize was not only to think but also to feel, not only to rationalize but also to poeticize.

9. Sansuikyō (*DZZ* 1:260–261).

10. See Suzuki, op. cit., pp. 17–188.

11. Suzuki's exposition of the psychological dynamics of kōan exercise is perhaps the only systematic one available at present, but it may be anticipated that the problem will be far more thoroughly and accurately explored in the future. The merit of Suzuki's interpretation for a full understanding of kōan dynamics must not be exaggerated. Katsuki Sekida, in his aforementioned work, advances a highly suggestive notion of "language samādhi" in relation to the dynamics of kōan meditation.

12. In his *Zen Comments on the Mumonkan* (New York: Harper & Row, 1974), Zenkei Shibayama appears to be much more appreciative than Suzuki of the legitimate use of kōan study in the spirit very similar to the realizationist view. Yet Shibayama's interpretation of the kōan and its language is still essentially instrumentalist and, as a result, fails to see the dynamic forces of language in the context of realization. See pp. 27, 87, 92, 100–101, 151, 266, 347, etc., for his view on the kōan.

At this point a qualification is in order: While the instrumentalist view maintains that the finger points to the moon, the realizationist view holds that the finger not only points to the moon but *is* the moon. To put it differently, the finger, according to the realizationist view, is not the moon, but the moon is invariably the finger, because it completes itself as the finger. Thus the realizationist view does not and should not reject the instrumentalist view; it only perfects it.

13. In total exertion ascesis and play are inseparably one. Accordingly, exertion and relaxation go together in *zazen;* by the same token, ascesis and artistic freedom are conjoined in art.
14. Dōtoku (*DZZ* 1:301–305).
15. Sansuikyō (*DZZ* 1:262).
16. Sansuikyō (*DZZ* 1:262–264).
17. I am indebted to Kagamishima Genryū, *Dōgen zenji to in'yō kyōten-goroku no kenkyū* (Tokyo: Mokujisha, 1965), and Terada Tōru, *Dōgen no gengo uchū* (Tokyo: Iwanami shoten, 1974). The latter has been extremely helpful for this study. Terada, however, does not sufficiently delve into the intrinsic relationship between spiritual discipline and linguistic activity in Dōgen's thought, or between Dōgen the practicer and Dōger the thinker. The present investigation and analysis are a modest attempt to go beyond Terada by showing that linguistic activity is an indispensable part of the spiritual discipline demanded by the logic of the Buddha-dharma.

    In addition, I would like to acknowledge my indebtedness to the following: Chung-ying Cheng, "On Zen (Ch'an) Language and Zen Paradoxes," *Journal of Chinese Philosophy* 1 (1973), pp. 77–102; Kurebayashi Kōdō, "*Shōbōgenzō* ni okeru kōan kaisetsu no ishitsusei," *Journal of Indian and Buddhist Studies* 14 (1, December 1965), pp. 1–12; Ueda Shizuteru, "Zen to kotoba," *Kōza Zen* 7 (Tokyo: Chikuma shobō, 1968), pp. 7–50; and Takemura Makio, "Dōgen no gengo-tetsugaku," *Kōza Dōgen* 4 (Tokyo: Shunjūsha, 1980), pp. 192–215.
18. Sokushin-zebutsu (*DZZ* 1:44). Quotation marks in the translated text indicate, aside from their customary applications, those instances where Dōgen applies various methods of linguistic transformation. To explicate the underlying transformative processes, I have, wherever feasible, used the device of quotation marks.
19. Not only does this observation have a very important implication for our understanding of Dōgen, but it is a great challenge to the translator of the *Shōbōgenzō.* Confronted with such expressions as the present one, he is better off not to oblige himself to restate them in more facile language, but to try to participate in the symbolic play.
20. Kūge (*DZZ* 1:114).
21. Loc. cit.
22. Shohō-jissō (*DZZ* 1:365).
23. Bukkyō (*DZZ* 1:311).
24. Mujō-seppō (*DZZ* 1:397).
25. To take just one example: The two Chinese characters *katachi* ("form") and *gotoku* ("like") in *kedashi musō-zammai no katachi mangatsu no gotoku naruo motte nari* (". . . because the formless samadhi has its form just like the full moon") are combined together and rendered as *gyō-nyo* ("to embody thusness," "to form thusness," "form-thusness"). The quite ordinary characters meaning nothing more than "a form just like" are dramatically altered in their signification; as a result, form is no longer likeness but thusness itself. See Busshō (*DZZ* 1:23–24).
26. See Masao Abe, "Dōgen on Buddha Nature," *EB* 4(1):28–71.
27. Zenki (*DZZ* 1:204).
28. Busshō (*DZZ* 1:–22–23).
29. Kembutsu (*DZZ* 1:480).
30. Daigo (*DZZ* 1:85).
31. As for the problem of Japanese thought patterns in relation to language and

culture, see Hajime Nakamura, *Ways of Thinking of Eastern Peoples* (Honolulu: University of Hawaii Press, 1964), pp. 345–587.

32. Juki (*DZZ* 1:200).
33. Kaiin-zammai (*DZZ* 1:103).
34. Gabyō (*DZZ* 1:210).
35. Kūge (*DZZ* 1:108–115).
36. Kūge (*DZZ* 1:111).
37. Mitsugo (*DZZ* 1:395).
38. Tsuki (*DZZ* 1:206).
39. Baika (*DZZ* 1:459).
40. Loc. cit.
41. Dōtoku (*DZZ* 1:302).
42. Uji (*DZZ* 1:189–194).
43. Uji (*DZZ* 1:192).
44. *Vajracchedikā-prajñāpāramitā-sūtra.* See Edward Conze, *Buddhist Wisdom Books* (London: Allen & Unwin, 1958), pp. 17–74.
45. Busshō (*DZZ* 1:19).
46. Sansuikyō (*DZZ* 1:267).
47. Uji (*DZZ* 1:193).
48. Although I here use "intra-dharmic" and "inter-dharmic," I do so advisedly, with full awareness that these expressions are at best only an approximation.
49. Bukkōjōji (*DZZ* 1:224–225).
50. Uji (*DZZ* 1:193).
51. Kattō (*DZZ* 1:331).
52. Shisho (*DZZ* 1:337).
53. Muchū-setsumu (*DZZ* 1:244).
54. Kattō (*DZZ* 1:334).
55. Kattō (*DZZ* 1:335).
56. Shohō-jissō (*DZZ* 1:368–369).
57. Muchū-setsumu (*DZZ* 1:244).
58. Sansuikyō (*DZZ* 1:261).
59. Gabyō (*DZZ* 1:210).
60. Shisho (*DZZ* 1:338).
61. Takasaki Jikidō and Umehara Takeshi, *Kobutsu no manebi: Dōgen,* Bukkyō no shisō 11 (Tokyo: Kadokawa shoten, 1969), pp. 43–52. Dōgen is said to have been enlightened by Ju-ching's utterance.
62. Busshō (*DZZ* 1:17).
63. Tashintsū (*DZZ* 1:585–593).
64. Kattō (*DZZ* 1:332–333).
65. Bendōwa (*DZZ* 1:737).
66. Hotsu-bodaishin (*DZZ* 1:646).
67. Kokyō (*DZZ* 1:187).
68. See Kagamishima, op. cit., pp. 69–71.
69. Shoaku-makusa (*DZZ* 1:278).
70. Shin-fukatoku (*DZZ* 1:64–67).
71. Zazenshin (*DZZ* 1:90–101).
72. Zazenshin (*DZZ* 1:90).

The Incomparable Philosopher: Dōgen on How to Read the *Shōbōgenzō*

Thomas P. Kasulis

In viewing Dōgen from a philosophical standpoint, there is the temptation to juxtapose his thought with modern Western philosophy. That is, one might write a comparative piece on such topics as, for example, "Dōgen and Searle on Speech Acts," or "Dōgen and Marcel on the Mystery of Being," or "Dōgen and Derrida on Interpretation." East-West comparisons involving Dōgen abound in Japanese and can be found ever more frequently in English.

The popularity of these comparative topics deserves our attention. Why is Dōgen so often examined alongside modern, usually twentieth-century, philosophers? We should also bear in mind that from the early fourteenth to the early eighteenth centuries, there was a dearth of commentaries on the *Shōbōgenzō* even in Japan and the study of this masterpiece among Buddhist specialists has peaked only in our century.[1] Thus, it seems that the *Shōbōgenzō* must be, in some respect, distinctively modern and appropriate to our own time. But what exactly constitutes this almost unique relevance? There are admittedly many factors, but here we will consider just two.

The relevance of Dōgen's philosophy today

First, the twentieth century is characterized by a concern for language. Having discovered the clarity of logically pure expression (such as computer languages), we have been impressed with the possibility of unambiguous denotation. In other words, we have become expert in technical, precise ways of speaking. At the same time, by understanding how language can denote, we have come to recognize that much of our ordinary speaking is connotative, symbolic, or performative. We often mean more than we explicitly say; we intentionally use words to evoke new meanings; we speak in order to do things as well as to talk about things. In short, we are acutely aware of both the limitations of language (we cannot think what our language does not allow us to say) as well as its manifold possibilities (to refer, to suggest, to create, to do).

Over seven centuries ago, in a distant part of the world, in a radically different cultural and historical context, Dōgen was also sensitive to, and a master of, the many dimensions of language. The twentieth-century Japanese philosopher Tanabe Hajime recognized this quality in the Master:

> . . . viewed from the philosophical standpoint, Dōgen's *Shōbōgenzō* is matchless in its command of Japanese language and logic with the power to realize the ineffable in and through speech and discussion.[2]

As Tanabe's comment suggests, Dōgen's analysis and creative use of expression are provocative to modern thinkers concerned with the limits and possibilities of language.

A second aspect of Dōgen's thought relevant to twentieth-century Western philosophy is the issue of presence or givenness. Dissatisfied with the abstractions, generalities, and psychologism of German Idealism, twentieth-century philosophers have sought a new foundation for their discipline. Thus, contemporary philosophy has tried to return to concrete experience and to use it as a ground for all knowledge, whether analytic or synthesizing. Of course, logical positivism, pragmatism, and phenomenology, for example, each has its own version of what constitutes concreteness, but what characterizes all of them is their trust in what is directly experienced. The world we perceive is not an illusion. If our beliefs are untrue, it is because we have misguided ourselves through our own delusive interpretations. Knowledge begins and ends in the comprehension of what is immediately presented. The authority of texts, the observations of the past, and what is known through abstract logic alone are all of secondary, if any, importance. Be it the "simples" of G. E. Moore's common sense, the "pure experience" of William James's radical empiricism, or Husserl's phenomenological "primordial givenness," philosophical truth is grounded in what is experientially present.

Of course, like all Zen Buddhists, Dōgen also seeks verification in the person's own experience. The *way* in which Dōgen discusses this issue is unique, however. From most of the Chinese Ch'an masters, we have either technical advice on the proper way to practice or *mondō* accounts of their dynamic interactions with students. In general, except perhaps for a poem or two, the Chinese Masters themselves seldom wrote down their own teachings. Instead, we usually have the record of their practice as written by their chief disciples. The Japanese Zen masters did not follow this tradition quite so strictly and many masters have themselves written important works. Even within this context, though, Dōgen's

Shōbōgenzō is unique. Dōgen does not merely teach technique, nor does he only give a psychological account of his own path to enlightenment. In this regard, Dōgen is obviously doing something different from Hakuin, for example. The *Shōbōgenzō* is more an *analysis*, a personal investigation into the nature of one's own experience.

But what is the ground of this experience? Obviously, that which is prereflectively, nonconceptually, immediately given—the direct encounter with dharmas as present in zazen, what Dōgen calls the "presence of things as they are" *(genjō-kōan)*. Dōgen is very much interested in the nature of presence *(genjō)* and its appearance on different specific occasions *(jisetsu)*. His starting point is, of course, zazen, a state which Dōgen characterizes as without-thinking *(hishiryō),* a state in which there is just presence in its purest form, presence experienced immediately with a oneness of body-mind *(shin-jin ichinyo).* On these issues concerning presence, direct experience, and different perspectives arising on different occasions, Dōgen has much to offer contemporary Western philosophy. Possible comparisons and contrasts abound.

These points about Dōgen's sensitivity to the problems of language and presence establish his credentials as a philosopher. Dōgen is clearly a profound thinker and he can surely enrich our consideration of philosophical issues current in the West today. There are, however, difficulties with any comparison that would try to cross the conceptual boundaries separating twentieth-century Western ideas from Dōgen's thirteenth-century Japanese thought.

Problems with comparative techniques

First, the ideas of one great thinker can never be precisely mapped on to those of another. At best, we can find some points of common concern and a shared terminology or methodology. Comparative analyses must, to some extent, separate individual ideas out from the total fabric of a philosopher's thought. In many cases, the general pattern of the fabric is repeated often enough so that a carefully selected piece is indeed representative of the whole. In the case of Dōgen's thought, however, we have something more like a tapestry depicting a single scene, rather than a fabric with a repeating pattern, so it is difficult to take any single, isolated idea as truly representative.

Consequently, comparisons between Dōgen and modern Western philosophers will often be unfair to Dōgen. If a single concept such as "being-time" *(uji),* for example, is compared to the philosophy of temporality in, say, Husserl or Heidegger, the Western thinker comes out of the analysis looking more complete, more developed, more "philosophical" than Dōgen. Dōgen's contribution may seem valuable, but only as a thought-provoking suggestion, not a fully developed philosophical position. There is something distasteful in this, something comparable to the old-fashioned Western treatment of so-called "primitive religions." That is, it is again as if we modern Westerners are surprised to find that even primitives have profound ideas, or at least they are profound once we more advanced folk come along and help them articulate their own ideas on their behalf.

In making cross-cultural philosophical comparisons, we too frequently ignore certain of our own methodological assumptions. In what amounts to an instance of intellectual provincialism, we presume that *our* tradition is the one which stipulates the nature of philosophy and thinkers of other cultures are to be evaluated in terms of how well they help us understand and solve *our* problems. Perhaps this is even worse than provincialism and it might be better characterized as a form of philosophical imperialism: *we* are the manufacturers of philosophical ideas and foreign realms merely supply raw material for our own exploitation and development.

Perhaps the day has come for us to recognize the philosophical equivalent of national self-determination, that is, we ought to let each cultural tradition decide its own course of development. As philosophers, we may criticize the prudence of a chosen path and we may even criticize the enterprise as a whole if we believe it counterproductive, but once we have recognized each civilization's right to its own intellectual destiny, we can no longer criticize a foreign tradition simply because it is unlike ours. For example, the very fact that the Japanese intellectual tradition went on for a millenium and a half without having to develop certain classical philosophical problems found in the West should be a point of intense interest among Western philosophers. Instead, the peculiar twist of the Western mind has usually been to ignore that tradition as alien and less then philosophical because it did not develop the "right" problems.

Even if we accept the principle of national self-determination, philosophy may still, in some sense, be universal, but if so, it is because philosophizing, not philosophers, are universal. In other words, the ultimate criterion for identifying philosophy is not *what* is thought about, or even *how* it is thought, but *why* it is thought. To reduce philosophy to a *what* is to reduce its search for wisdom into just another form of knowledge. To consider philosophy a *how* is to make it into merely another technique or even a style of thinking. Philosophers may think about different things, they may even develop different general procedures for carrying out their investigations, but what they truly share is their common motivation and vision. Philosophers address themselves to what cannot yet be known through empirical and logical procedures, but which must be at least tentatively answered as the basis of a worldview and a personal value system to be utilized within the decisions of daily life.

Given the differences in cultural and historical situation, therefore, we should not expect to find in Dōgen's writings a fully developed Western theory on freedom vs. determinism, or the relationship between universals and particulars, or a solution to the is-ought problem. Indeed, we should probably be suspicious of anyone who claims we could. Dōgen is not doing Western philosophy; in fact, he is not even doing modern Japanese philosophy. Still, he is *philosophizing*; he is thinking through the questions of his own society and his own personal context. To appreciate Dōgen as a philosopher, we must meet him on his own turf, not ours.

Perhaps this analogy is helpful. Consider a traditional Kanō school painting with its gold-colored background. When I first saw these paintings in Western museums, I found them garish and overly ornate. Where was the famed Japanese aesthetic of simplicity, naturalness, and rusticity? When I later saw these works in their intended Japanese surroundings, however, my impression was totally different. In the shadowy, softly illumined quarters of a traditional Japanese building, the gold was barely visible. Rather, it was a quiet, luminous quality giving the painting life and depth. Analogously, Dōgen's ideas in the *Shōbōgenzō* are best seen in their own natural setting—the softly shaded nuances and conceptual contexts of Dōgen's own remarkable style. Taken to the bright glare of Western philosophical analysis, they seem merely ornate, unnecessarily contrived, or even odd. Since I do not want to create such an impression of Dōgen, I will not here make that kind of comparison.

In other words, it is a mistake to be defensive. It is not necessary to *prove* Dōgen is a philosopher and, unfortunately, East-West philosophical comparisons have often adopted this defensive stance. It is as if we wanted to show Dōgen's philosophical nature by virtue of the company we can make him keep: Dōgen shares one concern with Plato, a certain analysis with Heidegger, a line of thought with Austin. This is unconvincing; if we do not accept guilt by association, we should not recognize wisdom by association either. Much worse, however, this is a disservice to Dōgen's thought itself. Imagine, for example how distorted and disjointed a picture of Kant we would have if we focused mainly on how he was like and how he was unlike other philosophers. If we were to analyze Kant only in that way, we would never get to the aspect of Kant which is perhaps his greatest virtue: his completeness and his philosophical integration of diverse aspects of human experience (the epistemic, religious, ethical, and aesthetic). In a parallel way, Dōgen often suffers more from comparisons than he is helped by them. In his writings, one point leads into the next, one insight expands into another, a third circles back to readdress the conclusion of the first. This organic, fluid sense of reflection is a mark of Dōgen's philosophical style and it is often an injustice to Dōgen to cut this thread of internal consistency for the sake of tying Dōgen to some other, disconnected philosophical tradition.

In approaching Dōgen on his own terms, we must turn our attention to his magnum opus, the *Shōbōgenzō*. In analyzing Dōgen's philosophy, though, we should not only think about his supposedly discrete ideas, but we should also join him in his philosophizing process. It is not easy to communicate Dōgen's mode of thought in English, especially in a paper as short as this one must be. In order to demonstrate this process, however, we can choose a topic in which style and content come together. Specifically, we can ask Dōgen how we should read the *Shōbōgenzō*. We will find, not surprisingly, that a philosopher as insightful and thorough as Dōgen addresses this very issue. In his discussion he brings us into the very heart of his theory of meaning and his interest in writing such a work.

The Shōbōgenzō: *Language*

⌐The *Shōbōgenzō* is obviously a written document expressed in language. Therefore, to understand how Dōgen wishes his text to be read, we must begin with his view of language. Dōgen knows language or true "expression" *(dōtoku)* to be an extraordinarily rich, yet commonplace, event. He recognizes that the Buddha's truth *(buppō)* is communicated at times discursively in ordinary words that can be rationally understood and at other times esoterically in "intimate words" *(mitsugo)* that must be grasped immediately without discursive thinking. Dōgen believes that *both* are equally legitimate means of transmitting the correct Dharma *(shōbō)*.

An illuminating discussion occurs in the fascicle "Mitsugo" [Intimate (or esoteric) words] wherein Dōgen discusses the traditional story of the birth of Zen—Śākyamuni's twirling of a flower and winking, a gesture by which the Dharma was directly transmitted to Mahākāśyapa. Some interpret this episode to mean the Dharma, at least the Zen Dharma, can only be transmitted nonverbally. Dōgen disagrees.

> Those [who have not heard a genuine master's instructions] arbitrarily regard the twirling of the flower and winking at the great assembly of monks to be Śākyamuni's "esoteric language" *(mitsugo)*. By that reasoning, the Buddha's verbal exposition would be superficial, as in what can be conveyed by names and forms. Twirling the flower and winking in nonverbal exposition would itself be an occasion for the technique of esoteric language.

> . . .

> [But] Śākyamuni says after that, "I have the treasury of the correct Dharma-eye *(shōbōgenzō)* and the wondrous mind of nirvana. I transmit these to Mahākāśyapa." Is such an utterance verbal or nonverbal? If

Śākyamuni dislikes the verbal and prefers to twirl the flower, he should save the twirling for after [speaking].[3]

That is, Dōgen acknowledges the special intimacy of direct, nonverbal transmission, but this does not mean he rejects verbal teachings. The following passage explains this point more fully:

> If you regard Śākyamuni's verbalization as superficial, then twirling the flower and winking must also be superficial. If you regard Śākyamuni's verbalization as [just] names and forms, then you are not modeling yourself after the Buddha's truth *(buppō)*. Although you have known verbalization to be names and forms, you do not yet know that there are no names and forms for Śākyamuni—your unenlightened feelings have not yet been molted. The Buddhas and Patriarchs, having completely penetrated their body-minds and molted them, expound the Dharma, do so verbally, and turn the Dharma wheel. Many are those who see or hear them and who derive benefit from them.[4]

In short, Dōgen is very much a part of the Zen tradition in recognizing that discursive language is not necessary for enlightenment, yet he also grants the value of verbal exposition. In fact, in the final analysis, the fascicle maintains that the two means of transmission are not at all separate, but are two dimensions of the same reality. The esoteric *(mitsu)* is an intimacy *(shinmitsu)* with what is seen and heard in the everyday:

> The esoteric words, meanings, and actions of the Buddha's truth *(buppō)* are not the way [that the anti-verbalists argue]. On the occasion when you meet someone, you hear and express esoteric words. When you know yourself, you know esoteric activity.[5]

> This word *esoteric (mitsu)* is the fact of *intimacy (shinmitsu)*. . . . Esoteric action is not knowledge of self and other [in that] I alone can know my private self and do not understand each other private person. Because "intimacy is what is near you," everything exists through intimacy; each half exists through intimacy. Personally investigate such facts with clarity and diligence in your practice.[6]

Dōgen is keenly aware of the richness of language. Language is a primary human activity. Insofar as Zen touches on and vitalizes every dimension of life, its spirit must pervade language in *all* its uses, both esoteric and discursive.

The Shōbōgenzō: *Audience*

Now that we have some clearer understanding of Dōgen's view of language, we may ask for whom the *Shōbōgenzō* was written. The first fascicle, "Genjōkōan," was supposedly composed, for example, as a letter to a layman, Yōkōshū, in 1233. Yet, it is hard to imagine a layman's receiving a copy of "Genjōkōan" in the mail. What would he make of it? If it were merely meant to be practical advice for a layman in Kyūshū, why is the Japanese so often difficult and technical? Could Dōgen really have been so out of touch with reality that he thought a layperson like Yōkōshū, probably a bureaucrat for the military government, would be able to fathom the complexities of such a "letter"? Compare, for instance, the contemporary letters of Shinran or Nichiren, or even the later Zen letters of Hakuin. These examples are clearly more personal and give more concrete, practical advice than "Genjōkōan." Furthermore, if it were merely a letter, why did Dōgen save a copy and, two decades later, place it first in his edition of the *Shōbōgenzō?*

To read the *Shōbōgenzō* carefully is hard work. At first, one may suspect there is a linguistic problem: perhaps one is shaky in medieval Japanese grammar or perhaps one is being confused by the Sung Chinese colloquialisms Dōgen sprinkles throughout. On the other hand, the difficulty may be more historical: more study of the intellectual climate of Kamakura Japan may be required. Then, again, there could be buddhological complexities and one may need more background in the development of Buddhist doctrine or the subtle nuances of Buddhist terminology. The reference works—commentaries, dictionaries, glossaries, histories, grammars—begin to pile up on the desk. Individual lines assume unfathomable depth, but somehow the basic meaning is still elusive.

When I personally reached this point of desperation, I went for guidance to one of the finest Dōgen scholars in Japan. To begin the conversation, I simply asked why Dōgen wrote in Japanese instead of Chinese (*kanbun,* that is), the language favored by his Japanese predecessors in writing philosophical treatises. The answer of this scholar transformed my relationship to the text: "Dōgen did not write the *Shōbōgenzō* in Japanese. No other Japanese before or after Dōgen wrote in the language of the *Shōbōgenzō.* It is Dōgen's own language." Later, the scholar said something else equally significant: "In the final analysis, no one—not any commentary, not I, no other scholar—can teach you. The correct Dharma *(shōbō)* is in you."

It follows from this comment that since Dōgen wrote the *Shōbōgenzō* in his own, personal language, part of his audience would seem to be himself. That is, part of the riddle of the idiosyncrasies in the book lies in the fact that, to some extent at least, Dōgen was writing for himself as well as for others. Since Dōgen himself probably compiled the first edition, obviously the *Shōbōgenzō* was intended to be a public document. Yet it is also an intensely personal, intimate record. As the "Mitsugo" fascicle showed, the Dharma does not depend on words for its transmission; but neither does it depend on silence. That is, the language of the

Dharma can be simultaneously discursive and esoteric, simultaneously public and intimate. To fathom the full meaning of *Shōbōgenzō*, we must encounter and comprehend it in both dimensions.

The discursive is plain enough—at least once we have referred to the previously mentioned commentaries, dictionaries, glossaries, histories, and grammars. But how do we fathom the esoteric level, the level of intimacy? We have already seen one of Dōgen's suggestions in the fascicle "Mitsugo": "On the occasion when you meet someone, you hear and express esoteric words. When you know yourself, you know the esoteric actions." By extrapolation, to penetrate the intimacy of Dōgen's words, we must come face to face with the Master himself. The *Shōbōgenzō* is Dōgen's own esoteric action, that is, it expresses his own self-knowledge.[7] In this respect, it is written by himself, for himself, in intimacy with himself.

At the same time, the *Shōbōgenzō* is half of a dialogue, a most extraordinary dialogue, a verbal presence to be taken up as soon as the reader is ready and willing to meet the person who wrote it. In this respect, the *Shōbōgenzō* is written for us, or more precisely, for each of us, for *me* personally. It is a literary *dokusan,* the personal interview between master and disciple. We refer again to our previous quote from "Mitsugo":

> Because "the intimate is what is near you," everything exists through intimacy; each half exists through intimacy. Personally investigate such facts with clarity and diligence in your practice.

For me to achieve intimacy with Dōgen, I myself must make an intimate, esoteric act, that is, I must know myself by "investigating such facts with clarity and diligence in my practice." In short, the *Shōbōgenzō* is Dōgen himself, who by his esoteric act has created the "half which exists through intimacy." In a remarkable sense, the *Shōbōgenzō* is Dōgen's own presence—a discursive account of his own self-knowledge as presence and also the intimate presence of Dōgen himself, in oneness of body-mind *(shinjin ichinyo).* To separate Dōgen (the physical presence) from his ideas (his mental presence) is to deny that oneness. Conversely, I must bring my whole self, body and mind, to the text in order to create my own esoteric act, my own "half which exists through intimacy." The very act of interpretation, then, involves the whole person, the body-mind unified through intensity of focus and held *(ji)* together in the personal act *(gyō),* the continuous practice *(gyōji)* inseparable from enlightenment.

If this mode of interpretation involving the unified body-mind is achieved, the Dharma is directly transmitted. Then my body-mind itself is molted *(shinjin datsuraku);* so is Dōgen's. Furthermore, the act of transmission is not a single historical moment. Each reading of the *Shōbōgenzō* reopens the dialogue.[8] The transmission is unceasing and, when it occurs, there is the discovery of primordial personhood *(hon-bunnin):*

> To model yourself after the way of the Buddhas [and certainly Dōgen is a buddha] is to model yourself after yourself. To model yourself after yourself is to forget yourself. To forget yourself is to be authenticated by all dharmas. To be authenticated by all dharmas is to effect the molting of body-mind, both yours and others'. The distinguishing marks of enlightenment dissolve and [the molting of body-mind] causes those dissolving marks of enlightenment to emerge continuously.
>
> At first, when you *seek* the Dharma, you have distanced yourself from its domain. Finally, when the Dharma is correctly transmitted to you, you are immediately the primordial person.[9]

But who is the primordial person? If Dōgen and I can establish an intimacy through *Shōbōgenzō,* can we really be distinguished? This issue is directly discussed in the fascicle "Kattō" ["Vines" or "(Verbal) entanglements" or "Intertwinings"]. Like the fascicle "Mitsugo," the focus of "Kattō" is Zen transmission, this time the transmission from Bodhidharma to Hui-k'o rather than the transmission from Śākyamuni to Mahākāśyapa—which, incidentally, is mentioned in the opening of the fascicle. The familiar story concerns Bodhidharma's asking his four disciples what they have attained. After the first gives his answer, Bodhidharma replies, "You have attained me in my skin." To the second disciple's reply, Bodhidharma says, "You have attained me in my flesh." To the third he says, "You have attained me in my bones." The fourth, Hui-k'o, says nothing and merely bows three times. Bodhidharma tells him, "You have attained me in my marrow." He gives Hui-k'o his robe and names him the second patriarch.

Usually, it is assumed that the answers are arranged in order of increasing profundity. Dōgen's interpretation of the exchange is, however, radically different.

> Bear this in mind: the Patriarch's words about skin-flesh-bones-marrow are neither shallow nor deep. Even if there were qualitative differences among their views, the Patriarch only says ". . . attaining me . . ." That doctrine —the device of saying "attaining me in my marrow" or "attaining me in my bones"—is suited to each person, is just picked up and discarded. Here there is no matter of being good enough or not. It is like [Śākyamuni's] twirling the flower or [Bodhidharma's] passing down his robe, for example. [Bodhidharma's] speaking for the sake of the four is, from the start, on the same level. Although the Patriarch's words may be on the same level, the four views should not necessarily be the same. The four views may be dis-

tinct, but the Patriarch's words are just the Patriarch's words. There is no general rule that the utterance and the views necessarily agree. When the Patriarch was instructing his four monks, for example, he uttered, "You have attained me in my skin." If there were hundreds or thousands of monks after the Second Patriarch, there should be hundreds or thousands of interpretations for the monks.[10]

Thus, however one may grasp the meaning of the Master's utterance, if the interpretation is appropriate to one's perspective, and if one incorporates that interpretation fully into one's own life, that interpretation is valid.

Even the "in my skin" must be a transmission of the Dharma. The Patriarch's body-mind is the Patriarch—his skin-flesh-bones-marrow. It is not the case that the marrow is intimate and the skin distant.[11]

That is, just as Bodhidharma is a oneness of body-mind, he also is a oneness of skin-flesh-bones-marrow. To attain any of these truly is to attain the whole of Bodhidharma's presence. Hence, there is not just one route to the intimate or esoteric. There are as many approaches to the Dharma as there are people who seriously undertake the Zen way. Ultimately, though, the goal is to become one with the Master. Thus, Dōgen advises:

You should be aware of the phrases "you attain me," "I attain you," "attaining both me and you," and "attaining both you and me." In personally viewing the Patriarch's body-mind, if we speak of there being no oneness of internal and external, or if we speak of the whole body's not being completely penetrated, then that is not the realm of the Patriarch's presence.[12]

When one's intimate act becomes intertwined with that of the Master, we have true *kattō.*[13]

Therefore, the very utterances are lines that leap out of themselves; student and master personally practice together. The very listenings are lines that leap out of themselves; student and master personally practice together. The common personal investigation of master and disciple is the patriarchal intertwining [*kattō*]. The patriarchal intertwining is the life of the skin-flesh-bones-marrow. The very twirling of the flower and winking are the intertwining.[14]

This analysis can be applied to reading *Shōbōgenzō* itself. To read *Shōbōgenzō* is to be ensnared in the vines of words *(kattō),* yet at the same time, its very complexity reveals Dōgen's own personal presence and gives us the opportunity to entangle our own entanglements with his entanglements. Then, at that point of great unity, *kattō* cuts through *kattō* and the Dharma is transmitted:

> Generally, saints set out in their personal practice to cut off the roots of *kattō,* but they do not personally practice this as slicing through *kattō* with *kattō.* They do not know about entangling *kattō* with *kattō,* to say nothing of knowing how to inherit *kattō* through *kattō.* Knowing the inheritance of the Dharma itself to be *kattō* is rare—no one has heard of this. It has yet to be uttered. So few have authenticated it.[15]

That is, Zen is often taken to be the enemy of words. Yet, as we saw in "Mitsugo" and again here in "Kattō," Dōgen entangles himself in words, inviting us to join him intimately in his entanglement. To join him is to achieve the act of intimacy by knowing oneself and molting both one's own and Dōgen's body-mind, that is, by eliminating all barriers separating oneself from the immediate apprehension of the Dharma.

Dōgen as philosopher

Having examined Dōgen's view of language and its relevance to interpreting the *Shōbōgenzō,* we can turn now to Dōgen himself as philosopher. In one sense, we could easily argue that Dōgen has presented a hermeneutic theory and that he has struck a distinctively twentieth-century chord. He has, to put it briefly, claimed that there is no objective, neutral standpoint from which the *Shōbōgenzō* may be read and critically evaluated. To read the text and to attempt an understanding of it, we must involve ourselves in it, seeing it from our own cultural, historical, and personal perspectives. Understanding involves the interaction of writer and reader, text and interpretation. In short, the text has no intrinsic, objective, and independent meaning until it is read by someone and that someone interacts with it. This, of course, is a theory of interpretation much developed by such twentieth-century members of the hermeneutic movement as Gadamer, Ricoeur, and Derrida. Again, though, to make such a comparison is ultimately a disservice to Dōgen. If we are looking for a systematic hermeneutic, any of the Western figures would give us a view more developed and more pertinent to today's philosophical climate than Dōgen could. If we were to stack up Dōgen's hermeneutic against, say, Gadamer's, Dōgen would come in a poor second. Why, then, should we make the comparison at all? Is it not enough to say Dōgen is thought-provoking in his own right, without our making him an honorary member of some twentieth-century movement? No, that is not enough. It is as much a disservice to Dōgen to isolate his thought as it is to make it the grist for comparisons and contrasts.

The undeniable fact is simply that reading Dōgen reminded *me* of reading the modern Western hermeneuticists. I cannot take myself out of the equation: Dōgen + Kasulis = hermeneutics. That is, there is something in me that makes the connection and that something should become the basis of my own philosophizing as well as my own Zen practice. "To model yourself after the way of the buddhas is to model yourself after yourself." The connection between Dōgen and modern hermeneutics is not objective in the sense that it is publicly verifiable. If hermeneutics had not already been invented, I doubt that I would have invented it upon reading Dōgen. Quite probably, I would have read the same fascicles and found some other passages to be the most interesting. Perhaps even the same passages would have said to me something quite different. The point, however, is that I am an inextricable part of the equation. Something already stimulated by hermeneutics also responded to Dōgen's ideas of *mitsugo* and *kattō*. To try to escape that fact is to flee from an insight into my own thinking. To reduce that fact to an objective comparison between the two traditions is to live in bad faith, to live in self-deception, to project my inner experience as a standard for the public world.

What, then, is required of the interpreter? One should not stop at *what* Dōgen and the hermeneuticists have in common. Nor should one stop at the similarities in their *method*. Rather, one must press to uncover the motivation in their philosophizing. In doing so, one also reveals the trend in one's own philosophizing that allowed one to connect the two traditions in the first place. In the pragmatist's terms, one should examine the common problematic situation out of which Dōgen's text, hermeneutics, and one's own philosophical reflection arise. In the present instance, that problematic seems to be one of knowing the correctness of an interpretation. As already noted, Dōgen is not easy to read. Whenever I pick up the *Shōbōgenzō,* there is a sense of enormous distance. For me the *Shōbōgenzō* is written in a foreign language over seven centuries old. Furthermore, Dōgen's style is highly idiosyncratic; he writes, as we have said, in *his own* language. On a more personal level, Dōgen was a Zen master and I am a secular philosopher. His society was highly hierarchical and group oriented, whereas mine is egalitarian and individualistic. Yet, despite the distance, the text may sometimes strike me and I believe I know exactly what Dōgen means. What gives me the right to say that, however? Admittedly, the text does not have an independent, self-existent meaning ensconced somehow in the inkspots on the page, but neither is its meaning simply whatever I make of it. In short, how can I distinguish what I read in the text from what I may have read into it?

Dōgen does not set any publicly verifiable criteria for interpretation. Rather, the true knowledge of the text comes about through an intimate connection between writer and reader. The specific content of this intimacy will vary with the audience—some will, as it were, be intimate with Dōgen's skin, some his bones, some his marrow. But insofar as one intimately contacts Dōgen on *any* of these planes, one becomes intimate with the whole of Dōgen himself. This intimate contact is the ultimate criterion for the interpretation's correctness. In a true interpretation, the speaker and audience reveal themselves to each other through each other. This intimacy is not describable in discursive terms; hence, it is "mysterious"—*mitsu*. Nor can it be authenticated by the text alone (that is only "half" of the intimacy). The true interpreter is one in whom and through whom the text speaks ("the true Dharma [*shōbō*] is in you"). The interpretation should speak *for* Dōgen, not about him.

It is now clearer why Dōgen should not be the object of East-West comparisons. A comparison can only juxtapose what two philosophers may say; it cannot speak for them. Allusions to other traditions may be helpful as an explanatory device in some cases, but at best they can only be a prelude to the real philosophizing. In the end, Dōgen himself must speak through the interpreter—that is, the interpreter as translator, not as objective critic. Yet, as Derrida says, "translation is transformation" and we cannot be neutral in our interpretations. We are intrinsically part of the message as we choose this or that word to communicate Dōgen's idea or this or that point to communicate Dōgen's view in a given context.

A consequence of this theory of comparative philosophizing is that the writer and interpreter become so intertwined that is it impossible to separate fully the thought of one from that of the other. If I, for example, am a legitimate interpreter of Dōgen, I say what Dōgen says. I cannot separate myself from his position. This runs against the grain of philosophy as it has typically been done in the modern Western tradition. This tradition has developed such that the interpreter is expected to be critical of the interpreted, that is, to read the text with the goal of criticizing, in part, whatever is untrue therein. This is only possible to the extent the interpreter distances oneself from the text, but how then can the text speak through the interpreter? The words of the text include *mitsugo,* "esoteric words," and the interpreter must be initiated into them in order to know their true meaning. Initiation at a distance is impossible.

In fact, this essay itself is an example of the theory just outlined. I have interpreted Dōgen in such a way that Dōgen cannot be wrong and Kasulis right, or vice versa. In speaking for Dōgen, I am also speaking for myself. Thus, to criticize my interpretation is to criticize what I have said. From my perspective as interpreter, the criticism applies to Dōgen as well as to me. Dōgen (through his text) and I (through my interpretation) are equally responsible for defending the content of the statements I have made. We have each contributed our half of the intimacy.

Can there be more than one interpretation that is correct? Certainly. In fact, as I change, my interpretation will change and, in effect, the meaning of the text itself will change with me. At each point, however, I am required to interpret Dōgen in a way that makes what he says true. I cannot separate what I find in the text from the truth, since I am seeking the truth in the text. In terms of comparative philosophy, therefore, my role is to bring Dōgen to the forum of philosophy and to interpret him so that I can speak for him. Whatever motivates Dōgen's philosophizing must also motivate my philosophizing. I must be responsible and continually return to the text to show how my words are based in Dōgen's own words, but I must also own up to the fact that the words are mine as well as Dōgen's. In this way, my entanglements become entangled in Dōgen's entanglements.

This profound sense of interpretation can be readily overlooked. One can easily forget that one must not only say what one sees in the text, but also where one stands when one sees it. To forget this is to be like the little boy who, seeing the harvest moon glistening on a still lake, tries to scoop up the luminous water so he can take it home to show his family. When he opens his hands, the shining water is gone. The meaning I find shining through the text is only visible from where I stand. If that vista is not available to you, you must return to the source itself to discover what you can see from your own intimately known place. Dōgen of the *Shōbō-genzō* is waiting. His half of the intimacy is an open book.

Notes

1. For a brief, but excellent, discussion of the Dōgen commentarial tradition, see Hee-jin Kim, *Dōgen Kigen: Mystical Realist* (Tucson: University of Arizona Press, 1975), chap. 1.
2. Ibid., p. 320, fn. 14. Original can be found in Tanabe Hajime, *Tanabe Hajime Zenshū* (Tokyo, Chikuma shobō, 1963), vol. 5, p. 456.
3. *DZZ* 1:393–394.
4. *DZZ* 1:394.
5. *DZZ* 1:395.
6. *DZZ* 1:395.
7. Compare this account of action and expression with this passage from the twentieth-century philosopher Nishida Kitarō:

    The world of the active self is a world of expression. The world of expression has been conceived in the past merely as an objective world of the understanding; but as I have said above, it must also determine the person. As I said in the opening of 'Preface to Metaphysics,' entities in the world of the present must be mutually related through expression, and mutually determined through action, as the self-identity of absolute contradictories.

    David A. Dilworth, trans., *Nishida Kitaro's Fundamental Problems of Philosophy* (Tokyo: Sophia University Press, 1970), p. 99.
8. For Dōgen there can never be a final interpretation of any spiritual text. The truth of interpretation depends not on content, but on the attitude of the interpreter. Thus, even though one's interpretation of a passage may change

radically through the years of practice, each interpretation may be true on the occasion it was developed. See the fascicle "Shoakumakusa" or the brief discussion of it in T. P. Kasulis, *Zen Action/Zen Person* (Honolulu: University Press of Hawaii, 1981), pp. 93–97.

9.   Genjōkōan, (*DZZ* 1:7–8).
10. Kattō, (*DZZ* 1:332–333).
11. Ibid., (*DZZ* 1:333).
12. Ibid., (*DZZ* 1:333).
13. Nishida again seems to have a similar relationship in mind.

> My concept of the personal world of mutual determination of I and Thou must be seen in the direction of the determination of the *noesis* of the above self-determining world. Therefore, that which stands over against the I as a *noema* in the social and historical world is not a Thou. It must rather be infinite expression. . . .
>
> Thus the I can never see the Thou as a *noema*, but at the same time it does see the Thou in the form of *noesis*. The I becomes the I by recognizing the Thou, and vice versa. Such personal determination in terms of noesis as the self-identity of absolute contradictories means at the same time to see the infinitely deep world of expression in the form of the *noema*.

> From Dilworth, trans., *Nishida Kitaro's Fundamental Problems of Philosophy,* pp. 102–103.
>
> In other words, Dōgen and I achieve our personal identity by being opposed and yet identified. The mediation of this dialectical relationship is the "infinite expression" (in this case, the *Shōbōgenzō* itself), an object of discovery and interpretive action for both Dōgen and me. Hence, the text is the object (noema) for our respective noetic acts and forms the place for our mutual determination.

14. Kattō, (*DZZ* 1:334).
15. Ibid., (*DZZ* 1:331).

The Oneness of Practice and Attainment: Implications for the Relation between Means and Ends

Masao Abe

In the beginning of this essay, a question young Dōgen encountered concerning "original awakening" is analyzed. Then the author tries to clarify Dōgen's solution, which is his notion of the "oneness of practice and attainment." Finally, the significance of Dōgen's idea for us today is discussed.

According to such biographical accounts of Dōgen's life as *Sansogyōgōki*[1] and *Kenzeiki,*[2] Dōgen in his younger days encountered a serious question in his study of Tendai Buddhism on Mt. Hiei. It was expressed as follows:

> Both exoteric and esoteric Buddhism teach the primal Buddha-nature and the original self-awakening of all sentient beings. If this is the case, why then in the Buddhas of all ages did the longing for awakening arise and they engage in ascetic practice?[3]

This question concerns the Tendai idea of "original awakening" *(hongaku)* as opposed to "acquired awakening" *(shikaku)*. Tendai Buddhism emphasizes "original awakening," the doctrine that everyone is originally awakened or enlightened. It rejects "acquired awakening" as unauthentic because that doctrine indicates that awakening can be acquired only as a result of sustained practice. Dōgen came to doubt this fundamental standpoint of Tendai Buddhism, and asked, "Why should people engage in religious practice to overcome delusion if they are originally enlightened?"

This was the most crucial question for the young truth-seeker, and it finally led him to China. The solution realized during that journey provided the foundation for Dōgen's later religion and thought.

Dōgen's initial question may be restated as follows:

If, as Tendai Buddhism expounds, all sentient being are originally endowed with Buddha-nature and are inherently awakened to their true nature, why is it necessary for so many Buddhists in the past, present, and future to set upon a religious quest and practice various forms of Buddhist discipline to attain enlightenment? Are not that resolve and practice unnecessary?

This question is unavoidable for Tendai Buddhism in its expounding of "original awakening." When young Dōgen came across this question, however, he apparently took the Buddha-nature, or one's true nature, to be Reality as it exists immediately without the mediation of practice. He apparently grasped original awakening simply as something beyond time and space, something with a real existence independent of all practice. It must be said that in such an understanding there lurks a kind of idealization and conceptualization of "original awakening." Strictly speaking, not only the Buddha-nature and original awakening, but also religious resolution and practice, are idealized in that understanding. But as Chih-i, the founder of Tendai Buddhism, had said: "Where can there be an innate Maitreya and a naturally enlightened Śākyamuni Buddha?" The Buddha-nature or original awakening does not exist immediately without the mediation of practice in time and space. Rather, it discloses itself only in our own resolution and practice in time and space. Resolution and practice are therefore indispensable factors in the disclosure of the Buddha-nature.

In contrast to the question encountered by Dōgen concerning the standpoint of original awakening, there is another question which could arise from a totally opposite direction. It may be expressed as follows:

If our own resolution and practice are indispensable, we cannot legitimately say that we are originally endowed with the Buddha-nature or that all sentient beings are originally enlightened. Why then does Tendai Buddhism expound the primal Buddha-nature and the original awakening of all sentient beings?

This question is posed from the standpoint of 'acquired awakening.' In that standpoint, Buddha-nature and one's true nature, seen as not originally endowed, are taken as something to be realized only as a result of resolution and practice and are not understood as existing directly without the mediation of practice in time and space. It must be said, however, that here again there lurks a kind of idealization and conceptualization. Although it is from a direction totally opposite that of the previous case, Buddha-nature is now equally idealized as the ideal to be reached, and resolution and practice are conceptualized as the means to reach it. And so, by taking our own resolution and practice in time and space as indispensable, we misconceive them as the indispensable *basis* for attaining Buddha-nature or awakening to one's true nature.

Both of the above questions are nothing but the idealization, conceptualization, and objectification of the Buddha-nature in Mahayana Buddhism from opposite directions. Both of them abstract equally in taking as an object the Reality of the Buddha-nature or awakening, which is fundamentally unobjectifiable and cannot be idealized.

In order to overcome this error of abstraction, we must clearly realize the distinction between that which must be a *ground* or *basis* and that which must be a *condition* or *occasion*. From the Mahayana Buddhist perspective, both Buddha-nature and resolution-practice are indispensable and necessary for awakening. They are, however, indispensable in two different senses. Buddha-nature is indispensable as the *ground* or *basis* of awakening, whereas resolution-practice is necessary as the *condition* or *occasion* for awakening. The aforementioned errors of abstraction stem from the confusion of ground and occasion (or basis and condition); in this confusion, only one side is recognized while the significance of the other side is neglected. Either that or the two are mistaken for each other.

Put more concretely, in the case of young Dōgen, Buddha-nature or one's true nature is recognized as the Reality which is the ground of awakening for all sentient beings and beyond the limitations of time and space. But that the necessity of our own resolution-practice in time and space is the indispensable condition for realizing that ground as the ground is doubted. The Buddha-nature as ground is grasped abstractly by Dōgen as something existing immediately without the mediation of resolution-practice as a condition. The other standpoint, however, over-emphasizes the necessity of our own resolution-practice in time and space and treats it as if it were the ground. This view thereby commits the abstraction of conceiving of the Buddha-nature as a direct extension of our own resolution-practice. In this case the Buddha-nature, which should originally be the ground, loses its reality and its character as the ground and is grasped merely as a sign to lead our resolution and practice; that is, it is grasped as nothing more than a condition or occasion. Even though the Buddha-nature is understood to be realized at the last extremity of time and space, it is not seen as beyond the limitations of time and space.

As we saw before, the question young Dōgen encountered was that of why resolution-practice is necessary if we are originally endowed with Buddha-nature. To Dōgen it was an existential and subjective question. At least intellectually, however, Dōgen must have fully realized the existence of another question, that of how the primal Buddha-nature can be seen as fundamental if resolution-practice is indispensable. For these questions are the two sides of the same issue of Buddha-nature or 'awakening,' and they are essentially connected with one another. Among novices and monks at Mt. Hiei, where Dōgen was studying, there must have been many who encountered one or the other of these two questions, even thought their doubts might not have been as clear and acute as Dōgen's.

At any rate, while studying Tendai Buddhism at Mt. Hiei, Dōgen unconsciously idealized the Buddha-nature and doubted the necessity of practice. And yet, precisely at that point, he could not help feeling restlessness and anxiety over his own existence, which was somewhat separated from the fundamental Reality. This may be why in the opening pages of *Hōkyōki,* a record of Dōgen's dialogues with his Chinese teacher Ju-ching, Dōgen says:

> The mind that aspires to enlightenment arose in me at an early age. In my search for the Way I visited various religious teachers in my own land and gained some understanding of the causal nature of the world. Yet the real end of the three treasures (Buddha, Dharma, and Sangha) was still unclear. I clung vainly to the banner of mere names and forms.[4]

By this Dōgen means that he was shackled by doctrinal concepts and formulations and, in his understanding, was unable to penetrate to Reality. It must have been this anxiety stemming from his feeling of separation from the fundamental Reality that motivated him to sail to China even at the risk of his life.

In China, Dōgen "visited many leading priests of Liang-che, and learned of the different characteristics of the Five Gates."[5] Dōgen wrote: "Ultimately, I went to T'ai-pai peak and engaged in religious practice under the Zen master Ju-ching until I had resolved the one great matter of Zen practice for my entire life."[6] He means that he had overcome all idealization, conceptualization, and objectification of the Buddha-nature. There was not even an inch of separation between the Buddha-nature and Dōgen's existence. Dōgen's statement "The practice of Zen is body and mind casting off"[7] implies that all possible idealization, conceptualization, and objectification of practice and attainment, discipline and the Buddha-nature, had been completely cast off. Herein is a complete realization of the primal Buddha-nature as the cast-off body and mind.

How was the problem of the relationship between resolution-practice and the Buddha-nature solved at the very moment of "body and mind casting off" *(shinjin datsuraku),* which is immediately "the cast-off body and mind" *(datsuraku shinjin)?* His solution is shown here and there in his writings":

> This Dharma is amply present in every person, but unless one practices, it is not manifested; unless there is realization, it is not attained.[8]

> To think practice and realization are not one is a heretical view. In the Buddha Dharma, practice and realization are identical. Because one's present practice is practice in realization, one's initial negotiation of the Way in itself is the whole of original realization. Thus, even while one is directed to practice, he is told not to anticipate realization apart from practice, because practice points directly to original realization. As it is already realization in

practice, realization is endless; as it is practice in realization, practice is beginningless.[9]

As for the truth of the Buddha-nature: the Buddha-nature is not incorporated prior to attaining Buddhahood; it is incorporated upon the attainment of Buddhahood. The Buddha-nature is always manifested simultaneously with the attainment of Buddhahood. This truth should be deeply, deeply penetrated in concentrated practice. There has to be twenty or even thirty years of diligent Zen Practice.[10]

In the Great Way of Buddhas and patriarchs there is always continuous practice which is supreme. It is the way which is circulating ceaselessly. There is not even the slightest gap between resolution, practice, enlightenment, and nirvana. The way of continuous practice is ever circulating.[11]

These statements all show that awakening is not subordinate to practice, attainment to discipline, Buddha-nature to becoming a Buddha, or vice versa. Both sides of such contraries are indispensable and dynamically related to each other. Such of Dōgen's expressions as "Oneness of practice and attainment," "the simultaneous realization" of Buddha-nature and the attainment of Buddhahood, and "the unceasing circulation of continuous practice" clearly indicate this dynamic and indispensable relation. Unless one becomes a Buddha, the Buddha-nature is not realized as the Buddha-nature, and yet at the same time one can become a Buddha only because one is originally endowed with the Buddha-nature. It is at this point that the dynamic truth of the simultaneous realization of the Buddha-nature and its attainment can be seen.

As we see in diagram 1, the standpoint of "acquired awakening" may be illustrated by a horizontal line, for it presupposes a process of resolution and practice leading to attainment as its end. It indicates the dimension of time and space. On the other hand, the standpoint of "original awakening" may be illustrated by a vertical line, because by completely overcoming the notions of process and time and space implied by "acquired awakening," it indicates the transspatial and transtemporal dimension, not process but depth.

Diagram I

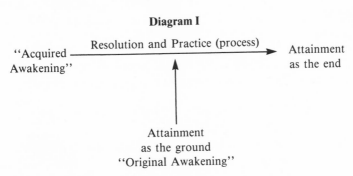

As already discussed, in Mahayana Buddhism, especially in Tendai Buddhism, both resolution and practice as the condition (occasion) and attainment as the ground (basis) are indispensable. Nevertheless, the standpoint of acquired awakening takes resolution and practice as the necessary ground for attainment, which is seen as the end. It takes only the horizontal dimension as the real and overlooks the vertical dimension, which is actually the indispensable ground for resolution and practice. On the other hand, the standpoint of original awakening as understood by the young Dōgen takes attainment as the one true reality and doubts the significance of resolution and practice. That view takes only the vertical dimension as the real and neglects the horizontal dimension, which is seen as something unnecessary.

However, as Dōgen realized through his experience of "body and mind casting off," practice and attainment are not two but one and constitute a dynamic whole in which the horizontal dimension (practice) and the vertical dimension (attainment) are inseparably united. Thus he emphasizes, "As it is already *realization in practice,* realization is endless; as it is *practice in realization,* practice is beginningless."[12] This dynamic relation of practice and realization (attainment) may be illustrated as in diagram 2.

Diagram II

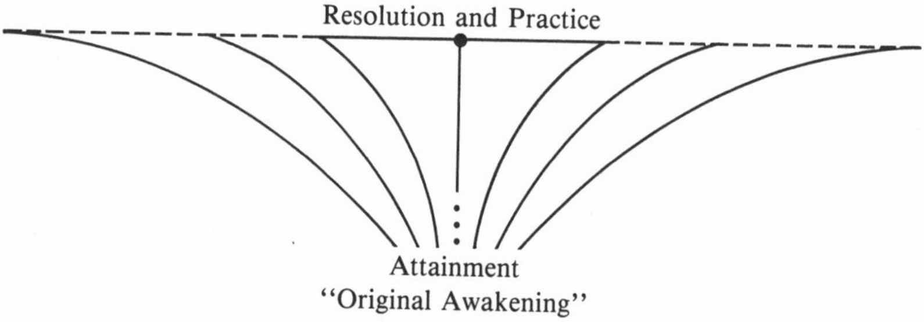

Resolution and Practice

Attainment
"Original Awakening"

The center of this dynamic whole is the intersection of the horizontal dimension and the vertical dimension. We are always living in, and living as, this intersection. Since the horizontal process of practice is beginningless and endless, *any point* of the process of practice is *equally* a point of intersection with the vertical line attainment, which is infinitely deep. This means that attainment, as the ground, supports and embraces the whole process of practice, and the *any point* of practice points *directly* to original attainment.

In order to properly grasp this matter, however, it may be necessary to clarify the issue by dividing it into two aspects as follows:

(1) Both attainment (awakening or the Buddha-nature) and practice (Discipline or becoming a Buddha) are indispensable; but the former is

indispensable as the ground or basis whereas the latter is indispensable as the condition or occasion. In this regard, their distinction, and especially the irreversible relationship between them, must be clearly realized; attainment (awakening) is more fundamental than practice, not the other way around.

The young Dōgen recognized the indispensability and the reality of attainment of the Buddha-nature. Precisely because he did so, however, the indispensability and necessity of practice in becoming a Buddha was doubted. He clearly realized the transcendental reality of attainment (the Buddha-nature) which is beyond time and space, but could not help doubting the reality of resolution, practice, and becoming a Buddha which do not escape the limitations of time and space. This is because Dōgen was trying to understand the reality of the latter by only taking the reality of the former as the standard. In other words, at that point, without distinguishing between 'that which must be a ground' and 'that which must be a condition,' Dōgen was trying to grasp both attainment and practice, the Buddha-nature and becoming a Buddha, in one and the same dimension. It is, however, an abstraction to grasp both of them in that way, for the standpoint of attainment (or the Buddha-nature) which is beyond time and space is clearly different in its dimension from the standpoint of practice (becoming a Buddha) which is inseparable from the limitations of time and space. The former is 'that which must be a ground' of human existence whereas the latter is not. But, even so, one should not immediately say that only the former has reality whereas the latter lacks it. If one were to understand the issue in that way, it would be yet another form of abstraction and conceptualization of the matter, and would not arrive at the reality of the issue. The standpoint of resolution, practice, and becoming a Buddha is an indispensable reality in a different sense than Buddhahood. It is indispensable not as 'that which must be a ground' but as 'that which must be a condition' which realizes the ground as the ground. Resolution or practice is indispensable as a condition or occasion for Buddhahood. Further, 'that which must be a ground' is more fundamental than 'that which must be a condition,' and thus there is an irreversible relationship between them. That is to say, attainment or the Buddha-nature is more fundamental than resolution and practice, and this relationship should not be reversed.

In short, although both attainment (the Buddha-nature) and practice (becoming a Buddha) are equally real and equally indispensable to human existence, the former is so as a ground, whereas the latter is so as a condition or occasion. Attainment and practice—the Buddha-nature and becoming a Buddha—are inseparable from one another, and yet the former has priority over the latter. In order not to abstract frrm the concreteness of the matter, however, one must not miss the distinction between 'that which must be a ground' and 'that which must be an occasion' and their irreversible relationship. This is precisely because, as quoted before, Dōgen says: "This Dharma is amply present in every person, but unless one practices, it is not manifested; unless there is realization, it is not attained."[13] This is one of the things Dōgen awakened to at the point of body and mind casting off.

A question opposite to the one young Dōgen faced was the question of why the primal Buddha-nature is emphasized if resolution and practice are indispensable? In this question, the questioner understands resolution, practice, and becoming a Buddha as if they were the ground of the Buddha-nature, for he overemphasizes their indispensability. Here again, there is a confusion between 'that which must be a ground' and 'that which must be an occasion.' That this standpoint, too, has fallen into an abstraction distant from the Reality must have been clearly recognized by Dōgen in his realization of body and mind casting off.

(2) As stated above, there is an irreversible relationship between attainment (the Buddha-nature) which is indispensable as the ground of one's awakening, and practice (becoming a Buddha), which is indispensable as the condition of attainment. Attainment (the Buddha-nature), however, is not something substantial; in itself it is non-substantial and non-objectifiable no-thingness. Accordingly, through a realization of the non-substantiality of its ground, practice as a condition is realized as something real in terms of the ground. Thus, going beyond the irreversible relationship between attainment (the Buddha-nature) and practice (becoming a Buddha), these two aspects come to be grasped in terms of a reversible identity.

As Dōgen says, "Because the Buddha-nature is empty it is said to be no-thing."[14] Attainment (the Buddha-nature), indispensable as the ground of human existence, is not a being or something substantial, but is in itself empty and no-thing. Accordingly, even though the Buddha-nature is the ground which is realized only through practice as its condition, it is not a substantial ground or a ground which is something, but a ground as no-thing, a non-substantial, unobjectifiable ground. It is a ground which is different from a ground in the ordinary sense as something simply distinguished from a condition. In this way, the distinction between ground and condition in the ordinary sense is overcome. Further, the irreversibility between them is also overcome. At that point, that which is a condition is immediately realized as a ground. This is the reason why Dōgen expounds 'impermanence–Buddha-nature' *(mujō bus-shō)* by saying, "Impermanence is in itself Buddha-nature."[15] In other words, at that point impermanence itself, which is strictly limited by time and space, is realized in its suchness as the Buddha-nature which is beyond time and space. Accordingly, resolution, practice, and becoming a Buddha are not only occasions or conditions for attaining the Buddha-nature, but also come to have the meaning of original attainment. Conversely, original attainment, which must be the ground, cannot be attained apart from resolution, practice, and becoming a Buddha, which are usually understood as conditions. Therefore, a reversible relationship between attainment and practice, the Buddha-nature and becoming a Buddha, is realized. This is the reason Dōgen says:

> In the Buddha Dharma, practice and realization are identical. Because one's present practice is practice in realization, one's initial negotiation of the Way in itself is the whole of original realization. . . . As it is already realization in practice, realization is endless; as it is practice in realization, practice is beginningless.[16]

Again, it is for this reason that Dōgen says, "There is not even the slightest gap between resolution, practice, enlightenment, and nirvana. The way of continuous practice is ever circulating."[17] Practice now is not mere practice but 'practice in realization.' Accordingly, it is realized as 'wondrous practice' and is not different from 'original realization pointed to directly.' In other words, the Buddha-nature is not merely "incorporated prior to attaining Buddhahood." There is an aspect in which we must say, "It is incorporated *upon* the attainment of Buddhahood." And so, in the final analysis, as Dōgen said, "the Buddha-nature is always manifested simultaneously with the attainment of Buddhahood." This is what Dōgen calls "the truth of the Buddha-nature."[18]

In this, we see Dōgen's emphasis on the oneness of practice and attainment, Buddha-nature, and the ever-circulating way of continuous practice. This is precisely what Dōgen awakened to at the moment of body and mind casting off, and it was a complete solution to the question which arose in him on Mt. Hiei. This emphasis, however, does not indicate an immediate identity between practice and attainment—or the Buddha-nature and becoming a Buddha—which exists apart from the mediation of any negativity. One should not overlook the fact that Dōgen's realization of 'the oneness of practice and attainment' includes a dynamism mediated by negation—a dynamic, nondualistic identity between practice and attainment which is mediated by the realization of 'impermanence–Buddha-nature.' That realization includes, as stated before, (1) an aspect in which attainment (the Buddha-nature) as ground and practice (becoming a Buddha) as condition are both indispensable and must be distinguished from one another, and (2) an aspect in which attainment is nothing but the attainment of 'impermanence–Buddha-nature.' Attainment as ground, and practice as condition, are nondualistically identical in the realization of 'impermanence–Buddha-nature.' In other words, Dōgen's view of the oneness of practice and attainment, i.e., the ever circulating way of continuous practice, does not indicate a mere reversible identity between attainment and practice, the Buddha-nature and becoming a Buddha. Rather, it indicates a reversible identity, in which an absolute irreversibility between attainment and practice, the Buddha-nature and becoming a Buddha, can be reversed by virtue of the nonsubstantiality of attainment and the emptiness of the Buddha-nature. This point must not be overlooked. Involved here is a reversible identity which is always inseparably connected with the irreversibility. Dōgen's realization of the oneness of practice and attainment consciously includes within itself this sort of reversible identity.

This means that Dōgen, and all of us, are always standing at the intersection of the temporal-spatial horizontal dimension and the trans-temporal-transspatial vertical dimension insofar as we awaken to the oneness of practice and attainment. We are also always standing at a dynamic intersection of irreversibility and reversibility, between practice as a means and attainment as a ground. Each and every moment of our life is such a dynamic intersection. We are living such moments from one to the next, realizing that impermanence is in itself Buddha-nature.

What significance does Dōgen's idea of the oneness of practice and attainment have for us today? Needless to say, it has undeniable significance for our religious life. First of all, in our *zazen* practice and religious life in the narrow sense, we must clearly realize the dynamic oneness of practice and attainment. Dōgen's idea of the oneness of practice and attainment, however, has rich implications which are applicable, in terms of the oneness of means and ends, to a much wider domain of our human life than just religious life in the narrow sense. I would now like to discuss two areas to which the idea of the oneness of means and ends may be significantly applied. One area is the understanding of the present and future in our individual and social life; the other is the understanding of one's personality and its relationship to other persons and other things.

The understanding of the present and future

In our individual and social lives we tend to set up an end or purpose in the future and think about how to live the present in order to attain that end. This aim-seeking approach or teleological approach has been quite prevalent throughout history, but it is most evident in the modern West. In the West, the notion of "progress" has been strongly emphasized, and the progressionist view of history has been predominant. (Even Marxism may be regarded as a sort of progressionism.) In this view of history, and in the aim-seeking approach, the present is regarded simply as a step toward a future goal. This implies at least the following three points:

(1) The present is not grasped as something meaningful in itself, but

as something significant only as a "means" to arrive at the end projected in the future.

(2) We are always "on the way" to the attainment of a goal and, though we may approach the projected goal, we cannot completely arrive at it. Thus we are not free from a basic restlessness.

(3) This basic restlessness stems from the fact that in the aim-seeking approach we objectify or conceptualize not only the future but also the present, and thus we are separated from reality.

In contrast to the aim-seeking approach, the realization of the oneness of means and ends implied in Dōgen's idea of the oneness of practice and attainment provides an entirely different view of the present and future. In the realization of the oneness of means and end, each and every step of the present is fully realized as the end itself, not as a means to reach the end. And yet, at the same time, each and every step of the present is totally realized as a means toward a future goal because we are living at the dynamic intersection of the temporal-spatial dimension and the transtemporal-transspatial dimension. In this way, firmly grounding ourselves on reality, we can live our lives creatively and constructively toward the future.

In order to realize the oneness of means and end, and the dynamic intersection of the temporal-spatial and transtemporal-transspatial dimensions, we must turn over the aim-seeking progressionist approach from its base. Only when we clearly realize the unrealistic, illusory nature of the aim-seeking, progressionist view of life and history do we come to the realization of the dynamic oneness of means and end.

The understanding of one's personality

Unlike a thing, which is usually regarded as existence which is a means, a person is regarded as existence with the self as its own end. This is especially clear in Kantian ethics, which gave a philosophical foundation to the modern notions of personality, freedom, and responsibility. Kant distinguishes things and human personality, and insists that while things can only have value as existence which is a means, human personality has dignity and grace as existence with self-purpose. Although a human being can be used as a means, at the same time he or she must always be treated as an end. In the Kantian framework, this superiority of people over things, and end over means, should not be overcome. Thus Kant talks about the "Kingdom of ends" as the community of personality. Viewed in the light of Dōgen, this Kantian notion of personality is not only limited by anthropocentrism but also is not completely free from reification of the human self. In Dōgen, people are not essentially distinguised from other beings, but are grasped as a part of the realm of beings. People and other beings are equally subject to impermanency or transiency. Although only people who have self-consciousness can realize the impermanency common to all beings as 'impermanency,' they can overcome the problem of life and death only when they can overcome the impermanency common to all beings. In Dōgen both suffering and emancipation from it are grasped on this trans-anthropocentric dimension. Hence Dōgen's emphasis on the simultaneous attainment of Buddha-nature for self and others, and for man and nature. In this simultaneous attainment, each person becomes an occasion or means for the attainment of others while each person respectively realizes his or her own attainment. Here self-awakening and the awakening of others take place at the same time. While maintaining one's individuality in terms of self-awakening, one serves as the means for the awakening of others. This dynamic mutuality takes place not only between the self and others, but also between man and nature. This is the reason Dōgen emphasizes in *Bendowa* that

> trees and grasses, wall and fence, expound and exalt the Dharma for the sake of ordinary people, sages, and all living beings. Ordinary people, sages, and all living beings in turn preach and exalt the Dharma for the sake of trees, grasses, wall, and fence. The dimension of self-enlightenment-qua-enlightening-others basically is fully replete with the characteristics of realization, and causes the principle of realization to function unceasingly.[19]

This mutual help for enlightenment between man and nature, however, cannot take place insofar as man takes only himself as the end. As Dōgen maintains,

> To practice and confirm all things by conveying one's self to them, is illusion; for all things to advance forward and practice and confirm the self, is enlightenment.[20]

The self must be emptied for all things to advance and confirm the self. Accordingly, "to forget one's self" is crucial. "To forget one's self" is nothing other than "body and mind casting off." And when body and mind are cast off, the world and history are also cast off. If body and mind are cast off without the world and history being cast off, it is not an authentic "body and mind casting off." Further, "body and mind casting off" is not something negative. It is immediately "the cast-off body and mind," that is, the awakened body and mind which are freed from self-attachment and are ready to save others. In the same way, the casting off of the world and history, which takes place at the same time as the casting off of body and mind, is not something negative. It is directly the cast-off world and history, that is, the awakened world and awakened history which "advance forward and practice and confirm the self."

Such are the implications of the notion of the oneness of means and end when that notion is applied to the understanding of one's personality and its relationship to other persons and other things. Here we can see Dōgen's challenge to the contemporary issues of ecology and history. The crucial point of this dynamic mutuality between the self and others, and man and the world, is "to forget one's self" or "body and mind casting off." Only when one forgets one's own self and one's body and mind are cast off is self-awakening-qua-awakening-others fully realized. This is not the "Kingdom of ends," but the "Kingdom of dependent co-origination."

Notes

1. *Eiheiji sanso gyōgō-ki, SSZ* 16:16.
2. *Kenzeiki, SSZ* 17:16a.
3. Heinrich Dumoulin, *A History of Zen Buddhism,* trans. Paul Peachey (Boston:Beacon Press, 1969), p. 153 (with adaptation).
4. *Hōkyōki,* trans. N. A. Waddell, *EB* 10 (2):117.
5. *Bendowa,* trans. N. A. Waddell and Masao Abe, *EB* 4 (1):130.
6. Ibid.
7. *Hōkyōki,* op. cit., p. 131.
8. *Bendowa,* op. cit., p. 129.
9. Ibid., p. 144.
10. *Buddha-nature,* trans. N. A. Waddell and Masao Abe, *EB* 9 (1):88.
11. *Gyōji I, DZZ* 1:122.
12. *Bendowa,* op. cit., p. 144.
13. Ibid., p. 129.
14. *Buddha-nature, EB* 8 (2):108.
15. *EB* 9 (1):91.
16. *Bendowa,* op. cit., p. 129.
17. *Gyōji I,* op. cit.
18. See note 10. *Buddha-nature, EB* 9 (1): 88.
19. *Bendowa,* op. cit., p. 136.
20. *Genjōkōan,* trans. Norman Waddell and Masao Abe, *EB* 5 (2):133.

The Practice of Body-Mind: Dōgen's *Shinjingakudō* and Comparative philosophy

John C. Maraldo

Introduction

Investigating an issue in the light of comparative philosophy poses questions which compel us to re-think the way we conceive of typical problems. One example is the body-mind problem, which has been formulated as follows: if the mind is a spiritual thing and the body a material thing, how do they interact? Is the mind a thing, a substance, at all? Is the mind rather only a metaphor for what the brain does? What do words signifying mental events really mean?

There are, of course, alternative ways of posing the problem; there are even accounts which deny that a real problem exists, or which declare all its formulations to be themselves problematic.[1] Despite the controversy, however, or perhaps because of it and of recent findings in brain research, there is a burgeoning interest today in the body-mind issue.[2] The task of the comparative philosopher in addressing this issue is not so much to solve or dissolve the problem as to uncover the presuppositions which have traditionally nurtured it, perhaps for hundreds of years. The comparative philosopher does not simply assume that a problem is perennial or universal, and then go on to compare approaches and solutions to it. Rather he or she attempts first and foremost to investigate the sets of guiding questions which cluster around an issue, to define the shifting boundaries of problems in differing traditions, and to raise new questions which challenge those boundaries.

In the arguments of contemporary philosophers and cognitive scientists, the "body-mind problem" may be exposed as a whole cluster of problems, or as no problem at all. But a contrast of such arguments and their terms with the texts and contexts of a vastly different tradition or time might reveal a definable problem after all, one that is unique to the modern West.[3] This could happen only if a jarring contrast revealed something that was utterly unthought of (or forgotten) in current argumentation—an aspect or dimension that offered a radical alternative to modern Western thinking. Whether anything so radically different turns up or not, such contrast can provide mutual illumination of the ways we read texts of divergent traditions.

Thus we might better gauge the bounds of the mind-body problem if we address the question of body and mind from the standpoint of an entirely different tradition, such as that conveyed by Dōgen. The Zen master's writing entitled *Shinjingakudō,* "Body-Mind Studying the Way," is a paradigmatic text for an inquiry proceeding from contrast rather than from an assumption of parity. This thirteenth-century Sino-Japanese Buddhist text, seemingly so remote from us today, not only inherits the formative questions of a contrasting tradition; it also explicates and often transforms them. In turn, our investigation should suggest alternative formulations of the body-mind issue, new methods for comparative philosophy, and new possibilities for the reading of ancient or alien texts.

To pursue this path of contrast, I propose to examine some of Dōgen's views on body and mind as expressed in his *Shinjingakudō* and to juxtapose these views with themes in Western philosophy of mind. In the following I offer a tentative reading of Dōgen's text—more accurately, a series of tentative readings which take successive parts of the text as their anchor and use them as a foil to highlight the bounds of the body-mind problem. Reciprocally, I attempt to throw light (and shadows) on Dōgen's procedure from the stance of modern philosophy. I suggest that the phrase *shinjingakudō* has several senses which replace and transform one another, in dialectical fashion and, when applied to the West, turn the body-mind issue inside out. Finally I return to the question of our vantage point and hermeneutical procedure to comment on the open task of body-mind inquiry.

Questions raised by context and method

In 1242, shortly before Dōgen left his suburban temple Kōshō-hōrinji for the remote mountains of Echizen, he composed *Shinjingakudō.* The text opens by echoing parts of earlier compositions: the beginning of the *Fukanzazengi* and several passages in the *Bendōwa.* I translate freely:[4]

> The Buddha Way is not attained by endeavoring to not call it the Way; it grows ever more remote by endeavoring to not study. As Nagaku Daie said, it is not that there is no practice and realization, just that they are not to be defiled. If one were not to study the Buddha Way, one would fall into heresy

outside the Way and into the ways of *icchantika*. For this reason the buddhas of past and future practice the Buddha Way without fail.

It can be said that the immediate context for these statements is
Dōgen's reformist position vis à vis the eclectic practices of Zen during
his day and Hieizan Tendai's notions that no practice was necessary.[5]
Hence Dōgen once again seems to be insisting solely on the *zazen* practice
and justifying the institution he is about to establish in Japan. But rather
than take these historical circumstances to be the context of Dōgen's
opening statements, I wish to consider the statements themselves as the
context of his views on body and mind, and to contrast that context with
the typical framework of the Western body-mind problem.

In the *Shinjingakudō* ("Body-Mind Studying the Way"), the order
in which Dōgen discusses topics is the reverse of that of the lexical elements named in the title: first comes the Way *(dō)*, then study *(gaku);*
and, though named together originally, mind *(shin)* will be dealt with
before body *(shin)*. Study is specified as practice, and practice, as we
learn in the passages to follow, is exemplified by the actions of the buddhas and patriarchs. Dōgen's consideration of body and mind serves to
elucidate the Buddha Way, something that is at once an ultimate reality
and a path in need of realization. The opening lines of the text make it
clear, then, that the primary concern and object of study is the Buddha
Way; *shinjingakudō* first of all means to study the Way, not the body and
mind. Dōgen's consideration of body and mind begins with a negation of
their priority.

Arising as it does amidst medieval Sino-Japanese controversies
about the nature and necessity of practice for accomplishment of the
Buddha Way, the text's opening affirmation of the primacy of the Way
has no strict counterpart in traditional Western philosophy. Though the
opening lines clearly intimate that this practice *(shugyō)* is a bodily
accomplishment (the term connotes bodily endeavor), body and mind are
not presented as central objects of study. This difference will prove to be
heuristically significant for our reading of contrasting modern Western
formulations as well as of Dōgen's text. The text forces not a detour
around body-mind considerations in Dōgen, but a transference or transposition of the connotations these terms carry. Indeed, in an arena of
contrast the text will suggest that the terms body and mind in philosophical usage are already transpositions; they act more as metaphors than as
names.[6]

In Western philosophy of mind, body-mind considerations have
assumed the central position, from whose vantage point the bounds of
man's knowledge were to be fixed. Insofar as theories of knowledge were
derived from considerations of body and mind, or senses and intellect,
the latter were accorded primacy as objects of study. To be sure, intellect

and senses were more often regarded as faculties or powers than as things; and it was their functions and functioning which interested philosophers. But this functioning was itself consistently taken as an object of reflection; the mind of the philosophers was more the mind thought-about than the mind thinking. Hence the epistemologies which were developed were epistemologies of representation: on the primary level mind became mind thought-about, and secondarily, all other things thought-about or known became objects of that mind. Hence in idealism the mind comes to "represent" or take the place of all the objects of the world. And in realism and empiricism, the mind re-presents or reflects objects in the world as a mirror reflects whatever stands before it. "To know means to reflect accurately what is outside the mind," as Richard Rorty puts it in his critical study of the epistemologies of representation.[7]

Rorty's work shows that one need not read texts such as Dōgen's to link the mind-body problem with theories of knowledge based upon representation. But when we do read traditional Western formulations in juxtaposition with Dōgen's text, their context and consequences emerge more clearly. Body-mind considerations which found theories of knowledge tend to focus on the nature, scope and limits of reason as a mental power, on the ability of the mind to reflect and the nature of the world reflected. We can find a diversity of positions, ranging from idealism to empiricism, on the autonomy of mind and the foundations of knowledge. But is not a predominant mentalism in all these positions apparent when we contrast their focus on mental reflection with Dōgen's emphasis on practice and exemplary human activities? To clarify this question, let us return again to *Shinjingakudō*.

"In learning the Buddha Way," Dōgen continues, "we may provisionally distinguish study by way of the mind and study by way of the body." Here the sense of *gakudō* becomes "study by way of." Considering first study via the so-called "mind," Dōgen mentions its various aspects. Borrowing expressions from Tendai philosophy and old Chinese Zen records, Dōgen includes the reflecting or self-conscious mind *(citta)* and dimensions which transcend self-consciousness: ubiquitous mind and all-comprehending mind;[8] the aroused bodhi-mind, bits and pieces of straightforward mind, mind of ancient buddhas, ordinary mind, three worlds-one mind. I will leave the interpretation of these various aspects of mind open for the time being, and proceed to the more important question of the method of study.

Dōgen writes that "there is study of the Way by discarding or letting go of all these [aspects of] mind and study by taking up or employing them; there is, then, study by way of thinking *(shiryō)* and by way of not thinking *(fushiryō)*." Here any distinction between means of study and object of study dissolves, so that *shinjingakudō* also comes to connote the way of studying mind and body. The "thinking of not-thinking," or release of objects of thought, is of course mentioned in the *Fukanzazengi* in the context of practical *zazen* instruction; but Dōgen goes a step further here when he connects it with various incidents in Zen history. To illustrate "the study of mind with mind" *(isshin gakushin),* he mentions (though with ellipsis of proper names) Śākyamuni's transmitting and Kāśyapa's receiving the golden brocade robe, Hui-k'o's grasping the marrow of Bodhidharma's teaching, and the Sixth Patriarch's study by way of pounding rice. Then, after citing such incidents, Dōgen makes the relevant connection: "To think of not-thinking is to enter the mountains [of practice], and non-thinking *(hishiryō)* is discarding the world [of attachments]."

Dōgen's appeal here to traditional Zen history is significant because it takes something likely to be considered merely a mental technique and places it in the context of social practices. Even if one considers this method of thinking, not thinking, and not-thinking as a method engaging mind, the mind engaged is more than the conscious or reflecting mind, as Dōgen's list of the various aspects of mind makes clear. And, as the various expressions of mind illustrate, the mind totally engaged and totally disengaged is the pivot of study. Mental reflection, while not excluded, is not the only aspect of mind engaged in study; and its nature, scope and limits are not the only object of consideration. Dōgen will go on to imply that mind *(shin)* is not merely mental, much less merely rational.

Now let us shift back to Western philosophy of mind, bracketing the sense of body, as does Dōgen, for the time being. "To know is to represent accurately what is outside the mind," Rorty sums up the traditional stance, "so to understand the possibility and nature of knowledge is to understand the way in which the mind is able to construct such representations."[9] But if we were to take this "mind" and place it within Dōgen's context, it would fit nowhere except under the category of *citta* or reflecting mind. Likewise, the method of understanding how the mind works would fall in the domain of study by way of thinking (Dōgen's *shiryō*). Specifically, this mind itself would appear as an object of reflection or representation, and the activity of representation would actually have a double object: first the world represented by mind and then mind itself, represented as the power to represent. There is, then, a double process of externalization involved in reflecting accurately what is outside the mind. Not only is world outside mind, but mind is outside the mind. Not only is world outside mind, but mind itself, as an object of philosophic reflection, is made to be "outside," or at least on the other side of, the invisible activity of reflecting. Ironically, the view that placed mind inside ended up externalizing it, taking it as object or concept and forgetting it as living activity.

It is true that existential phenomenologists such as Heidegger, Sartre and Merleau-Ponty criticize this tradition and place mind originally in the world, collapsing a rigid distinction between inside and outside. Heidegger's critique of representational or objectifying thinking reminds us of what had been forgotten and recalls some non-objectifying ways of study: musing, poeticizing, questioning, conversing.[10] Sartre suggests that the thinker or ego as subject of thoughts is constructed post factum, after the act of thinking, and belongs to the world of objects.[11] Merleau-Ponty lets us see that mind and world are reversible: mind thought-about and mind thinking must be parts of a whole, itself beyond objectification.[12] These philosophers break through the limits of representational theories of mind and stress its pre-reflective aspects. They approach Dōgen's primacy of practice, in which mind as the way or method of study exceeds mind as object of study, where mind is a matter to be practiced and realized and not simply thought about. Heidegger in particular has implied that thinking is first and foremost a practice, and not a condition or an object of representation.[13]

But does Heidegger's thinking attain Dōgen's "thinking of not-thinking," either as a technique of practice or as an interpretation of exemplary human activity? I think not. The existential phenomenologists may "take up" in their study "various aspects of the mind" (as Dōgen has in part described "thinking"), including those which transcend consciousness and incorporate the world. But their study does not include the practice which consists in letting go of thoughts, "discarding all aspects of mind" (as Dōgen has paraphrased "not-thinking"); Dōgen himself, however, never gives specific instructions on how to perform "not-thinking," either as mental technique or as exemplary action. Does he leave its meaning open because it is a meaning to be realized, a koan like the expressions of transmission of mind he cites from Zen history, or like "entering the mountains and discarding the world"? Do such statements serve a double grammatical function, proclaiming the nature of the study almost as a matter of fact, but at the same time enjoining upon the reader a task to be accomplished? Are they imperative as well as declarative statements?

Questions posed by manner of argument and allusion

If we can answer yes to these questions, then the open, hortatory character of many of Dōgen's statements would temper the authoritative, self-assured, even dogmatic tone one is likely to hear in them. To clarify this point and contrast it with Western modes of argument, let us turn to the main themes in the next part of the text.

Echoing the *Awakening of Faith* and innumerable Yogācāra and Zen texts, Dōgen proclaims mind to be "mountains, rivers, earth, sun, moon, and stars." Here Dōgen alludes to common Buddhist teachings and expressions concerning the mind, as he has done before in the text. But he does not simply repeat them without applying a kind of Mādhyamika logic and interpreting them from his own vantage point. "Mountains, rivers, earth," etc. "exceed the forms that appear to us; they are boundless phenomena of all the worlds [of Buddhist cosmology]; they appear differently to us than to other beings, according to different viewpoints; and therefore," as Dōgen twists ordinary logic, "the view of one mind is one and the same. Are not all these mind in its universal form? Shall we construe this mind as inside or outside, coming or going, increasing with life or decreasing with death? As attained or not attained, known or not known? . . . Beyond our grasp, mind is such that we must resolve to let it study of itself, and must accept on faith or trust that this is *shingakudō,* the mind studying the way and the way the mind studies."

Leaving aside the task of tracing Dōgen's references and questions of the uniqueness of his interpretation here, I will merely comment on it as a mode of argument. A series of statements is given, and though their grammar at times suggests an interrogative, the questions seem rhetorical and the statements sound definitive. Allusions made in this passage and throughout the text, particularly when the speaker is named, strengthen the impression that other, perhaps inaccessible, sources are taken as authoritative. There is hardly a sense of a rational argument being developed, something which would consider various possible views of mind, raise objections, and defend one view against others for certain explicit reasons. I will not cite here any passages from Western philosophy of mind which illustrate the discursive mode of argument, but assume that we are all familiar enough with it. What then is the nature of Dōgen's argument, be it argument at all?

Dōgen does allude to various views concerning the nature of mind and does not always accept them uncritically. When he speaks of the mind neither increasing during life nor decreasing upon death, he refers implicitly to a view denounced by name in the *Bendōwa,* i.e., to the so-called Senika heresy of a personal, individual mind or soul which lives on after the death of the body. When he questions whether that mind (and mountains, rivers, earth, sun, moon, stars) are inside or outside, he implicitly criticizes those idealistic Yogācāra interpretations which would see phenomena as creations of the imagination *(parikalpita).* Later in the *Shinjingakudō* he directly implores young students not to concede to innatism *(jinenken)* the heretical view that bodily practice is unnecessary. But even there he cites as authoritative the words of Pai-chang, to the effect that liberation *(gedatsu)* itself is buddha, but attachment to liberation belongs to the heresy of naturalism or spontaneous enlightenment.[14] Dōgen offers no reasons against various false views; he merely states that they are wrong.

Yet we may ask whether this lack of reasons does not suggest a manner of argument which parallels the content of the text. Some criticisms are offered, just as consciousness and reason are included as part of mind; but not to the exclusion of other, universal dimensions. Authority is appealed to, just as acceptance by faith is invoked to complement a rational grasp of the dimensions of mind. Allusions interconnect the text with other texts in the tradition, just as mind and aspects of the world are said to be interdependent. Finally, attributes and descriptions of mind are consequently affirmed, negated, and emptied, just as non-thinking and release *(hōge)* are named—and non-discrimination is implied—as ways of study. I am asking whether the *form* of Dōgen's argument recapitulates its content, whether what Dōgen is *doing* with words and statements reflects what he is saying (and not saying). But this question arises for me only by way of contrast to the discursive arguments, based upon reasons and formal rules independent of content, which are typical of Western philosophy of mind.

Questions posed by metaphor

It is remarkable that Richard Rorty's own argument against the traditional mind-body problem concludes that "pictures rather than propositions, metaphors rather than statements, determine most of our philosophical convictions." He suggests, then, that something has been more persuasive than rational argumentation in the tradition, namely, the images and comparisons presupposed by the arguments. I want to say a few words about metaphors for the mind and the mind that makes metaphors.

The controlling metaphor in the Western tradition, Rorty finds, is

> . . . the mind as a great mirror, containing various representations—some accurate, some not—and capable of being studied by pure nonempirical methods. Without the notion of the mind as mirror, the notion of knowledge as accuracy of representation would not have suggested itself. Without this latter notion, the strategy common to Descartes and Kant—getting more accurate representations by inspecting, repairing, and polishing the mirror, so to speak—would not have made sense. Without this strategy in mind, recent claims that philosophy could consist of "conceptual analysis" or "phenomenological analysis" or "explication of meanings" or examination of the "logic of our language" or of "the structure of the constituting activity of consciousness" would not have made sense.[15]

The mirror metaphor and the image of cleansing (vs. sharpening) the mind by polishing the mirror can of course be found in Taoist and Zen texts,[16] but I will not comment on this interesting likeness here. Instead, let me add other, more recent comparisons to the list.

One controlling metaphor today is the mind as the brain. There are important variations of this image: (1) The brain is a computer, the mind its software. One's behavior is determined by the way the brain has been "programmed."[17] (2) The brain is a biosystem, not a machine, and the mind is the neural functioning of that system; one's behavior is the motor outcome of biological events in the central nervous system.[18] (3) The brain is a hologram, and the mind consists of interference patterns of waves encoded on it;[19] one's behavior is a decoded and projected pattern. Still another school would look in the mirror and see no mind at all; the brain is real enough, but the "mind" is nothing but behavior or dispositions to behave.[20]

Phenomenologists will resist such metaphors, take a more holistic approach, and insist on the irreducibility of consciousness and its intentional, intersubjective and intramundane aspects. They will be less likely to forget that the program-mind, the neuron mind, the hologramic mind, etc., are parts of a whole which includes the very activities of programming computers, investigating the brain, observing behavior, proposing theories of mind, and creating metaphors. Thus the metaphors they employ will cover more than what the term "mind" conveys in traditional philosophy of mind. Merleau-Ponty, for example, uses the words "intertwining" and "chiasm" to indicate the intersection and reversibility of parts: I am of such a nature that I can both see and be seen, touch and be touched, etc.; as embodied consciousness I am a visible seer, an audible hearer, a tactile/tactual being. He chooses the word "flesh" to speak of something more elemental and relational, more concrete and yet universal, than what words like "matter," "spirit," "body" and "mind" convey.[21]

Nevertheless, Merleau-Ponty's metaphors seem abstract and recondite when compared with Dōgen's statement in the next phrase of the *Shinjingakudō:* "the mind is fences, walls, tiles and stones." Itself an allusion to a saying of Zen master Su-shan Kuang-jen and unnamed others,[22] this metaphor dislodges that of mind as mountains, rivers, earth, sun, moon and stars; and empties the "three worlds–mind only" view of any remnant of abstraction and idealism. "It is not three worlds–mind only, it is not dharma realm–mind only; it is fences, walls, tiles and stones."

We certainly cannot suppose that the term "mind" is univocal in all the descriptions I have mentioned. Yet I wonder if they do not share an underlying preconception of mind as something internal, invisible, and individual or individuated—even if that sense if to be dislodged. Thus the metaphor of "three worlds–mind only" implies but turns against the sense of mind as internal and individual, and of world as external and independent. Likewise, Dōgen knows that we take things to be objects in the world, so his walls, tiles and stones, like Chao-chou's oak tree, turns on the presumption that mind can be differentiated, and reality objectified.

Just as we cannot suppose that the term "mind" is used univocally, we cannot assume that the metaphors are used in the same sense. Indeed, some people will balk at calling the descriptions metaphors at all, and insist that they are to be taken literally. When the contemporary psychobiologist Mario Bunge says the mind is a set of brain functions, he means it literally; when Dōgen says mind is walls, tiles and stones, he means just that.[23] But Bunge abandons this literalism when he goes on to develop formal definitions, postulates, and mathematical formulae to specify his sense of mind.[24] And Dōgen refuses a fixation of his meaning when he goes on to say (actually quoting Su-shan): "before the year Kantsu [of the T'ang era] mind is built of fences, walls, tiles and stones; after the year Kantsu it is torn down." As if just to make sure, Dōgen later declares that "the mind of ancient buddhas is not fences, walls, tiles and stones, and these do not mean the mind of ancient buddhas."

In his *Zuimonki* Dōgen remarks that expressions like "mind–mountains, rivers and the great earth" as possible as *kakekotoba,* i.e., pivot or turning words that evoke enlightenment.[25] This term may be a more appropriate one than "metaphor" to describe the expressions of mind in the *Shinjingakudō.* But perhaps these expressions also tell us that we ordinarily understand metaphors in a very restricted sense. A metaphor, we think, is comparison of two things, one thing standing for something else. This view itself is an example of representational thinking. One thing (e.g., mind) is understood in terms of another, more basic or better-known thing (e.g., brain); and the metaphor of comparison is derivative of the literal meaning of the base term (e.g., "we know that the brain really is, and we can say the mind is [like] the brain").

This manner of understanding metaphors does not work for "the mind is walls, tiles and stones." Rather, expressions like this expose certain preconceptions and turn our sense of metaphor around. Could metaphors perhaps turn out to be connectives more basic than literal meanings, to be concrete embodiments of a whole which devaluate a language of fixed concepts referring to independent entities? In this sense, mind as mirror, mind as brain, and mind as walls, tiles and stones would all be metaphors, whether meant "literally" or not. They are transpositions, as intimated at the beginning of our reading, in which the nature of mirrors, brains, and concrete pieces becomes as enigmatic as that of minds, in which each side of the equation becomes metaphoric and mutually illuminating/obfuscating. Views which would objectify mind (or denigrate metaphor) would conceal the relativity of language and the reference to a sustaining whole, whereas Dōgen first points out the primacy of the Way, then jolts the mind and dislodges the ordinary connotations of words. In the *Shinjingakudō,* "mind" *(shin)* becomes a cipher whose meaning is to be filled by accomplishing the Way, i.e., through bodily practice.

Questions posed by point of departure

Although the question of metaphor in Dōgen must be left for further study,[26] we can draw some consequences of the significance of the Way for an understanding of mind by returning for a moment to the opening passage of Dōgen's piece. At the beginning of *Shinjingakudō,* Dōgen writes that the buddhas of past and future, so as not to fall into false views, have all practiced the Buddha Way—i.e., attained it bodily.[27] Up to now I have been following the bias of traditional Western philosophy of mind and ignoring the body. Dōgen also postpones his discussion of the body until the last third of his piece. He has told us in the opening passage of the text that there are, *provisionally,* two ways of study: via the mind and via the body. This simple remark, which suggests that the two will be taken up one at a time, is a tacit allusion to the doctrine of *shinjin-ichinyō,* oneness of body and mind. We find this principle affirmed throughout Dōgen's works and discussed especially in the *Bendōwa* in connection with the Senika heresy. The gist of the discussion there is that to believe the mind to be eternal or immutable and the body perishable, or indeed to assume any real separation between them, is heretical and self-defeating. From the perspective of perishability, all things are perishable; from the perspective of immutability, all things are immutable. Body and mind are not two.[28]

I take this position to be the point of departure for the separate discussions of mind and body in the *Shinjingakudō.* Fundamentally, human practice *(gyō)* is oneness of body and mind, and practice-realization *(shushō)* must not separate them. Their separate treatment in the text, however, indicates that a provisional distinction between them is appropriate not only for purposes of discussion, but also for bringing home the point that body and mind signify a unity to be practiced and achieved; they are neither merely conceptual opposites nor a pre-given identity.[29] Once again, an examination of Dōgen's text will show that its very form reflects this transposed unity. The later section of the text that begins with the phrase *shingakudō* ("body-studying Way") recapitulates the main points and procedures expressed previously. Let me highlight part of its content, although I will shuffle the order of presentation somewhat.

Shingakudō means: . . . to study the Way with the body, with the whole naked flesh. What the body is emerges from the study of the Way, and what emerges from the study of the Way is the body. All worlds in the ten directions are this very human body; birth and death, coming and going, the four elements, the five skandhas[30] are this true human body. To study with the body is to cut oneself off from the ten evils, uphold the eight precepts, convert to the three treasures, leave home and renounce the world.

Here Dōgen expresses the concrete, universal, phenomenal, boundless, practical and social dimensions of the body, in parallel with expressions concerning the mind. And again, the manner of argument is to let the style or mode of presentation itself demonstrate the meaning of the content. Dōgen displaces more abstract metaphors (the ten directions) with more concrete ones (a grain of dust); more static images (a grain of dust) with more active, social ones (to construct a practice hall is to incorporate the whole world in a grain of dust; this of itself is the true human body). Even concepts signifying active practice and realization, like liberation *(gedatsu),* become like broken furniture in an empty house when attachments to them form, i.e., when they become concepts. Just as there is practice with the body and expressions of that practice, there is also practice by discarding the body and discarding expressions: "to drop the body is to raise the voice that stops all echoes."

As in the mind section of the text, the body section embeds numerous allusions and quotations. The image of practice by stopping the echo (perhaps itself an allusion) is followed by the phrase "cutting an arm and attaining the marrow," an allusion to Hui-k'o's transmission from Bodhidharma, and hence to the practice of cutting off objectifications of mind, the "mind" that Hui-k'o cannot find.[31] The allusions refer to teachings which Dōgen sometimes affirms, sometimes criticizes, sometimes reinterprets: "Broken furniture in an empty house," for example, criticizes innatism, the heresy Dōgen identifies by quoting Pai-chang's words about attachment to liberation. These allusions and quotations seem to make Dōgen's own contribution more elusive. In a sense they break down a strict distinction between his own position and that of others. It becomes impossible at times to distinguish his originality—his self—from others, so that Dōgen's very style illustrates the message he alludes to and quotes: the true human body is beyond selfness and otherness.

What can Dōgen's starting point, the non-dual transposable nature of body-mind, then tell us about the mind-body issue in modern philosophy? Perhaps a more stark contrast could not be imagined, both in content and style of thinking. I find that the juxtaposition brings to light two biases inherent in current presentations of the body-mind problem. Most solutions and dissolutions presuppose dualism and mentalism, even when they are monist and materialist. In order to explain this strange accusation, it may be helpful to repeat a typical formulation of the problem. If the mind is a spiritual thing, and the body a material thing, how can they interact? Is the mind a thing, a substance, at all? Is the mind, rather, only a metaphor for what the brain does? What do words for mental events ("feeling sad," "thinking about supper," etc.) really signify?

While other formulations of the problem occur, it is difficult to find one which does not initially *oppose* body to mind, even if the solution is to reduce one to the other. The philosophical problem, then, concerns the relationship of two terms, or realities, or realms of signification. Let us consider two philosophies which seem to dismiss the opposition outright: conceptual behaviorism and materialism. Behaviorism avowedly rejects the term "mind" as meaningless. It admits only of publicly observable entities and events, assumes that the body belongs entirely to the public realm, and attempts to explain in terms of conditioned bodily responses the more private, hidden human experiences formerly attributed to "mind." But just this persistent attempt belies a mind-body opposition posited initially, if implicitly. In behaviorism, "mind" *means* such and such, e.g., it signifies events such as feeling emotions and thinking thoughts, or it mistakenly purports to signify the substratum of such events. But these events can be explained in terms of verbal or non-verbal behavior, and no subject or substrate other than body is necessary. In behaviorism the reality of mind may be dismissed, but a notion of mind opposed to body is not; otherwise there would be nothing to explain.[32]

Likewise, a mind-body opposition is presumed, before it is dissolved, by all the strong and weak forms of materialism, ranging from the simple identification of mind with brain-events to the sophisticated views of mind as a qualitatively different "emergent property" of the brain. "Mind" is shown to be brain, or a product of the organization of the brain; "spirit" is shown to be matter-energy: this is the position of the psychoneural monists.[33] Reductions of "mind" to brain, however, in whatever form they occur, presuppose a notion of mind whose functions can be shown to be identical with those of the brain. The conceptual terms and models in modern solutions may have changed (one may speak of covert verbal behavior instead of private thoughts, or of plastic neural systems instead of "mind"); but such solutions come in the wake of the historical opposition of body and mind and derive their cogency from that opposition. They remain dualist solutions, then, insofar as a body-mind duality, to be explained or explained away, remains their point of departure.

A glance at what mind and body denote in the *Shinjingakudō* suggests by way of contrast another bias in modern philosophy of mind. In addition to terms signifying the universal, boundless, and formless dimensions of body and mind, there are expressions which identify the mind or body as a particular, concrete, and social action. "Leaving home and renouncing the world" is just as much a metaphor for mind (and body) as is "thinking or not-thinking"; "constructing a meditation hall" describes body (and mind) just as much as does "the four elements," or "a grain of dust."

One might interpret such actions merely as examples of behavior, and conclude that for Dōgen too mind is behavior. But surely no behaviorist would concur with Dōgen that "mind" (or whatever substitutes for "mind") can be totally exhausted by, or manifest in, *one* concrete action, here and now. The behaviorist's position is actually mentalist, insofar as "mind" means for him a set of internal functions explainable as covert and overt behavior; and it is representational insofar as "behavior" for him does not include his own activity of observing and testing the behavior of others. He takes a different stance toward others than he does toward himself; somehow, he retains mind, where others exhibit behavior. Likewise the materialist, who demonstrates that what we call "mind" is identical with functions of the brain. The meaning of "brain" (its logical intension), and therefore of "mind," does not include for him the very activity of researching the properties of the physical organ. If such activity engages his "whole body and mind," to put it metaphorically, and cannot be reduced to neural occurrences in the brain, then the materialist too remains, paradoxically, a "mentalist." He locates "mind" in the brain and excludes, from its sense, activity in the world. The methodologies of both the materialist and behaviorist permit evidence only from the realm of objects and objectification: brains, object-bodies, and observable behaviors. They too share in the fundamental bias of traditional philosophy of mind, which I have called the mentalism of representational thinking. This is the mentalism which, ironically, has externalized mind by placing it inside and world outside, indeed, by *placing* it at all. Contrary to Dōgen's deliberate practice of affirming, negating and emptying the identities of mind and body, the modern tradition would fix the meaning of mind to *something definite*.

I have let Dōgen's *Shinjingakudō* turn two solutions to the modern body-mind problem on their head. The behaviorist denial of mind is mentalist, and psychoneural monism presupposes a dualist starting point. I think it would be possible to see other solutions and procedures in the same light, i.e., as representative of representational thinking and defensive of an inner territory once called mind.

Once again, phenomenologists have come closer to Dōgen's approach to body and mind. Marcel, Sartre and Merleau-Ponty resurrected the body as a theme of philosophic discourse, developed a terminology which did not presuppose a body-mind duality, and exposed some basic prejudices in the tradition.[34] They refused the language that implied I *am* my mind and I *have* a body, and sought alternatives to the metaphors of mind as self, body as property, and both as object. In particular, Merleau-Ponty spoke of the subject body and the "flesh" which defied objectification. He intentionally spoke in metaphors and drew his examples from concrete activity in the world. But he also labored to overcome Cartesian dualism and chose his metaphors and examples in conscious opposition to the tradition. Universal dimensions of mind which had been spoken of in pre-Socratic philosophy were as foreign to him as to most of the tradition,[35] so the idealism he opposed was that of Kant and Husserl, not that of Yogācāra. And starkly concrete metaphors, like "wall, tiles and stones," could not express the total embodiment of mind or of world for Merleau-Ponty, who had no contact with the sort of thinking (and non-thinking) which is practiced in Dōgen's writings.

Concluding questions

For our investigation of Dōgen's *Shinjingakudō* and the issue of body and mind, I have employed the method of jarring contrast, pitting a thirteenth-century Sino-Japanese text and current Western formulations against one another. The contrast showed us remarkable divergencies in the priority of themes, forms of argument, status of language and points of departure; but perhaps it also misled us into forgetting that the divergent texts arise from separate traditions and address quite different questions. This method escapes the danger of being ahistorical only upon recollection that the terms of contrast themselves relate metaphorically. They are deliberately dislodged from their comfortable home in history to confront one another in contemporary arena of inquiry. They do take part in originally different questions, and any unification of themes or traditions must come, like Dōgen's unit of body and mind, as an achievement. That achievement, however, is likely to be not a fusion of traditions, but a transposition of barriers.

Still, before the achievement, or along its way, further historical retrieval and open questioning are called for. Let me point the way by recalling Richard Rorty's masterly summation of traditional Western philosophy of mind and my difference from it. Rorty discusses "solutions to the mind-body problem" not, he says, to propose one but to illustrate why he does not think there is a problem. The mind-body problem belongs to history for Rorty, in the sense both of being historically determined and of being obsolete. Specifically, our notions of the mental belong to a philosophical game which "links up with no issues in daily life, empirical science, morals, or religion."[36] Rorty intends his work to be therapeutic, rather than constructive, and to restore conversation and not a tribunal of reason, as the context of knowledge. Alluding to Aristotle's and Plato's "wonder" indirectly by way of Heidegger, he would evict from the great conversation of mankind technical and determinate questions which are poor substitutes for that "openness to strangeness which initially tempted us to begin thinking."[37]

Certainly one would have to be open to strangeness to listen to a conversation between Dōgen and modern philosophy of mind. Like Rorty, I have offered no solution to the mind-body problem as I formulated it at the outset; I have not even attempted a reformulation. But maybe by "playing" with that problem, by bouncing it against walls, tiles, stones and other strange pivots, I have caught some bits and pieces of Dōgen's mind whole before they dissolved in my grasp. I turned the body and mind's study of the Way into a study by way of body and mind, into the way the body-mind studies, into a study of body-mind, forgetting the Way. I found that a behaviorist and a materialist have a mind of their own which they seem unwilling to share with mountains, rivers and the great earth. I found the phenomenologist's body not exhausted by constructing metaphors, and not exhaustively embodied in any one grain of dust.

Unlike Rorty, I cannot renounce the practical and social consequences of the mind-body problem and view it as a retreat to the mountains of words better forgotten, as a remote language game long played out. Although I have not touched upon these issues here, I think that other, urgent problems hinge in part on conceptions of body and mind, their sameness and their difference. Whether we ascribe rights to the unborn; whether we find limits to behavioral modification; whether we divide responsibility for acts bodily committed under mental incompetence; even how we relate to our environment—as property or as self—these are social issues which depend upon how we conceptualize, and how we practice, oneness of body and mind.

Notes

1. A major work exploring the status of the problem is Richard Rorty, *Philosophy and the Mirror of Nature* (Princeton: Princeton University Press, 1979). Allusions to Rorty in this essay refer to this work.
2. Among the plethora of literature on the body-mind issue are these books published since Rorty's work: R. W. Rieber, ed., *Body and Mind - Past, Present and Future* (New York: Academic Press, 1980); Mario Bunge, *The Mind-Body Problem: A Psychobiological Approach* (New York: Pergamon Press, 1980); Julian M. Davidson and Richard J. Davidson, eds., *The Psychobiology of Consciousness* (New York: Plenum Press, 1980); Daniel C. Dennett, *Brainstorms: Philosophical Essays on Mind and Psychology* (Cambridge: MIT Press, 1981); Douglas R. Hofstadter and Daniel C. Dennett, eds., *The Mind's I* (New York: Basic Books, 1981); John Haugeland, ed., *Mind Design* (Cambridge: MIT Press, 1981); Hilary Putnam, "Mind and Body" in his *Reason, Truth and History* (New York: Cambridge University Press, 1981); and Noam Chomsky, "Mind and Body" in his *Rules and Representations* (New York: Columbia University Press, 1980).
3. For a contrast with the ancient and early medieval West see the fascinating study of the Hebrew and Hellenistic notions of the body by Margaret R. Miles: *Fullness of Life: Historical Foundations for a New Asceticism* (Phil-

adelphia: Westminster Press, 1981). It is unfortunate that the author does not critically examine her use of the term "soul" in the book.

4. *DZZ* 1:36–41.
5. Historical background to Dōgen's views can be found in Martin Collcut, *Five Mountains: The Rinzai Monastic Institution in Medieval Japan* (Cambridge: Harvard University Press, 1981), pp. 49–56.
6. For an examination of the terms and connotations relating to body practice in Dōgen, see my essay, "The Hermeneutics of Practice in Dōgen and Francis of Assisi," *EB* 14 (2): 22–46.
7. Rorty, op. cit., p. 3.
8. The three terms Dōgen uses are almost as ambiguous as the English "mind." *Shittashin,* a transliteration of the Sanskrit *citta,* most likely denotes discriminating mind *(ryochishin). Karidashin,* Sanskrit *hṛdaya,* is probably equivalent to *sōmokushin,* the mind of plants and trees, connoting universal, omnipresent buddha nature. *Iridashin,* Sanskrit *vṛddha,* is probably *shushushōyoshin,* the wisdom mind grasping and extracting the essence of the entire body or universe. See Nakamura Sōichi, *Shōbōgenzō Yōgojiten* (Tokyo: Seishinshōhō, 1975). For a discussion of body-mind terms in Dōgen's works, see Hee-Jin Kim, *Dōgen Kigen: Mystical Realist* (Tucson: University of Arizona Press, 1975), pp. 127–135.
9. Rorty, loc. cit.
10. Although Heidegger does not discuss anything like a "mind-body" problem, his insights concerning being-in-the-world have laid the foundation for an alternative view of human being. See especially *Being and Time,* trans. John Macquarrie and Edward Robinson (New York: Harper and Row, 1962), pp. 78–90. Critiques of representational or objectifying thinking are found in *What Is Called Thinking,* trans. J. Glenn Gray (New York: Harper and Row, 1968) and "The Theological Discussion of the Problem of a Non-Objectifying Thinking and Speaking" in *The Piety of Thinking,* trans. James G. Hart and John C. Maraldo (Bloomington: Indiana University Press, 1976), pp. 22–33.
11. Jean-Paul Sartre, *The Transcendence of the Ego,* trans. Forrest Williams and Robert Kirkpatrick (New York: Noonday Press, 1957).
12. Maurice Merleau-Ponty, *The Visible and the Invisible,* trans. Alphonso Lingis (Evanston: Northwestern University Press, 1968), esp. pp. 135ff.
13. A sustained attempt to practice thinking is his series of university lectures presented as *Was heisst Denken?,* trans. J. Glenn Gray, op. cit.
14. See Kim, op. cit., p. 155, for a discussion of naturalism, spontaneous enlightenment—or innatism. I will leave it an open question whether this innatism is synonymous with that criticized in the *Sesshin Sessho* as the position of Ta-hui Tsung-kuo, namely, the view that mind is only intellect and perception, Dōgen's *citta.*
15. Rorty, op. cit., p. 12.
16. The locus classicus of mirror imagery in Zen literature is the Sixth Patriarch controversy, where contender Shen-hsiu composes this verse: "The body is the bodhi tree,/The mind is like a clear mirror./At all times we must strive to polish it,/And must not let the dust collect." Hui-neng replies, "Bodhi originally has no tree,/The mirror also has no stand./Buddha nature is always clean and pure;/Where is there room for dust?" See Philip B. Yampolsky, *The Platform Sutra of the Sixth Patriarch* (New York: Columbia University Press, 1967), pp. 130ff. Compare the ancient Taoist texts, *Lao Tzu: Tao te Ching,* trans. D. C. Lau (Harmondsworth, Middlesex: Pen-

guin, 1963), chap. 10: "Can you polish your mysterious mirror? [i.e., mind]"; and *Chuang Tzu*, trans. Burton Watson (New York: Columbia University Press, 1964), p. 66 (chap. 5), ". . . . if the mirror is bright, no dust settles on it; if the dust settles, it isn't really bright" and p. 95 (chap. 7), "The Perfect Man uses his mind like a mirror—going after nothing, welcoming nothing, responding but not storing."

17. This imagery is pervasive at present; a classic statement can be found in John Lilly, *The Human Biocomputer: Programming and Metaprogramming* (Miami: Communication Research Institute, 1967).

18. A recent defense of this position is Mario Bunge, op. cit.

19. Karl H. Pribram is the most energetic advocate of the hologramic theory; see his "Mind, Brain, and Consciousness," in Davidson and Davidson, op. cit. My statement of this metaphor is taken from Paul Pietsch, *Shuffle-brain: The Quest for the Hologramic Mind* (Boston: Houghton Mifflin, 1981).

20. The adamant defender of the behaviorist position is B. F. Skinner; see his popular books *Beyond Freedom and Dignity* (New York: Bantam Books, 1972) and *About Behaviorism* (New York: Vintage Books, 1976).

21. Merleau-Ponty, op. cit., esp. pp. 139f.

22. This metaphor is almost ubiquitous in Ch'an literature and is found again in the *Shōbōgenzō* (*DZZ* 2:462–463).

23. Dōgen is even more explicit in *Zuimonki*, talks delivered in 1235–1237 at Kōshō-hōrinji: "Without knowing who taught them these things, students consider the mind to be thought and perceptions, and do not believe it when they are told that the mind is plants and trees. . . . Therefore, when the Buddhas and the Patriarchs categorically state that the mind is plants and trees, revise your preconceptions and understand plants and trees as mind. If the Buddha is said to be tiles and pebbles, consider tiles and pebbles as the Buddha. If you change your basic preconceptions, you will be able to gain the Way." From Masunaga Reihō, trans., *A Primer of Sōtō Zen* (Honolulu: East-West Center Press, 1971), pp. 65f.

24. Compare one of his postulates on thinking, an activity mistakenly thought to be a property of "mind": "POSTULATE 7.4. A sequence of thoughts about propositions is (identical with) the sequential activation of the psychons whose activities are the propositions in the sequence" and "DEFINITION 7.3. Two thoughts are equivalent if they consist in thinking of the same constructs. That is, (C) (C') if C = C' for any animals a and b." Bunge, op. cit., pp. 159–161.

25. *Kakekotoba,* ubiquitous in Zen literature, are also a literary convention in classical Japanese, especially court poetry, where they function as a kind of pun. See the discussion in Earl Miner, *An Introduction to Japanese Court Poetry* (Stanford: Stanford University Press, 1968), pp. 23f. A potent example of the phrase "mind—no other than mountains, rivers and the great earth" functioning as a *kakekotoba* is the enlightenment experience of Yamada Kōun Roshi, reported in Philip Kapleau, *The Three Pillars of Zen* (Boston: Beacon Press, 1965), pp. 205ff.

26. For penetrating studies on the functioning of metaphor in general, see George Lakoff and Mark Johnson, *Metaphors We Live By* (Chicago: University of Chicago Press, 1980), and Mark Johnson, ed., *Philosophical Perspectives on Metaphor* (Minneapolis: University of Minnesota Press, 1981). Other essays in the present volume discuss Dōgen's peculiar use of language; see esp. the introduction and the essay by Kim.

27. In the *Zuimonki* Dōgen says, "Is the Way attained through the mind or through the body? . . . In Zen the Way is attained with both body and mind. . . . Therefore, if you cast aside completely the thoughts and concepts of the mind and concentrate on *zazen* alone, you attain to an intimacy with the Way. The attainment of the Way is truly accomplished with the body. For this reason, I urge you to concentrate on *zazen*." Cited in Masunaga, op. cit., p. 47.

28. See "Dōgen's Bendōwa," trans. Norman Waddell and Abe Masao, *EB* 4 (1): 146.

29. The contemporary Japanese philosopher Yuasa Yasuo expands on the theme of mind-body unity accomplished through practice in his recent work *Shintai: Tōyōteki shinjinron no Kokoromi* (Tokyo: Sōbunsha, 1979).

30. Note that classical Buddhist classifications identify the body only with the first skandha, *rūpa* or matter.

31. Hui-k'o's story forms the 41st case of the *Mumonkan*. Standing outside in the snow, the future Second Patriarch begs Bodhidharma to set his mind at rest. Bodhidharma replies, "Bring me your mind and I will put it to rest." Hui-k'o: "I have searched for the mind but cannot find it anywhere." Bodhidharma: "I have now set it to rest for you."

32. See Skinner's intransigent defense of behaviorism, op. cit.

33. Bunge, op. cit., declared himself to be a psychoneural monist. A classic defence of materialism in general is D. M. Armstrong, *A Materialist Theory of the Mind* (London and New York: Routledge and Kegan Paul, 1968).

34. A summary and critical examination of the role of the body in these phenomenologists is Richard M. Zaner, *The Problem of Embodiment* (The Hague: M. Nijhoff, 1964).

35. The philosophy of A. N. Whitehead is an exception. See his discussion of mind extending throughout the natural universe in *Modes of Thought* (New York: Capricorn Books, 1958).

36. Rorty, op. cit., p. 22.

37. Rorty, op, cit., p. 9.

Dōgen's View of Authentic Selfhood and Its Socio-ethical Implications

Francis H. Cook

Writing in the first half of the thirteenth century, the Zen master Dōgen looked at the deficiencies of the human society he knew and as the antidote prescribed the forgetting of the self (*shinjin datsuraku,* "dropping off mind and body"). His language to this end was unique, and to some extent his interpretation was his own, but despite this he was continuing to articulate a Buddhist teaching concerning individual and social well-being which began with the ministry of Śākyamuni, continued in the forceful arguments of Nāgārjuna in the second century, and has been continued by all Buddhist spokesmen down to the present time. The understanding of Buddhist self-forgetting has passed through several phases in the West, ranging from early reactions of shocked disbelief and horror to a more recent understanding of its nature and spiritual implications. However, usually still missing from discussions of this doctrine is the understanding that the process of self-forgetting involves a paradox which contains very interesting implications for human society: this is that the process of self-forgetting is simultaneously a process of encompassing more and more of experience as "self," and that such a process in the individual promotes an enhanced humanness, not a diminished humanness. The Buddhist injunction to "forget the self" may therefore be seen as an injunction to become more human, with all the implications this has for living in the world.

However, that human beings are not yet human enough or authentically human implies not a need for greater self-assertion as individuals or as members of the human species but rather for less. Though Buddhist literature does not speak of religious liberation in terms of the realization of full human potential, it is implicit in Buddhist thought that true humanness is attainable with self-transcendence, or with "forgetting the self," as Dōgen called it. This simply means that from the Buddhist perspective man will be at his best when he has forgotten the self, and "being at his best" means *best as a human being* inasmuch as self-forgetting takes place within the framework of humanity. Consequently, man can achieve his fullest humanness in the process of self-forgetting, but the paradox is that he can achieve this potential only by transcending what he usually affirms as the essence of his humanity. What does it mean to actualize full humanness by transcending humanness, and what is the active expression of this actualization in the world?

Dōgen had much to say about these matters in the first half of the thirteenth century, but does he still speak to twentieth- and twenty-first-century people? I would like to propose in this paper that he does, and he does so for the reason that his understanding of the nature of authentic selfhood is more satisfying philosophically and has more value existentially than does the traditional Western definition of selfhood. It is worth noting that during the twentieth century in the West, particularly in the thinking of Martin Heidegger and Alfred North Whitehead, a new formulation of selfhood has emerged which has already had a significant impact on Christian theology, to name only one area, and this new formulation parallels Dōgen's in great part. To the extent that Dōgen's understanding of authentic selfhood is in many ways consonant with, and in many ways an even more radical statement of, recent trends in Western thought, his writings concerning the problems of inauthentic selfhood and the value of authentic selfhood remain as tools to aid contemporary man in his own reflections on egocentrism and anthropocentrism. It was, after all, Whitehead in the twentieth century who said that all the problems of the present time could be traced to the belief in substance—which I believe is the "self" which Buddhism has traditionally criticized. If he was correct, then perhaps Dōgen's reformulation of what the true self is may serve still as a guide to our own reflections.

This paper is an attempt to suggest that the two closely related ideas of the authentic self and that self's active participation in the world, as they are found in Dōgen's writings, serve as powerful criticisms of arrogant attitudes, assumptions, and actions which still characterize the twentieth century. I believe the two ideas are closely related because Dōgen's understanding of authentic selfhood is necessarily that of a self which is fully ingredient in the whole world, an active participant in the world, and a self which is committed to the world. My approach will be that of a Buddhologian, by which I mean the Buddhist equivalent of a theologian. The task of the Buddhologian, as I see it, is that of exploring and unpacking the symbols and images of a text in such a way as to make them more meaningful to contemporaries. By "meaningful" I intend two things: that the reader is able to grasp the essential idea or concept conveyed by the language, and that the reader is better able to understand what the meaning of the text may be for him. This essay is based on the belief that Dōgen's relevance to the present time lies in the challenge he presents to naive and unexamined assumptions concerning what a self is and how the self should function in the world. That challenge has always existed. When he left Kyoto to build Eihei-ji in Echizen Province, Dōgen was not abandoning his early hope of changing the world. It was only the tactic that changed. Feeling that his teachings were being resisted by a recalcitrant populace and realizing he was unlikely to see any great spiritual change in the foreseeable future, he left Kyoto to establish an elite community of men singlemindedly devoted to the achievement of an authentic selfhood which would be a model and constant reminder of what was ideally attainable by all people. At the same time, the model life of Eihei-ji and his voluminous writings would serve as a constant criticism of inauthentic selfhood and its corollary, social turmoil.

I will begin with two well-known passages from *Shōbōgenzō genjō-kōan,* which will serve as the basis for the comments I wish to make.

Conveying the self to the myriad beings to authenticate them is delusion;
The myriad things advancing to authenticate the self is enlightenment.

To study the Buddha Way is to study the self;
To study the self is to forget the self;
To forget the self is to be authenticated by the myriad things.[1]

As one Dōgen expert has pointed out, these lines concern the difference between delusion and enlightenment.[2] But these lines may also be read—and it is the same thing—as the difference between inauthentic and authentic selfhood, and I will discuss them in these terms. Dōgen's understanding of inauthentic selfhood is expressed in a manner not very different from the way it is in almost all Buddhist literature; that is, that inauthentic selfhood derives from the human tendency to superimpose patterns of thinking, categories, and concepts onto experience in order to manipulate it. But the process of superimposition, or "conveying the self to the myriad things," is not something that simply happens in the nature of things. The heavily vested interest of the self is forcibly brought out by means of a visual image of the self being carried or conveyed *(hakobu)* out to the experience *(jiko o hakobite).* The parallelism of these first two lines is interesting in the way it reveals how carefully Dōgen used language to convey precise meaning and nuance. The first line has *jiko,* self, as the object of the transitive verb *hakobu,* indicating that something conveys the self out to the objective event, and, of course, it is the self which conveys itself to the objective event. To understand why the self conveys itself out to the experience and imposes meaning on it is to understand why in fact it is an inauthentic self. On the other hand, the second line contains the intransitive verb *susumu,* advance, and here it is said that the experience *(mampō,* myriad things) advances to authenticate the self. Here, the self is not actively involved in the process of experiencing in the way it is in the previous line. It does not convey itself to experience or convey experience to itself, but rather things-events advance of themselves, and this process constitutes enlightenment or the authentication of the self. What it means for the myriad things to advance and authenticate the self will be discussed in detail further on. Here it may suffice to point out that authentic selfhood results from things advancing to the self and, as I will argue further on, in fact constituting authentic selfhood, while inauthentic selfhood results from the self's conveying itself out to things. Authentic selfhood is made authentic by the myriad things in the first case, while in the second case inauthentic selfhood results from the attempt of the self to authenticate experience, or to give it meaning, through its own agency.

What is this self which achieves inauthenticity by imposing meaning on experience and which is the target of the Buddhist critique? It is not difficult to locate it. It is that function of the human mind which is oriented primarily towards its own gratification and protection at the expense of what is interpreted as "other." At the same time, it is that which the individual detects in the act of introspection. From the standpoint of Dōgen, such a self is also abstract rather than concrete, because whereas the concrete self is in fact just the immediacy of experience, as I shall argue further on, the abstract self is abstract because it arises from and is constituted by the self's memory of past concrete experiences. It is consequently an image constructed from memory and is quite abstract. In scholastic literature prior to Dōgen, this situation is discussed in terms of a split in consciousness or mind, whereby the original unity of consciousness becomes bifurcated and comes to take the form of mind as subject and mind as its own object—that is, self-consciousness of the type described by Piaget. The mind as object of itself is abstract because the mind as true subject can never catch itself in its own form as vibrant, concrete, lived experience. It can only seize a past image of itself in the form of memory, and thus there is a saying in Buddhism to the effect that "a knife can not cut itself."

Above, the terms "mind" and "self" have been used interchangeably because "self" is merely the mind's own self-image. That is, the mind in its bifurcated form comes to think of itself as "self," a self being defined as having the characteristics of unity, discreteness, endurance through time as self-identical and, perhaps, even permanence. What is challenging about Buddhism, and particularly Dōgen's version, is the recognition of this function of human consciousness, along with what its effects are on human—and nonhuman—societies. This function constitutes the problem of delusion, but there is more than delusion. In its analysis of the human problem Buddhism found three qualities of the mind—the so-called "three poisons"—which generate all problems. The fundamental quality is delusion, as shown in the traditional formula of the "dependent origination in twelve links." However, the other two are desire ("thirst") and hatred. To understand the nature of the mind-self and why it creates its own suffering, it is necessary to ask first why it is that the bifurcation of mind into mind as subject and mind as its own object should give rise to the deep desire and hatred which Buddhism considers to be the very characteristics of inauthentic selfhood and the source of all human problems.

Buddhism ordinarily halts its analysis of the human situation with the conclusion that the root problem is ignorance or desire.[3] However, there is abundant evidence in Buddhist literature, and in *Shōbōgenzō* in particular, to indicate that there has been from the beginning a keen awareness of a deep-rooted *anxiety*[4] which is expressed in the form of desire and hatred. Desire and hatred are rooted in the fear of impermanence and death and the pervasive insecurity that ensues from this fear. There are a number of well-known passages in Buddhist literature which attempt to encapsulate the spirit and practice of Buddhism in a short verse or prose formula, and they frequently dwell on the fact of *anitya,* impermanence, and imply that the perception of impermanence is the most dreadful of all perceptions and the motivation for undertaking the search for liberation. This is also clear from the episode of the "four sights" in the biographies of the Buddha and from the first of the "four noble truths," where *duḥkha,* which is an anxiety-ridden unrest or turmoil, is said to be universal human condition. With regard to Dōgen, various commentators have pointed out the importance of his early perception of impermanence to his own spiritual odyssey and how, in his thought, impermanence is linked with spiritual search in general.[5] Fear and insecurity in the face of impermanence and death not only drive the individual to search for a means of dealing with the problem, as they did with Śākyamuni himself, but are also the form taken by the inauthentic self.

In short, the inauthentic self is the self obsessed with fear for its own security and endurance, and authentic selfhood is the self which has been liberated from clinging to life and fearing death. Or, in other words, the change from inauthentic to authentic selfhood is the change from fear to assurance insofar as the life and death problem is concerned. In *Shōbōgenzō shōji,* for instance, Dōgen says that authentic selfhood—there called "enlightenment"—consists of ceasing to fear and hate the lifedeath process and searching for authenticity apart from it: "You only attain the mind of Buddha when there is no hating [of life and death] and no desiring [of nirvana]." Furthermore, "There is a very easy way to the Buddha. Those who do not create various evils; those who do not cling to life and death; . . . those who do not deny things or seek them; . . . they are called the Buddha."[6] Heidegger also, in his lifelong analysis of inauthenticity, saw that authenticity is very hard to achieve precisely because it entails a radical confrontation with one's own mortality.[7] For both Dōgen and Heidegger, inauthenticity results from the inability of the mind-self to realize its own impermanent nature and subsequently to live creatively and contentedly in the world in this self-knowledge. Thus, the root problem is ignorance, in the form of belief that one is a self, but the concrete day-to-day personal and social problems of such a self arise when, out of an anxiety-ridden fear for its own survival, it comes to thirst for things which will protect it and to hate those things which appear to menace it.

The inauthentic self, then, is the mind obsessed with self-survival *at all costs*. This is why delusion, in the first passage from *Genjō-kōan,* is defined in terms of the self being conveyed out to objective experience; the experience is never impersonal and abstract but rather is always interpreted in terms of the needs of the self preoccupied with self-survival. The mind is constantly colored with desire and hatred because any event is perceived as either beneficial or harmful to the self. Furthermore, pervaded with this deep anxiety, the self sees the difference between self and nonself as axiomatic, of the gravest import. Not only are individuals and even whole populations—human and nonhuman—destroyed for the sake of the insecure and fearful self, but a vast array of metaphysical systems, myths, "isms," and even religions are constructed and defended to the death in order to solace and defend minds which are primarily concerned with their own reality, importance, and survival. As Nāgārjuna argued in the second century, and as Dōgen continued to insist in the thirteenth, all positions and ideologies arise from and, in turn, nourish the inauthentic self and for that reason are to be abandoned—not excluding Buddhism itself. One of Dōgen's greatest challenges lies in the demand to recognize the possibility that everything we believe to be ultimate and of vast significance is no more than a projection of deep-seated insecurity, and nothing more than a projection from minds which resist death and diminution to the very end.

If the above is the nature of the inauthentic self, then what is the authentic self? The second line from *Genjō-kōan* says that when the self is authenticated by the myriad things, this is enlightenment. It needs to be said first that there are not two selves, an inauthentic one and an authentic one. It is rather a question of whether the self as an experiencing center of subjectivity functions authentically or not. In terms of the above-mentioned subject-object split in consciousness, authentic selfhood results from the restoration of the original unity. In terms used in *Genjō-kōan,* when the self in its assumed separateness imposes subjective meaning on experience, inauthenticity results ("Conveying the self to the myriad things to authenticate them is delusion"). On the other hand, when the self is made authentic by experience (the myriad things) or is made a self by them, the result is authentic selfhood. In this matter,

Heidegger says something similar about authenticity. According to Michael Zimmerman, Heidegger's lifelong search for authenticity disclosed that the authentic self is not revealed when one engages in theoretical self-reflection but rather is disclosed "in the worldly things with whom I concern myself."[8] I take this to mean something similar to what Dōgen means when he says that enlightenment is that condition in which the self is authenticated by the myriad things. The authentic self results from a *metanoia* which Dōgen calls "dropping off mind and body" *(shinjin datsuraku)* or "forgetting the self" *(jiko o wasururu)* and this *metanoia* is not a volitional act which antedates and makes possible the authentication of the self by the myriad things but rather is itself the very condition whereby the self is made authentic.

The inauthentic self is abstract because it is a mere image created out of the synthesis of past experiences which are no longer actual and concrete and because the world it experiences is an abstract, conceptual world. The authentic self, on the other hand, because it is constituted of immediate experience, is concrete. Because it *is* just immediate experience, there can be no real self prior to experience as the antecedent enjoyer of experience, or a real self which *has* experience. The concrete self cannot exist independent of experience or prior to it as simply a self which experiences objective facts in a different way but must be the "myriad things" themselves as felt immediacy. This is also implied in the overcoming of the subject-object split in consciousness, in which the unification of consciousness means that the subject is the object.

If the authentic self, which is to say the concrete self, is the form of the self as the unity of subject and object, then this has important implications for human self-understanding and the social expression of such understanding. If experience constantly changes, then the true self which is no more than a unit of immediate experience must constantly change also. If the word "I" can be used in any rigorous sense, then "I" must in fact be a series of selves which come into momentary existence in the form of unified experience and successively perish as experience changes. Now, though the discussion here has been in terms of the authentic self, it should be noted that this is only an alternate expression for what Dōgen called "Buddha" or "Buddha nature," which he says is both "permanent Buddha nature" and "impermanent Buddha nature." Bracketing the question of the meaning of permanent Buddha nature, can we not understand Buddha nature to be impermanent in the sense that, as the authentic self which is not apart from or other than experience, it must arise and perish in accordance with experience? This seems to be the implication in such essays from *Shōbōgenzō* as *Busshō* (Buddha nature), *Uji* (Being-time), *Genjō-kōan* (Presencing absolute reality) and others, where Dōgen discusses impermanent Buddha nature, the identity of being and time, and "dharma state" *(hōi)*. While such ideas are not linked to such questions as the status of the self, there is the very strong implication that the self is no different from other things in being constituted by a succession of states, each link of which perishes to be replaced by a new one.[9] Furthermore, Dōgen's understanding of what constitutes enlightenment or authentic selfhood cannot easily be grasped apart from an understanding of the true self as being impermanent, for in *Genjō-kōan* and elsewhere it is said that enlightenment itself is always and only enlightenment in a particular situation, and so consequently, rather than enlightenment being a once-and-for-all event, it must be actualized over and over as each new event is experienced. In *Genjō-kōan* it is said that enlightenment as the authentication of the self by the myriad things must be continued forever.[10] But what is especially suggestive to the modern reader of Dōgen is the idea that true selfhood is not permanent and unchanging, that it is not something which can or need be preserved from harm, that it is somehow privileged in being exempt from the impermanence to which everything else is subject. To be an authentic self must, Heidegger claimed, entail a graceful acquiescence to real impermanence and mortality, and one might speculate as to the impact on human institutions and other cultural forms by selves which are no longer motivated primarily by fear and insecurity in the face of change and death.

Part of the ordinary understanding of selfhood is that the self is permanent and substantial—an enduring object—and, therefore, in need of protection. Another part of the definition of the self is that it is discrete, and consequently one problem with the traditional definition lies in the way it is so limited. That is to say, the self is a small self, bounded by the skin of the individual. The very nature of this small self is that it is experienced as separated by a sharp, absolute line from everything else, and indeed, "self" means "not other." But if the authentic self is of the sort described above, two significant corollaries can be drawn which point to the essentially social nature of the self. First, the authentic self is actional and dynamic in a way impossible or at best difficult for the inauthentic self, for in contrast to the inauthentic self which merely observes and interprets, the authentic self as concrete immediate experience is profoundly immersed in experience, which is to say, the world. In other words, the life of the authentic self is none other than the life of everything, and therefore the authentic self is part of the world of everyday events in a way that is problematic for the inauthentic self. Second, and closely related to the activity of the authentic self, is the relational nature of such a self, because, as I have argued above, such a self has no existence prior to or apart from the experience which in fact constitutes it. Such a self is not "simply located" (in Whiteheadian terminology), enclosed absolutely within a particular body and separated from its objective world. It is rather the very "other" in a real way. Thus, when Dōgen says in *Shōbōgenzō kajō* (Everyday Life) that the everyday life of the enlightened patriarchs consists simply of eating plain boiled rice and drinking plain green tea, he means that authentic selfhood—i.e., the enlightenment of the patriarchs—is constituted of such ordinary, representative acts as these, and no real self exists independently of them. In *Yuibutsu yobutsu,* he says, "What the Buddha means by the self is precisely the entire universe *(jindaichi).* Thus, whether one is aware of it or not, there is no universe that is not this self. . . ."[11] And in another passage, he quotes Master Chang-sha as saying,

> The whole universe is the eye of a monk;
> The whole universe is a monk's everyday speech;
> The whole universe is a monk's entire body;
> The whole universe is the self's dazzling light *(kōmyō);*
> The whole universe is within the dazzling light of the self.[12]

Now, if the "dazzling light of the self" (which means the dazzling light which *is* the self) is what I have been referring to as the authentic self, such a self is not "simply located" and limited to a particular body-mind but must encompass the totality of events which comprise experience. To "drop off mind and body," as Dōgen says in the second passage from *Genjō-kōan* quoted earlier, involves, in the process of being authenticated by the myriad things, the realization that the true self is far greater in scope than previously imagined. Such a self is not absolutely discrete and separate from the world as is the inauthentic self; it is both truly ingredient in the world and at the same time encompasses the whole world. For this reason, recent translations of the Sanskrit Buddhist term *śūnyatā* as "boundless openness," "luminosity," and the like by Herbert Gunther, Masao Abe, and others is in many ways preferable to the older, widespread translation of the term as "emptiness." These newer translations avoid the negative flavor of "emptiness" and at the same time accurately capture the meaning of the experience as one of emcompassing more and more of experience as "oneself."

The relational nature of the authentic self precludes the possibility that selfhood is isolated and aloof from the larger world. To be an authentic self involves transcendence only in the sense that its achievement is coterminous with an abandonment of the self's drive for self-protection, comfort, domination, and the like. Transcendence is self-transcendence, not world-transcendence. Authentic selfhood as the *lived* experience of essential relationality points to a radically profound way of *being in the world* both existentially and socially. The limited nature of the inauthentic self consists, on the other hand, of not only an ontological restriction but also of an inability to be really in and of the world, and the paradox is that, as the inauthentic self is clung to more and more tenaciously, the self is experienced as more and more alienated from everything that is construed as not-self. If the authentic self is something like Nishida's "immediate experience," how could it be separate or aloof from its experience? The depth of this total immersion in experience is the theme of Dōgen's essay *Shunjū* (Spring and Fall), in which he comments on the *kōan* "Tozan's place where there is neither heat nor cold." There, the Zen life of complete freedom *within* the context of necessarily unavoidable conditions is framed in terms of an authentic selfhood in the form of a total participation in the world to the extent that when the "heat and cold" of experience come, there is no reactive, self-protective self confronting the experience but only the self *as* "heat and cold."[13] Thus, authentic selfhood is inseparable from a total living in the world, and this is the full implication of the line from *Genjō-kōan,* "The myriad things advancing to authenticate the self is enlightenment."

The individual breaks through the barrier of the inauthentic self to the ground which is the authentic and original self *(honrai no jiko)* through the process of self-forgetting, and this self-forgetting consists of the self's authentication by the myriad things of experience. In this way, the self is experienced as encompassing the "other" as self and there is the realization that the whole universe *(jindaichi)* just as it is is the absolute reality *(genjō-kōan)* or true self.[14] But this sense of identity is not the ultimate goal, for commitment and sympathy are not only involved in the process of authentication but are really the ultimate goal. Two essays in particular from *Shōbōgenzō* leave no doubt as to the nature of the real goal, which is that of commitment toward all beings and sympathy with their suffering. In the *Shōbōgenzō hotsu bodai shin* (Arousing the enlightened mind), Dōgen wrote:

> What is called "arousing the enlightened mind" means to make a vow to liberate all sentient beings at a time when oneself is not yet liberated. If one arouses this mind, no matter how humble in appearance one is, one is the guide of all beings.[15]

And in *Busshō* (Buddha nature):

> What is the essence of the World-honored One's words *"All sentient beings without exception have the Buddha nature"*? . . . You may speak of "living beings," "sentient beings," "all classes of living things," or "all varieties of living being," the words *whole being (shitsuu)* mean sentient beings and all beings. That is to say, *whole being* is the Buddha nature. I call one integral entity of whole being "sentient beings." Just when things are thus, both within and without sentient beings is in itself the *whole being* of Buddha nature.[16]

The passage from *Hotsu bodai shin* does not require much comment, since Zen as a form of Mahayana Buddhism incorporates the prominent Mahayana ideal of compassion and the Bodhisattva vow to liberate all sentient beings, that is, the teaching that enlightenment or authentic selhood is but a means, albeit a necessary means, to the end of liberating all sentient beings. However, it is important to point out here that Dōgen took this ideal most seriously, as is indicated by the fact that he devoted two whole essays to it, in *Hotsu bodai shin* and *Hotsu mujō shin* (Arousing the Supreme Mind). Therefore, for Dōgen, authentic selfhood is an authentic selfhood *for others*—that is, its proper function is that of eliminating suffering and struggle in the world. However, what is particularly noteworthy about this ideal as it is developed in Dōgen's writing, and what is particularly suggestive to modern man in his increasingly anthropocentric view of life and action, is Dōgen's radicalized version of what it means to commit oneself to the liberation of all beings. This radicalization is found in Dōgen's insistence, in the passage quoted from *Busshō,* to the effect that commitment is to all beings or actualities, *including* but also going beyond the human realm and even the realm of sentience. Dōgen's understanding of authentic selfhood is not easy for us to grasp, nor are such key terms as *genjō-kōan* and *gūjin,* unless it is realized that anthropocentrism is to be transcended no less than egocentrism.

The radicalization mentioned above occurs in the passage from *Busshō* in which Dōgen employs a quote from the *Nirvāṇa Sūtra* ("All sentient beings without exception possess Buddha nature") and interprets it as really saying, "*All* are sentient beings and the whole being is Buddha nature." Now, the Chinese term *(chung-sheng)* translated as "sentient beings" (Jap. *shujō*) is a Chinese translation of the Sanskrit *pṛthagjana,* which literally means "various births," in reference to the so-called "six realms" in which living things are reborn. *I-ch'ieh chung-sheng* (Jap. *issai shujō*) therefore has been accurately interpreted as meaning "all sentient beings," and consequently the Chinese text of the *Nirvāṇa Sūtra* really should be read as saying that "all sentient beings without exception possess Buddha nature." Dōgen's interpretation, on the other hand, is a radical broadening of the scope of Buddha nature, for he says that all beings, whether sentient or insentient, are (not *have*) Buddha. This broadening of scope is at once part of the history of the development of Japanese Buddhism,[17] perhaps the result of Dōgen's own religious experience, and also certainly the logical consequence of the Mahayana doctrines of *śūnyatā* and *samatā* (sameness). Yet, one may wonder why no one prior to Dōgen enunciated so clearly and unambiguously the all-encompassing scope of Buddha nature.[18]

Dōgen's extension of Buddha nature to all things is completely necessary to his understanding of authentic selfhood or enlightenment and, indeed, we are unable to understand just what authentic selfhood or enlightenment means in the context of Dōgen's Buddhism apart from the idea of the Buddhahood of all things. In Zen terminology, the actualization of the self as absolute nothingness *(zettai mu),* which I have been calling "authentic selfhood," is simultaneously the realization that everything else without exception is also this same absolute nothingness. Several key terms in *Shōbōgenzō* express this idea. *Zenki,* for instance, which means something like "total dynamic functioning," in an essay of the same title, expresses the idea that everything is the dynamic disclosure of absolute reality, and thus *zenki* is very similar to *genjō-kōan* in expressing, on the one hand, the idea that each entity is the absolute reality called "Buddha," and on the other hand, the denial that there are any hierarchies of reality, significance, or ultimacy insofar as endowment with Buddha nature is concerned.[19] Another term employed frequently is *gūjin,* which means either "total penetration" ("penetration" in the cognitive sense) or perhaps "total exertion," depending on whether *gūjin* is something being performed by an experiencing subject or is seen as the way an entity is the total disclosure of ultimate reality. In the first sense of the word, *gūjin* refers to the ability of an individual to totally penetrate the nature of an experience or entity, this ability being the hallmark of authentic selfhood.[20] In the second sense, *gūjin* is the same as *zenki* and *genjō-kōan.* With reference to the obliteration of absolute hierarchies of reality, it might be mentioned parenthetically that Justus Buchler's recent philosophy of "ontological parity" or "ordinal metaphysics," which denies any absolute hierarchy of reality and significance among "natural complexes," is a more recent form of the same idea, based, though, on different reasoning.[21] The point, though, to this excursus into terminology is to show that throughout Dōgen's writings there is evident a view that authentic selfhood and the vow to liberate all beings involves the perception of the Buddhahood of all things, the denial of human beings as an *absolute* locus of value, and consequently a necessity to extend concern beyond the human realm.

Authentic selfhood presupposes the understanding that all beings are the same self, the same reality, and this understanding has consequences as far as decision-making and action in the world are concerned. If authentic selfhood results in a broadening of concern for what lies, in a sense, beyond the narrowly defined self and its own projects, then the perception of all beings as endowed with Buddha nature implies that commitment must be transhuman in scope. What it means to liberate nonsentient beings would take us beyond the scope of this essay, but Masao Abe has remarked somewhere in his writing that there is an important sense in which everything suffers and is therefore in need of concern and help. Whatever bondage and liberation may mean from Dōgen's perspective, the achievement of authentic selfhood and the commitment to liberate all beings seem clearly to point to transcendence of anthropocentrism or "species-ism" as the sole basis for decision-making and altruistic action. Authentic selfhood thus must be a transcendence of

both egocentrism and anthropocentrism. This is one of the most challenging of the implications of authentic selfhood, because while it is possible to imagine self-transcendence, it is difficult to conceive of a mode
of being human in which one's organization of experience is not solely or
primarily determined by the conviction that human values and goals are
ultimate. In the West, even among those such as Heidegger and some
Christian mystics, for example, who speak of self-transcendence, the
ultimacy of human values, goals, and the like is never questioned. What
would it be like for humans to reject their most deeply held assumptions,
namely, that history has only human meaning, that humans are privileged by their nature, that the nonhuman world is solely a "resource" the
purpose of which is to serve human needs, that humans are the favorites
of the gods, that the teleological final cause of all history must be understood to have the human drama solely in mind?

To expand on the paradox mentioned at the beginning of this essay,
the full realization of man's potential as man depends on a liberation not
only from self-concern as individuals but also from anthropocentric self-
concern as a species, and this means liberation from anthropocentric
interpretations of value, meaning, and history. Thus, the essence of
humanness may not consist of an arrogant and uncritical assertion of
human drives, attitudes, goals, and so on but rather the cultivation of
human life arising out of a radically critical assessment of what a human
being is and the nature of human suppositions. This, in fact, involves
what "liberation" means in Buddhism, because liberation is in significant part a liberation from obstacles and self-confinement which prevent
the free use of creative potential in social life. A truly objective and
thoroughgoing assessment of what human beings are might free man
from a confining and self-destructive assumption concerning what he is
and his place in the whole, and it might free him *to* a new sense of his
continuity with the rest of nature, the essentially family nature of things,
a new sense of shared destiny, and a new appreciation for what is not
human. It might, in short, liberate him from a pitiful arrogance which
detracts from, rather than enhances, his humanness.

But to overcome this arrogance and abandon these fundamental
assumptions would be difficult to accomplish if, as I have argued, egocentrism and speciesism are both expressions of the human mind's fear
of insignificance, impermanence, and death. However, if fear and the
assumptions which it generates do indeed confine the individual and society and restrict the growth of true humanness, then authentic selfhood
would seem to involve both individual self-transcendence and species-
transcendence. Dōgen suggests that transcendence takes this dual form in
his expression for authentic selfhood, *shinjin datsuraku,* that is, the
dropping off *(datsuraku)* of mind and body *(shinjin).* The line in *Genjō-
kōan* following the line "To forget the self is to be authenticated by the

myriad things" is "To be authenticated by the myriad things is to drop off the minds and bodies of oneself and others." Two things are dropped off: the body and the mind. To drop off the *body* is basically the act of becoming free from the compulsive fear of death, and as was remarked earlier in this essay, this means a radical confrontation with one's own essential impermanence and mortality. To drop off *mind* means to let go of opinions, ideological positions, unsupported suppositions, and so on as absolute, insofar as they have no objective basis. This would involve commonly held assumptions concerning what human beings are and where they fit into nature. However, beyond this, to drop off mind would seem to involve a radical assessment of conceptual schemes which reinforce the human self's need for security and meaning, including metaphysical systems, political theories, and even religion, at least as they now exist. However, this is not a rejection of thought and imagination but rather their transformation, not a rejection of intellectual effort but a reformation of bad thinking. Dōgen calls this transformed thinking *hishiryo,* which is neither "thinking" nor "nonthinking" but what may be loosely translated as "true thinking."

A Buddhological reading from the passages from *Genjō-kōan* has generated a discussion of what has been called here "authentic selfhood" and its relationship with what is conventionally perceived as "not-self" or "other." This authentic self has been described as both relational by nature and as dynamically ingredient in its world. It was said also that self-transcendence must also involve a corollary species-transcendence insofar as self-transcendence occurs within the framework of humanness and because such a species-ism would not likely survive a letting go of the fear and insecurity which generate it. Insofar as much of human culture is the expression of anthropocentric assumptions, the transcendence of anthropocentrism would seem to imply a considerable revolution in human culture.

All this does not, however, imply a selfish individualism aloof from society, nor does it imply the "desertification" of human culture. The above explication of the lines from *Genjō-kōan* should have made it abundantly clear that Dōgen is advocating the abandonment of selfish individualism, not its intensification. If the authentic self is relational by nature, it must be a self which is acutely aware of its "family" or community life in the broadest sense of the words, since by definition it has no life apart from its community. However, though this self is aware of its intrinsically and profoundly relational nature, the question needs to be raised as to whether such a self-understanding is necessarily accompanied by a dynamic involvement with society. In fact, some Western observers of Buddhism in the West have answered in the negative. A prominent example is Paul Tillich in *Christianity and the Encounter of the World Religions,* where he typically argues that social-mindedness and concrete altruistic expressions of love depend on a strong sense of the unique personhood of oneself and others, and that the Buddhist process of self-forgetting must consequently diminish one's concern for others and also negate the possibilities of a democratic society with its underlying assumption of the necessity for mutual concern and aid.[22]

However, such a criticism overlooks both the essentially relational nature of the authentic self and what it is that is included in the sense of continuity with others. If the sense of continuity and that of shared nature and destiny were mere abstract ideas, then the sense of relationality would not necessarily result in a commitment to eliminate injustice, bondage, and suffering. This is evident in the fact that these things persist despite our sense of belonging to a single species, tribe, race, or religion. But the sense of commonality that results from the achievement of authentic selfhood, rather than being an abstract concept, is much more concrete and of the nature of feeling, for the "other" is *experienced* as the self in the overcoming of the subject-object split. More important than the mere experiencing of other beings as the self, though, is the act of feeling their feelings also. That is to say, the authentic self as the concrete unity of experience is not simply the unity in experience of mere physical entities but is also the inclusion of their concerns, their suffering and joys, and so on, in a manner perhaps analogous to Whitehead's understanding of a "prehension" as the "feeling of feelings." In Buddhist terminology this may be restated as saying that part of the conditions that make up the authentic self consist of the feelings of the other along with the other as physical presence. I believe that this is the basis for the Buddhist social emotions of sympathy and compassion and the reason why it is said that the Bodhisattva is said to feel the sufferings of others.

But does feeling necessarily lead to concrete social action—feeding the hungry, nursing the sick, and so on? I think that the answer is that it does not, at least as a *necessary* consequence. There is a large amount of evidence in Mahayana Buddhism to indicate that the individual needs to *decide* whether to act concretely on the basis of the new self-understanding. This implies further spiritual training. If he decides not to, this is presumably a falling short of the Mahayana idea; if he decides to, he will culminate his spiritual training. The history of Buddhism seems to indicate that some have chosen to put their understanding to work in the world while others did not. But the important point is that in Mahayana thinking authentic selfhood is the necessary foundation for true compassion, both as caring concern and as concrete social commitment, and, on the contrary, a strong sense of personal selfhood, rather than permitting compassion, makes it problematic. Compassion in Mahayana Buddhism is defined as the dynamic expression of enlightened understanding, or the treatment of other beings in accordance with reality (Sanskrit *tathatā*).

The individual who believes he is a substantial self in a world of other substantial selves and who is therefore motivated primarily by fear and insecurity is, from the Mahayana viewpoint, an unlikely embodiment of compassion.

Just as authentic selfhood does not imply an aloof individualism, neither does it imply the dismantling of human culture. Rather than the desertification of culture, a reshaping of culture as an expression of the collective creativity of individuals would seem to be implied. That is, instead of no art, science, education, technology, politics, law, and so on, these might be criticized in their present form and transformed. The reshaping of institutions might proceed along the lines of making them more human—politics, science, and law as truly responsive to the needs of beings—in the same way that E. F. Schumacher envisioned "economics as if people mattered" in his *Small is Beautiful,* in which he refers to such economics as "Buddhist economics." This is, in fact, nothing more than traditional Mahayana eschatology, which envisions an omega point in the evolution of human society when such a society would be made up of authentic selves creating a social life which would be a reflection of their new self-understanding. Western thought, too, has imagined the perfect human society, Christianity and Marxism being prominent examples. But whereas these have seen utopia as resulting from either divine intervention or social engineering, Dōgen and other Buddhists have argued that a better society and more adequate culture result only from the inner transformation of individuals, since "society" and "institutions" are in reality aggregates of individuals.

Finally, neither the self-transcendence nor species-transcendence I have discussed above imply an impoverishment of humanness. It is possible to see the whole Buddhist program of self-transformation as the theory that human perfection and happiness can be attained through the understanding of the true nature of one's own humanness, once arrogant, uncritical, and self-serving attitudes are abandoned. That is to say, rather than being the "self-annihilation" or "absolute death" earlier Western students of Buddhism perceived it to be, authentic selfhood has always been understood by Buddhism to be the highest development of which humans are capable. In Buddhism this perfection of human character is exemplified by the historical Buddha, who, as a model of religious life and human life, embodies the two qualities of perfect humanness, *prajñā* and *karuṇā.* The former is the quality of being able to see things as they really are *(yathā bhūtam);* the latter is the treatment of all beings in accordance with *prajñā*-insight. *Prajñā* is a *seeing* in which the distortions occasioned by fear and insecurity are absent. *Karuṇā,* compassion, is the *feeling* of the pain and confusion of other beings and a desire to eliminate it. In Buddhism man is thought to be at his best when he embodies these qualities in imitation of the historical Buddha.

It is clear from a close study of Buddhist praxis that Dōgen, as well as his predecessors, believed that an enhanced humanness is attainable only through the ruthless scrutiny of the conventional understanding of humanness and those attitudes and beliefs which express this understanding—for these attitudes, beliefs, and assumptions, which constitute a world view, are antithetical to those qualities of full humanness extolled by Dōgen and other Buddhists. *Prajñā*-insight is blocked by the belief in a substantial selfhood and the consequent adversarial attitude towards other beings. Consequently, in the *Shōbōgenzō* wrong views and attitudes come to an end with the dropping off of mind and body. At the same time, compassionate conduct is blocked when these assumptions, attitudes, and beliefs alienate one from the nonhuman world or other humans outside one's own race, nationality, religious group, and so on. Thus, if the union of insight and compassion is the distinguishing mark of an enhanced humanness, then it follows that a prerequisite for its attainment is the elimination of those antithetical qualities, even if these are conventionally and traditionally identified as integral to humanness, not excluding the basic concept of selfhood itself. Lin-chi's "True Man Without Rank" or Dōgen's "Dropped-off Mind-Body" is an authentic self which is non-deluded and motivated by a compassionate caring, but this authenticity is achieved at the expense of those attributes ordinarily identified with humanness.

In conclusion, it may be noted that Buddhism has always maintained that the greatest good is the realization of the true—that is, authentic—self. It is the greatest good because all other goods, such as ethical behavior and a humane, civilized culture in all its aspects, are impossible without it. It is, so to speak, the generating matrix for whatever else human beings value. In modern times this traditional teaching has been powerfully articulated by Nishida Kitaro in *A Study of Good*.[23] There, he argues both that the highest good is the realization of the true self and that, as a corollary, the false and evil of the world are to be understood as anything which impedes this greatest good. A physical, vocal, or mental act tends to impede this good because it arises out of a tendency to see things abstractly and conceptually and grasps at a mere piece of the total reality. Thus, falsehood and evil come into being "when one looks at one aspect of things abstractly and does not know the whole view, and where, leaning to one side, one goes against the entire unity."[24] In more concrete terms, evil and falsehood result, for instance, when one exalts something such as one's country, sex, race, or faith as the highest good, at the expense of authentic selfhood and those qualities which emerge with it. However, what must be stressed here is that the enhanced humanness of authentic selfhood and a culture which is its expression seem to imply a serious reassessment of every concept, beginning with that of selfhood and humanness itself. Thus, the view of selfhood and humanness envisioned over seven centuries ago by Dōgen still has very interesting implications for modern cultures and their underlying, unifying world views. What would tomorrow's world be like, inhabited and formed by Dōgenesque man? Dōgen's vision is not one of a diminished man creating an impoverished culture. On the contrary, it is a vision of an as-yet-unrealized humanness which emerges in the process of self-forgetting and proceeds to recreate a culture worthy of itself.

Notes

1. *Shōbōgenzō Genjō-kōan.* My translation of *DZZ* 1:7. English translation also by Masao Abe and Norman Waddell, *EB* 5 (2): 129–140.
2. Yasutani Hakuun, *Shōbōgenzō sankyū: Genjō-kōan* (Tokyo: Shunjūsha, 1967), pp. 40–42, 52–53.
3. Most discussions of turmoil or unrest *(duhkha)* in Buddhist literature trace the problem to ignorance *(avidyā)*. However, some texts trace the problem to desire or thirst. A modern work such as Nyanatiloka's *Buddhist Dictionary* (Columbo, 1956) explains this apparent inconsistency by saying that ignorance and desire are the same, ignorance being the name given to the cause of suffering in past lives and desire being the same cause in the present life.
4. I deliberately use the word translated from *Angst* in existentialist literature. *Angst* is an objectless fear or anxiety which is not consciously attached to a particular object, while fear is always fear of a particular thing. The abstract fear of death can be quite conscious, but usually it is vague and unconscious, though generating desire and hatred.
5. For instance, Hee-Jin Kim, *Dōgen Kigen, Mystical Realist* (Tucson: University of Arizona Press, 1975), p. 21 and *passim*. Also, Masunaga Reihō, *The Soto Approach to Zen* (Tokyo: Layman Buddhist Society Press, 1958), p. 75.
6. *Shōbōgenzō Shōji* (*DZZ* 1:779). English translation also in Masunaga, op.cit., p. 99.
7. Michael Zimmerman, *Eclipse of the Self* (Athens: Ohio University Press, 1981), p. 42.
8. Zimmerman, op.cit., p. 29.
9. See the discussion by Kim, op.cit., pp. 200–203, concerning *hōi*, "dharma state." See also the discussion of firewood and ashes in *Genjō-kōan*. In discussions of "dharma state," "being-time" *(uji)*, and similar terms, though the authentic self is not usually the issue, the implication is that the self, being no different from other realities, must be no less impermanent than they are. There is a strong similarity between this view of selfhood and that of Alfred North Whitehead in that both perceive the self to be a succession of drops of experience which arise and perish in a historical route.
10. *Genjō-kōan* (*DZZ* 1:8). See the translation of it in *EB* 5(2):135. T. P. Kasulis, in *Zen Person, Zen Action* (University Press of Hawaii, 1981), translates *datsuraku* as "molting," in order to capture accurately the meaning of repetition. While I appreciate the effort to capture this important idea, I feel that "molting" conveys an unfortunate or inelegant visual image.

11. Translation by Kim, op.cit., p. 217.
12. *Shōbōgenzō Kōmyō* (*DZZ* 1:116). See also the translation of Nishiyama Kōsen and John Stevens, *Shōbōgenzō*, vol. 1 (Tokyo: Daihokkaikaku, 1975), p. 53.
13. *DZZ* 1:327-330. See Francis Dojun Cook, *How to Raise an Ox* (Los Angeles: Center Publications, 1978), pp. 151-157.
14. An interpretative translation of the term *genjō-kōan* based on the discussion by Yasutani, op.cit., pp. 25-31.
15. *Shōbōgenzō Hotsu bodai shin* (*DZZ* 1:14). English translation also by Yokoi Yūhō and Daizen Victoria, *Zen Master Dōgen* (New York and Tokyo: Weatherhill, 1976), p. 107.
16. *Shōbōgenzō Busshō* (*DZZ* 1:14). English translation also by Waddell and Abe, *EB* 8 (2):97.
17. An excellent discussion of the Japanese Buddhist process of extending Buddhahood to include all beings can be found in William LaFleur, "Saigyō and the Buddhist Value of Nature," *History of Religions* 13 (2): 93-126, 13 (3):227-248.
18. In the above article, LaFleur shows that much of this kind of Buddhology did take place prior to Dōgen, but I believe that particularly in essays such as *Busshō*, Dōgen spoke out most comprehensively and clearly. LaFleur's article is very valuable in showing the work done by Tendai scholars, and perhaps Dōgen became aware of this work while he stayed on Mt. Hiei.
19. *Shōbōgenzō Zenki*. Translation by Waddell and Abe, *EB* 5 (1):74-77. Kim translates *zenki* as "total dynamism," "total function," and "total realization."
20. Kim translates *gūjin* as "total exertion," op.cit., p. 112.
21. Justus Buchler, *Metaphysics of Natural Complexes* (New York: Columbia University Press, 1966), pp. 30 ff.
22. Paul Tillich, *Christianity and the Encounter of the World Religions* (New York: Columbia University Press, 1963). See chapter 3.
23. Nishida Kitarō, *A Study of Good* [*Zen no Kenkyū*] (Tokyo: Printing Bureau, Japanese Government, 1960), especially chapter 13.
24. Ibid., p. 153.

The Meaning of
Dōgen Today

Robert N. Bellah

In this conference on "The Significance of Dōgen," we have considered what Dōgen meant in his own time, what modern Japanese philosophy made of him (even though we did not get much of that in the end), and, finally, what Dōgen's meaning is for the modern world. This structure somewhat loosely expresses the three moments of the hermeneutic process as Gadamer tells us it was traditionally conceived: understanding, interpretation, and application.[1] These three elements are not separate from each other. They require each other; they are profoundly and dialectically interrelated. It might seem that we have to understand the text before we can interpret it, and that we have to understand and interpret it before we can apply it, but there really is no understanding without interpretation and application. If there is to be a new understanding and interpretation of the real Dōgen, then we have to ask what that implies for those for whom Dōgen and his work are a matter of great importance—personally, religiously, humanly.

I want to talk mainly about application, but I am assuming the interpenetration of these three hermeneutic moments. Obviously, unless we have the most careful historical and philological study of the texts, so that we try to understand them as Dōgen meant them—even though we know that in the absolute sense that is never possible—we cannot even begin. But I want to stress (because in a sense this is my own competence relating to the rest of you, who are Dōgen scholars or Buddhologists) our horizon, to use Gadamerian language. We, as twentieth-century persons, and, most of us, Americans, bring our horizon to the text, and whatever comes out is the result of the meeting of Dōgen's horizon with our own horizon. Unless we are very conscious of what we are bringing to the text, we will not do a good job, no matter how careful our philology and our historical study. We obviously are not persons living in the Kamakura period. Yet we pick up the text and read it in English and maybe forget that there is a different world there. It is an incredible act of nerve to think that we can—across these centuries—understand each other.

There is an only slightly smaller gap for modern Japanese. Dōgen's language is not contemporary Japanese, as we have seen. Dōgen's world is not Japan in the 1980s. There are obviously certain continuities that make it a bit easier for modern Japanese to understand Dōgen, but it is not really easy for them either. For us Americans, the fact that our approach to Dōgen must inevitably come through contemporary Japanese scholars and religious thinkers adds a further degree of complexity to the whole process. Americans and Japanese share the same century, but in many ways not the same situation. We live in very different kinds of societies—that is one thing I want to develop later. We live in very different cultures with very different presuppositions.

I would like to begin with the opening chapter of Thomas Kasulis's book *Zen Action/Zen Person*.[2] There he quite wisely asks—before he says a word about Zen Buddhism or Dōgen or Hakuin—for some fundamental understanding of what it is to be a person in Japan. He develops an interesting discussion of the meaning of the word *ningen* as opposed to *kojin*. The traditional Japanese understanding of personhood, summed up in the word *ningen,* is that human beings are part of a social web, that they become who they are in social groups, that they find the meaning of their life in a social context, and that the notion of a radically discrete individual cut off from other human beings is strange. The Western idea of the individual *(kojin)* has been a problem ever since it first entered Japan in the Meiji period. Kasulis tells us that one way to think about Zen and its relation to the person is to see that Zen in the Japanese context accepts the notion that human beings are part of an encompassing world, and it restructures and restates that world in terms of the notion of *mu*. That, of course, is not a simple thing to do. It is in many respects a very radical thing to do. Various papers at this conference have considered how Zen breaks the tyranny of conceptual structures by various devices. We have seen how Dōgen in many remarkable, ingenious, and extraordinarily poetic ways opens us up to the immediacy of preconceptual experience. To become a person in the midst of *śūnyata* is a liberating and freeing experience.

One implication one might draw from Kasulis's discussion of Japanese personhood as embedded in a social web is that Zen practice involves a certain kind of liberation from that web. Even today the Japanese individual seems embedded in a society which is radically taken for granted. Through Zen practice, one can in a sense escape the radical embeddedness of the individual in society. Perhaps "escape" is not the right word, for Kasulis insists that through Zen practice one finds another kind of totality and another way of thinking about the social totality of one's daily life. But there is, at least in principle, the capacity for transcending what many modern Japanese have come to see as the strictures and constraints of an extraordinarily pervasive, powerful social group, and a culture which stresses social control over the individual more than most traditional societies. Throughout Japanese history there are archetypal examples like Ryōkan or Bashō, or, in a different way, Dōgen himself, who seem to have escaped those invisible steel wires that keep people where they are supposed to be in Japanese society. It is important to see Zen as not simply an expression of the taken-for-grantedness of Japanese culture and the way Japanese society works, but as in part a way of radically breaking through it.

I would like to suggest that the special resonance of Zen in general and Dōgen in particular in the twentieth century—both in Japan and in the United States—is closely linked to the question of modern individualism *(kojinshugi),* and to the central preoccupation in Western culture, but most of all in American culture, with the individual.

But there is something very different in our approach to Dōgen from that of modern Japanese. Zen has played a part for some Japanese in the effort to become a modern individual. Natsume Sōseki, for example, perhaps the most widely read of all modern Japanese novelists, was very preoccupied with individualism and found in Zen, very ambiguously and never with great satisfaction, one way of getting a handle on this problem. But we Americans are in a very different world from a culture that is first beginning to see what individualism is all about.

Modern Japanese are both scared to death of individualism and deeply attracted to it. One of the things that is clear, at least for Japanese intellectuals, is that there has been for nearly a century a deep hankering for something that would be a self in the Western sense, implying independence from society, as well as anxiety about such a self. But what happens when Zen—or a religious figure such as Dōgen—gets translated into a culture which has been moving in the direction of hyperindividualism for two or three centuries at an ever accelerating tempo? In the late twentieth century, our culture is moving into a phase of radical individualism, not just among a few isolated thinkers of world historical importance, like Heidegger or Sartre, but among the ordinary persons in the society. Almost the exclusive ground of meaning in our culture is the individual person, and virtually every social and cultural context that could previously be taken for granted is no longer so taken. For us, more and more, everything has to be authenticated in terms of what it is doing for me, or else it isn't legitimate at all. Kasulis in his paper points to one of the resonances between Dōgen and our world: both take the testing by individual experience as crucial. But I would suggest that while that is true and important, it means something very different when you are viewing things as Dōgen does in the midst of a traditional culture where 99.99 percent of everything social and cultural can be taken for granted and when you live in a culture where almost nothing can be.

Since Dōgen could take the social reality within which he lived pretty much for granted, his thought is concentrated elsewhere. As a number of the papers in this volume indicate, Dōgen's thought often seems to give us a picture of a world composed of a center of consciousness and a totality. The totality of meaning, the entire cosmos, exists in the immediacy of experience. I would like to bracket for the moment the religious validity of this way of thinking (I personally find it enormously attractive religiously) and look at it sociologically in terms of American society. Here I would like to introduce some findings coming out of my current research, which involves interviewing Americans in several parts of the country, particularly relatively well-off, relatively well-educated white middle class Americans. These are the sort of people from which the Zen centers draw almost exclusively. For many of these contemporary Americans there is almost nothing real except me right here and the whole cosmos. There is, therefore, a certain fit with Dōgen's explicit thought. But what Dōgen could take for granted, namely social reality, for many of the Americans to whom we have talked, is empty in a very un-Buddhist sense of the word. Social reality as anything that could be counted on, much less taken for granted, is simply not there.

Consider for a minute the fact that Dōgen did not live in that kind of world. For him there was a world which was, in very important respects, "there"—one that he could take for granted. For one thing, for Dōgen there are Buddhas and Patriarchs for us to model ourselves after. It is just assumed that we cannot do anything unless we have faith in them, unless we know that there is a tradition there, know that there is a Buddha-Dharma, Buddha Way, that we do not have to, in a sense, worry about, that is prior to us. We come to whatever enlightenment we are capable of through that. Dōgen says in numerous places that we practice for the sake of the Buddha-Dharma, not for our own sake. There is in that sense no isolated modern individual that is looking around and thinking, "Gee, I might try Zen as opposed to Hare Krishna or something." Dōgen is inside a tradition before he has to think about it. Of course he has to make decisions, of course he decides on this aspect of the tradition versus that, and so on, but relative to our situation, his is very different. He has a living and active content. There is the practice— that is, zazen; there is the life of the zendō; there is the presence of the Sangha; there is very importantly the crucial master/disciple relationship without which there is no practice. There is a social world that is part of the living Buddhist community out of which Dōgen comes. Now, he contributes to that, he reformulates that—I don't want to say that it is just a given—but he is working with something that is there and much less precariously there than it is either in modern Japan or certainly in the modern United States.

Beyond that, I think you see particularly in the *Zuimonki* the degree to which Dōgen takes for granted the *moral* universe of his society. It is essentially a Confucian moral universe. Since Buddhism has in most places had some difficulty in developing a fully articulated social-political morality for the whole society, it has frequently adopted one or another aspect of the non-Buddhist traditions with which it finds itself associated. In East Asia the link between Buddhism and Confucianism is close, and in Zen, especially close. In *Zuimonki* we see that Dōgen knows the Confucian classics by heart, he knows Chinese history forwards and backwards, he can give you anecdotes from virtually every period of Chinese history before him. In exhorting his monks, he loves to say: look at so and so who is so filial, behaves so nicely to his parents; look at this minister who is so loyal to his lord; or this general who served his king. How much more should you monks be loyal at doing what you are supposed to do if even laity can behave with such devotion, such commitment, such selflessness. What is that form of exhortation telling us? It is telling us that for Dōgen there is a real social world there that he can count on; there are virtues; there is a better and worse way to act. At some other level, of course, all these distinctions don't count, but I am now just talking sociologically and I am suggesting that there is some kind of dialectic that allows him to go to the heights of his intense experience of the unity of all being and that, at the same time, relates and articulates the social world he can count on.

Remember that Dōgen was living in a disrupted society with lots of social disturbance. I am not saying it was a period of great calmness. I am just saying that there were certain things that more or less everybody took for granted. In contrast, we are living in a society which is almost the opposite of that, where there is no tradition that can claim much authenticity for itself, where there is no institution, from the institution of marriage up to the state, that has much legitimacy. We live in a culture which has said, at least since the 17th century, that the only reality is the individual person. One of the appeals that Zen has had in our society is precisely that Zen was seen (first of all through D. T. Suzuki, but then through Philip Kapleau and others) as somehow fulfilling the end of that course of development. Zen seemed to be free of all the hangups, the metaphysical commitments, and the social absurdities of Western tradition and to validate the free individual to the fullest extreme. From some of the interviews that one of the members of my research group, Steven Tipton, carried out with a number of Zen students, it seems clear that many Americans came to Zen as a means for what we call self-realization. It is true that in their practice they learned that there was no self to be realized and so the whole cultural quest was turned around in a radically different direction. They learned to think differently from the expectations of our culture and to see that Zen has a lived practice in a communal context. I suspect that the recent emergence of the Zen *community* in America is the most important thing in the history of Buddhism in this country. But even here there is some ambiguity in relation to the central cultural theme that the only reality is the individual person. The Zen community, unlike some of the other exotic religions to which people have been attracted, has been, if I can use common cultural language, cool. It has not gone out and tried to pull you in like the Moonies and brainwash you. If you want to come, that is fine; if you want to leave, that is fine. It doesn't put pressure on you. It is open, it is ready, it is there, but it isn't, in a sense, laying its trip on you. And this is very appealing, particularly to the kind of well-educated people who become Zen students. They see the Zen community as a place where radical individualism might be worked out. It also is, of course, an enormous antidote to that, because the Zen community is, more than most of American society, a real community, where people live together in an organic way and take care of each other. But I would suggest that both of the components are there. There is both a "letting you be" to proceed with whatever it is that you are about, and a supportive context for you to do it in.

If there are some ambiguities in the institutionalized form of Zen, when we come to the larger cultural meaning of Zen, the ambiguities become enormous. By the larger cultural meaning, I think of the use of Zen by such culture heroes as Fritz Perls or Werner Erhardt, where Zen becomes a spiritual technology in the service of what I call utilitarian individualism—in a sense, the most radical perversion of Zen possible. There is something going on here that makes it possible to use Zen in this way. The irony is that Zen is being turned into a means for radical individualist self-seeking.

I would like to quote a bit from our interviews. One of our interviewees gave vivid expression to something that comes up again and again in our interviews: "In the end you are really alone, and you really have to answer to yourself. You're responsible for yourself and no one else." For many of the people we talked to that is the truth of the human condition. There is also commonly in our interview material a sense that that is the way it should be: "I am responsible for myself and I am not responsible for anyone else. In fact, it would be morally wrong for me to be."

We don't have a neutral interviewing technique. We learned something from Socrates about interviewing people. So we asked them, "Isn't there anybody you feel responsible for? What about your husband or wife?" "Oh, no. That would be really violating their personhood." And then, if they happened to be married and have children, "What about the children?" Well, that would give them some pause, because, especially in the case of little children, if they don't take any responsibility for them, they are not going to survive. But you get the kind of answer which says, "Yes, but as soon as they possibly can, they have to take responsibility for themselves." Almost the essence of evil is conforming to what other people want you to do, or letting other people take care of you.

It is hard to get this kind of American to take a strong moral stand.

The only sanction that you have, the only reason you can give for moral judgment, is "I feel good about that" or "I feel comfortable with that." There is even a rejection of the notion of rational argument about moral things because that would mean you are trying to force something down other people's throats. A frequent criticism of people who are too political or religious is that they are trying to force their opinions on other people. So my feeling about whether it feels good, whether I am comfortable with it, is the only criterion that is left. You would not get this kind of answer in Japan today. There may be a tendency to move in the same direction, but it is much less advanced.

What does it mean to talk about Zen in a world of radical individualists? Zen can easily be one more validation for so pathological a form of individualism that it undermines the capacity of the society even to survive. This extreme individualism undercuts every capacity to sustain loyalty in human relationships.

The Zen experience stresses the immediacy of my experience and the whole cosmos and leaves everything in between quite empty. When the in-between is filled with all kinds of traditional structures that everyone can count on, that is fine. When you are in a culture where everything in between is already undermined to the point that it is hardly functioning, there may be a problem. That is why, for instance, I think the stress that there is no hierarchy in the dharma is problematic. In one sense, that gives us a certain religious understanding that is right, and, even in one perspective, ethically right. But in another sense, if nothing is higher than anything else, if nothing is better than anything else, if there is no reason to choose one thing rather than another, then sociologically that is chaos. Of course in the context of monastic life, there is plenty of effective hierarchy. Dōgen has a whole little fascicle about how junior monks should treat senior monks, and we all know the respect that is owed to a roshi. Nobody assumes that everybody is exactly the same, even though in some ultimate sense it is true. In terms of practical action there are ways to make the distinctions that we have to make if we are going to live. No society can operate without organizing time, without thinking that some things have to come before other things. And again, obviously, in the monastic life time has been highly organized. But if you take the great religious truths and express them in a society which has lost its intermediate structures, which doesn't know that there are things that are noble and things that are just terrible, which says "If I feel it's good, don't tell me that it's terrible; that's your trip," then the meaning of the religious truth becomes problematic. It may even increase the very sickness that is going on in the society to tell people that everything is equal and that everthing is empty and so forth.

In one sense, the weakness of Japanese Buddhism in general, and even Zen, even Sōtō Zen, is that the taken-for-grantedness of Japanese society overwhelmed the radical religious insight. For centuries nobody knew that Dōgen really blew everything sky high, so to speak. The pattern of traditional relationships even within the religious life continued to predominate over the radical liberation. But I would suggest that that is the Japanese problem, and may still be the Japanese problem. There may still be a problem of how to bring the Buddhist message effectively into this tightly organized society in a way that will open up new possibilities. And yet this culture, which is more sensitive to nature, and where ordinary people are more sensitive to the nuances of the changes of the year than in any other culture in the world, has the worst record of pollution in the world. Somehow Buddhism hasn't had the capacity to translate religious insight into effective social action. I am not saying that anybody else has done much better, but that that is perhaps the specific Japanese problem. Our problem is: how can we reformulate or recreate some kinds of viable intermediate structures that can put our society together again?

The most important contribution that Zen can make in America is the kind of thing that is going on in the Los Angeles Zen Center and in the San Francisco Zen Center: the creation of actual communities. The embodiment of the Sangha in America can be a demonstration-experiment showing that there are other ways to live than the destructive ways of the larger society. That is one of the few things that gives me any sense of optimism about the present situation.

But still how to present in Zen American society, as a set of interpretations of the world, is very difficult. We can easily simply reinforce the very things that are the most problematic about our society if we are not careful. I noted at several points in this conference that it is not helpful to set up a simple contrast between East and West. Perhaps the central hope for us is some capacity to reappropriate what we broke off in the seventeenth century. There are resources in the Classical and Medieval West that we have long rejected and scorned, that have much to say to us about our present social reality. So a cultural symbiosis between the radicalism of Zen and some kind of modern Aristotelianism might even be thinkable.[3] The teachings of Dōgen might remind us not to reify metaphysical categories, while we reassert a teleological understanding of the order of human life and put back together those intermediate structures which make our few years on this planet bearable. I obviously can't spell out such a vision here. But I can say that a more sympathetic understanding of all the pre-modern traditions of the world, Western and Eastern, is desperately needed now.

The great cause of our difficulties is what has happened since the seventeenth century. It is *modern* Western culture that is destroying the natural habitat, undermining any kind of social solidarity, and creating a conception of the individual person which is utterly self-destructive. So, I

will conclude on the irenic note of a call for a more sympathetic understanding of the traditional cultures, which, in the face of the challenge—
as strong in Japan as it is here—of the destructiveness of modern culture,
are one of the few places we have to turn.

Notes

1.   Hans-Georg Gadamer, *Truth and Method* (New York: Seabury Press, 1975),
     pp. 274–305.
2.   Thomas P. Kasulis, *Zen Action/Zen Person* (Honolulu: University of
     Hawaii Press, 1981).
3.   By far the most helpful discussion of pre-modern Western moral thought
     and its relevance to our present situation is contained in Alasdair MacIn-
     tyre, *After Virtue* (Notre Dame: University of Notre Dame Press, 1981).

Contributors

MASAO ABE has been a visiting lecturer and professor of philosophy at a number of American universities, including the University of Chicago, Princeton, Claremont Graduate School, and the University of Hawaii. He has written widely on Buddhism and Western philosophy, most especially in his *Zen and Western Thought* (University of Hawaii Press, 1985). With Norman Waddell he has translated key fascicles of Dōgen's *Shōbōgenzō* for *The Eastern Buddhist*. His current principal interest is the dialogue between Buddhism and Christianity.

ROBERT N. BELLAH is Ford Professor of Sociology and Comparative Studies and vice chairman of the Center for Japanese Studies at the University of California at Berkeley. He was educated at Harvard University. His publications include *Tokugawa Religion, Beyond Belief, The New Religious Consciousness,* and *Varieties of Civil Religion.* He is currently completing a research project on American mores in collaboration with Steven Tipton, William Sullivan and two other younger scholars, the results of which will appear in a book entitled (borrowing a phrase from Tocqueville) *Habits of the Heart.*

CARL BIELEFELDT teaches Buddhism at Stanford University, where he is an assistant professor in the Department of Religious Studies. He received his Ph.D. from the Department of Oriental Languages at the University of California at Berkeley. Having published in the field of Ch'an and Zen, he is currently preparing a monograph on Dōgen's meditation writings

FRANCIS H. COOK teaches courses in Buddhism at the University of California at Riverside, where he is an associate professor in the Department of Religious Studies. He was a student of the late Richard Robinson at the University of Wisconsin and has published essays on various aspects of Buddhism. His books are *Hua-yen Buddhism: The Jewel Net of Indra* and *How to Raise an Ox: Zen Practice as Taught in Zen Master Dōgen's Shōbōgenzō.*

THOMAS P. KASULIS received his Ph.D. from Yale University and teaches philosophy at Northland College, where he has served as chairman of the Department of Philosophy. He has published *Zen Action/Zen Person* (University

Press of Hawaii, 1981), a review essay entitled "The Zen Philosopher: Dōgen Scholarship in English" (*Philosophy East and West,* July 1978), and essays in Japanese journals. He was the recipient of a Japan Foundation Grant during 1983 for a study in Japan of the development of Japanese values.

HEE-JIN KIM is professor of religious studies at the University of Oregon. Before that he taught at the University of Vermont, Wright State University, and Claremont Graduate School/School of Theology at Claremont. His scholarly interest revolves around Dōgen's thought in relation to broader issues —such as philosophy and religion, language and symbols, and mysticism and culture. He is the author of *Dōgen Kigen: Mystical Realist* (Scholars Press, 1975) and a forthcoming book, *The Flowers of Emptiness: Selections from Dōgen's Shōbōgenzō, Vol. I.*

WILLIAM R. LAFLEUR is professor of Japanese at the University of California at Los Angeles. His books are *Mirror for the Moon: Poetry by Saigyō (1118–1190)* and *The Karma of Words: Buddhism and the Literary Arts in Medieval Japan* (University of California Press, 1983). He has been involved in the Harvard/N.E.H. study of Buddhism in Japanese civilization and most recently, with a Japan Foundation grant, has begun an intellectual biography of Watsuji Tetsurō.

JOHN C. MARALDO is associate professor of philosophy at the University of North Florida. He received his Ph.D. from the University of Munich and has also taught at Sophia University in Japan. With James Hart he co-authored *The Piety of Thinking: Essays by Heidegger and Commentary* and with Heinrich Dumoulin he co-edited *Buddhism in the Modern World* (Macmillan, 1976). He is currently engaged in research on the formation of contemporary Japanese philosophy.

Glossary of Chinese and Japanese Terms

arakan 阿羅漢
A-yü-wang shan 阿育王山

baika/*Baika* 梅華
Benchō 辨長
bendōwa/*Bendōwa* 辨道話
Bodai ji 菩提寺
Bukkōjōji/*Bukkōjōji* [*Butsu kōjō ji*] 佛向上事
Bukkyō 佛經
Buppō 佛法
busshi 佛子
busshi 佛嗣
busshō/*Busshō* 佛性
Busso 佛祖
butsu-butsu 佛佛
Butsudō akiramezareba busshi ni arazu; busshi to iu wa busshi to iu kotonari 佛道あきらめざれば、佛嗣にあらず。佛嗣といふは、佛子といふことなり。
butsumen somen 佛面祖面

Ch'an/Zen 禪
Chao-chou 趙州
Che-weng Ju-yen 淅翁如琰
Chiang-hsi Ma-tsu 江西馬祖
chikujaku-katsujaku 築著蓋著
Ching-shan 徑山
Ching-te ssu 景德寺
Ch'ing-yüan Hsing-ssu 青原行思
chōnyū 跳入

chōshutsu 跳出
Cho-an Te-kuang 拙菴德光
chung-sheng 衆生

Daibutsu ji 大佛寺
daigo/*Daigo* 大悟
Daijō ji 大昭寺
Dainichi Nōnin 大日能忍
Dai shugyō 大修行
dangen dammyō 談玄談妙
darani/*Darani* 陀羅尼
datsuraku shinjin 脱落身心
Den'e 傳衣
Denkō roku 傳光錄
dō 道
Dōgen 道元
dōji jōdō 同時成道
dokusan 獨參
dōtoku/*Dōtoku* 道得

Eihei Gen zenji goroku 永平元禪師語錄
Eihei ji 永平寺
Eihei kōroku 永平廣錄
Eihei sanso gyōgōki 永平三祖行業記
Ekan 懷鑑
Enni Ben'en 圓爾辨圓

Fa-yen 法眼
Fukan zazen gi 普勸坐禪儀
fu-shiryō 不思量

fu-shiryō-tei ikan [no] shiryō/fu-
shiryō-tei ikanga shiryō sen
不思量底如何思量
fushō 不生

gabyō/*Gabyō* 畫餅
gabyō wa fu-jū-ki/gabyō wa ue ni
mitazu 畫餅不充饑
gaku 學
garan bō 伽藍法
gedatsu 解脫
Ge wa ge o sae ge o miru; ge wa ge o
gesurunari 礙は礙をさへ礙をみる。
礙は礙を礙するなり
genjō 現成
genjō-kōan/*Genjō-kōan* 現成公案／
現成公按
Gien 義演
Giin 義伊
Gikai 義介
goke 五家
Gokoku shōbō gi 護國正法義
go oku ri 吾屋裏
gozan 五山
gūjin 究盡
gyō 行
gyōji/*Gyōji* 行持
gyōji dōkan 行持道環
gyōnyo 形如

hakobu 運ぶ
Henzan 徧參
higan-tō 彼岸到
hiniku-kotsuzui 皮肉骨髓
hi-shiryō 非思量
hōbemmon 方便門
hōben 方便
hōge 放下
Hōkyō ki 寶慶記
honbunnin 本分人
Honchō kōsō den 本朝高僧傳
hongaku 本覺
honrai no jiko 本来の自己
hō-setsu 法說
hōtō 寶塔
Hsing-sheng wan-shou ssu
興聖萬壽寺

Hsüeh-tou Chih-chien 雪竇智鑑
Huang-po 黃檗
Hua-yen 華嚴
Hui-k'o 慧可
Hui-neng 慧能
Hung-chih Cheng-chüeh 宏智
正覺

i-ch'ieh chung-sheng 一切衆生
ichiei-zaigen kūge-rantsui/ichiei me
ni areba kūge midare ochin 一翳在
眼、空華亂墜
immo/*Immo* 恁麼
ippō-gūjin 一法究盡
iridashin 矣栗駄心
issai shujō 一切衆生
issai-shujō shitsuu busshō/issai no
shujō wa kotogotoku busshō ari
一切衆生、悉有佛性
isshin gakushin 以心學心

ji/toki 時
jigo 自悟
ji-ji 時時
jiji-muge/shih-shih wu ai 事事
無礙
jijuyū-zammai 自受用三昧
jiko 自己
jindaichi 盡大地
jinenken 自然見
Jinshin inga 深信因果
jinsoku 神足
jishō 自證
Jishō zammai 自證三昧
jinzū/*Jinzū* 神通
jisetsu 時節
jissō 實相
jōroku-konjin 丈六金身
jōtō 承當
Ju-ching 如淨
juki/*Juki* 授記

kaiin-zammai/*Kaiin-zammai*
海印三昧
ka-ka 果果
Kakuan 覺晏
k'an-hua 看話

kanna-zen 看話禪

kappappat/kappatsupatchi 活潑
潑(撥鱍)地

karidashin 汗栗馱心

kattō/*Kattō* 葛藤

kedashi musō-zammai no katachi
mangatsu no gotoku naru o
motte nari 蓋以無相三
昧形如滿月

Keiran shūyō shū 溪嵐拾葉集

keisei-sanshoku/*Keisei-sanshoku*
谿(溪)聲山色

Keizan Jōkin 瑩山紹瑾

kembutsu/*Kembutsu* 見佛

Kennin ji 建仁寺

Kenzei ki 建撕記

kōan 公案(按)

Kōfuku ji 興福寺

kokū/*Kokū* 虛空

kokyō/*Kokyō* 古鏡

kōmyō/*Kōmyō* 光明

Kōshō ji 興聖寺

kosoku-kōan 古則公案

Koun Ejō 孤雲懷弉

Kōzen gokoku ron 興禪護國論

Kuang Fo-chao 光佛照

Kuei-tsung 歸宗

Kuei-yang 潙仰

kūge/*Kūge* 空華

kung-an 公案

kū-ze-kū 空是空

kyōge-betsuden/chiao-wai-pieh-
ch'uan 教外別傳

kyōryaku 經歷

Lin-chi 臨濟

Lin-chi I-hsüan 臨濟義玄

mampō 萬法

Manzan Dōhaku 卍山道白

Ma-tsu 馬祖

Menju 面授

Menzan Zuihō 面山瑞芳

Miao-kao t'ai 妙高臺

mitsu 密

mitsugo/*Mitsugo* 密語

mokushō-zen 默照禪

mondō 問答

monji 文字

monji no dōri 文字の道理

monji no sentei 文字の筌蹄

moshi shosō wa hisō nari to mireba
sunawachi nyorai o miru nari 若見
諸相非相即見如來

mu 夢

muchū-setsumu/*Muchū-setsumu*
夢中說夢

mujō-busshō 無常佛性

mujō-seppō/*Mujō-seppō* 無情
說法

mushin 無心

musō 無相

musō 無想

Myōzen 明全

Nan-ch'üan 南泉

Nan-yang Hui-chung 南陽慧忠

Nan-yüeh Huai-jang 南嶽懷讓

nehan myōshin 涅槃妙心

Nichiren 日蓮

Nihon Daruma shū 日本達磨宗

nikon-tōsho/ima itaru tokoro ni
而今到處

ninpō 人法

Nishida Kitarō 西田幾多郎

nyo 如

Nyojō oshō goroku 如淨和尚
語錄

nyoze 如是

Ōbaku 黃檗

ōsaku-sendaba/*Ōsaku-sendaba*
王索仙陀婆

P'ang Yün 龐蘊

P'an-shan Ssu-cho 盤山思卓

Rinzai/Lin-chi 臨濟

ryochishin 慮知心

ryūgin/*Ryūgin* 龍吟

Sanbyaku soku 三百則

san chü 三句

Sanjūshichi hon bodai bunpō 三十七品菩提分法

san lu 三路

Sanso gyōgō ki 三祖行業記

sansui 山水

sansuikyō/*Sansuikyō* 山水經

san-ze-san 山是山

senshi kobutsu 先師古佛

seppō 說法

Sesshin sesshō 說心說性

shihō 嗣法

shihō-kiji/kono hō no okoru toki 此法起時

shikaku 始覺

shikan-taza 祇管打坐

shin 心

shin 身

shin-fukatoku/*Shin-fukatoku* 心不可得

shingakudō 身學道

shingen-engatsusō/mi ni engatsusō o genzu 身現圓月相

shinjin 身身

shinjin-datsuraku 身心脱落

shinjin-datsuraku 心塵脱落

Shinjingakudō 身心學道

shinjin ichinyo 身心一如

shinmitsu 親密

Shinran 親鸞

shiryō 思量

shiryō ko fu-shiryō tei/kono fu-shiryō-tei o shiryō su 思量箇 不思量底

Shisho 嗣書

shitsuu 悉有

shittashin 質多心

shoaku-makusa/*Shoaku makusa*/shoaku wa tsukuru koto nakare/shoaku wa nasu koto nakare/shoaku wa tsukuru koto nashi/shoaku wa nasu koto nashi 諸惡莫作

shōbō 正法

Shōbōgenzō 正法眼藏

Shōbōgenzō zuimonki 正法眼藏 隨問記

Shobutsu kore shō naru yue ni

shomotsu kore shō nari 諸佛これ證 なるゆゑに、諸物これ證なり

shōden no buppō 正傳の佛法

shōji 生死

shō jinsoku no doppo 正神足の 獨歩

shō-shō 生生

shosui 諸水

shozan 諸山

shugyō 修行

shujō 衆生

shunjū/*Shunjū* 春秋

shushō 修證

shushō-ichinyo 修證一如

shushō-ittō 修證一等

shuso 主座

shushushōyoshin 積聚精要心

sokushin-ze-butsu/*Sokushin-ze-butsu* 即心是佛

sōmokushin 草木心

Sōtō/Ts'ao-tung 曹洞

ssu liao-chien 四料簡

susumu 進む

sui-ze-sui 水是水

Ta-erh 大耳

Ta-hui Tsung-kuo 大慧宗果

Ta-kuei 大溈

Tanabe Hajime 田辺元

tanden 單傳

Tanni shō 歎異鈔

Tao-fu 道副

Tao-wei 道微

Tao-yü 道育

tashintsū/*Tashintsū* 他心通

teishō 提唱

tekishi 嫡嗣

Tendō san Keitoku ji Nyojō zenji zoku goroku 天童山景德寺如淨禪 師續語錄

Tenkei Denson 天桂傳尊

Tenzo kyōkun 典座敎訓

Te-shan Hsüan-chien 德山宣鑑

T'ien-t'ung Ju-ching 天童如淨

T'ien-t'ung shan 天童山

Tōdai ji 東大寺

Tōfuku ji 東福寺

tō-higan 到彼岸
tō-tō 等等
tōtoku anokutara-sammyaku-
    sambodai/masani anokutara-
    sammyaku-sambodai o ubeshi
    當得阿耨多羅三藐三菩提
tsuki/*Tsuki* 都機
Ts'ao-tung 曹洞
Tsung-chih 總持
Tung-shan Liang-chieh 洞山良介

udonge/*Udonge* 優曇花
uji/*Uji*/aru toki 有時

Watsuji Tetsurō 和辻哲郎
Wen-chun 文準
Wu-chi Liao-p'ai 無際了派
Wu-chun Shih-fan 無準師範
Wu shan 五山
wu wei 五位
wu-wei chen-jen 無位眞人

Yang-ch'i 楊岐
Yin-yüan 隱元
Yōsai 榮西
Yüan-wu K'o-ch'in 圜悟克勤
yuibutsu-yobutsu 唯佛與佛
yuibutsu-yobutsu nainō-gūjin
    shohō-jisso/tada hotoke o hotoke
    to nomi sunawachi yoku shohō-
    jissō o gūjin su 唯佛與佛, 乃能究盡,
    諸法實相
Yuň-men 雲門
Yuň-yen T'an-sheng 雲巖曇晟

Zammai o zammai 三昧王三昧
zazenshin/*Zazenshin* 坐禪箴
zenki/*Zenki* 全機
zettai mu 絕對無
Zuimonki 隨聞記
zusan 杜撰

Production Notes

This book was designed by Roger Eggers.
Composition and paging were done on the
Quadex Composing System and typesetting on
the Compugraphic 8400 by the design and production staff of University of Hawaii Press.

The text and display typeface is Compugraphic
Times Roman.

Offset presswork and binding were done by
Malloy Lithographing, Inc. Text paper is Glat-
felter Offset, basis 50.